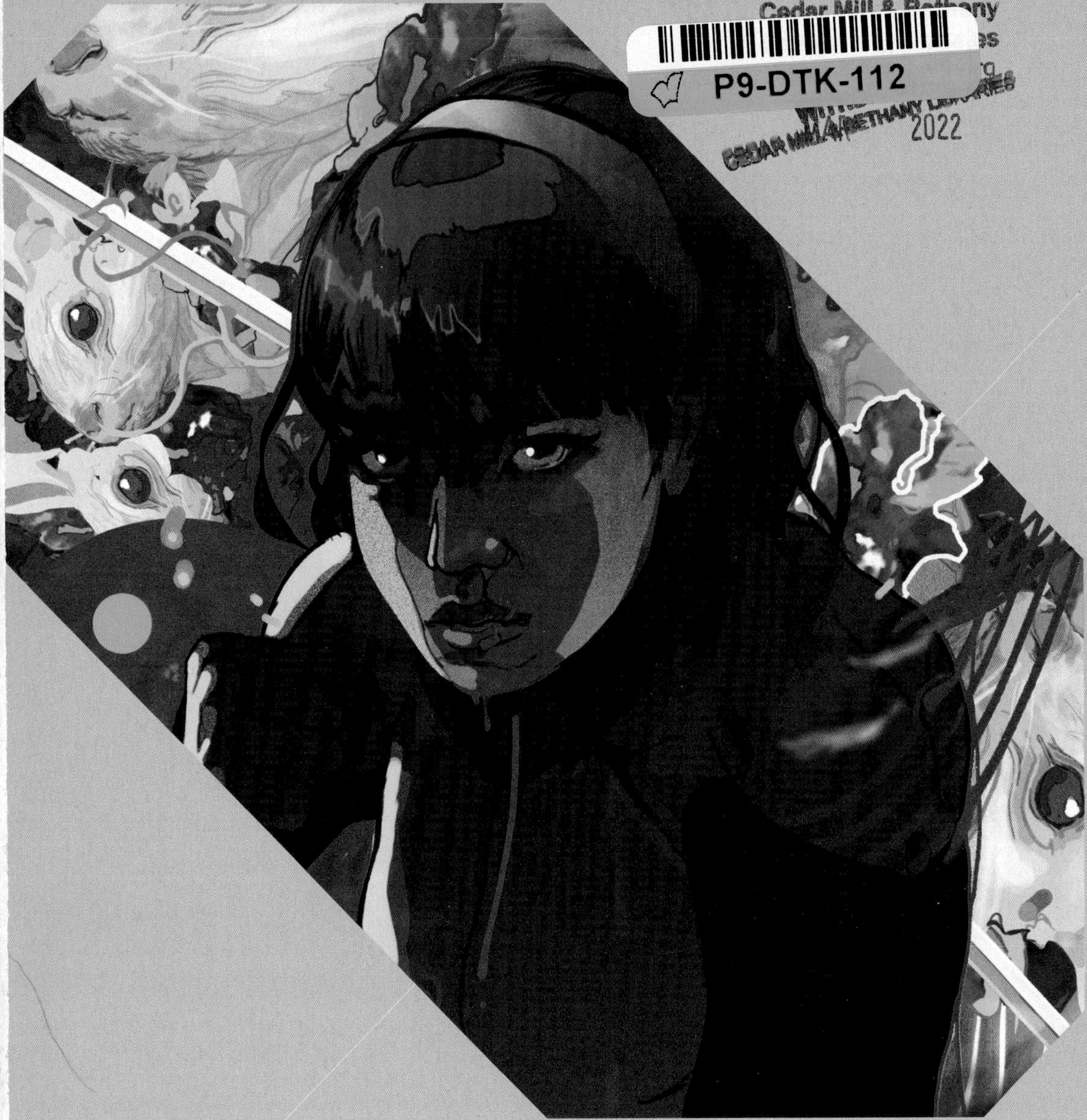

REIGN OF X VOL. 9. Contains material originally published in magazine form as HELLIONS (2020) #11, WOLVERINE (2020) #11-12, NEW MUTANTS (2019) #18, S.W.O.R.D. (2020) #5 and X-FACTOR (2020) #7. First printing 2021. ISBN 978-1-302-93382-1. Published by MARVEL WORLDWIDE, INC., a subsidiary of MARVEL ENTERTAINMENT, LLC. OFFICE OF PUBLICATION: 1290 Avenue of the Americas, New York, NY 10104. © 2021 MARVEL No similarity between any of the names, characters, persons, and/or institutions in this book with those of any living or dead person or institution is intended, and any such similarity which may exist is purely coincidental. **Printed in the Canada.** KEVIN FEIGE, Chief Creative Officer; DAN BUCKLEY, President, Marvel Entertainment; JOE QUESADA, EVP & Creative Director; DAVID BOGART, Associate Publisher & SVP of Talent Affairs; TOM BREVOORT, VP, Executive Editor; NICK LOWE, Executive Editor, VP of Content, Digital Publishing; DAVID GABRIEL, VP of Print & Digital Publishing; JEFF YOUNGQUIST, VP of Production & Special Projects; ALEX MORALES, Director of Publishing Operations; DAN EDINGTON, Managing Editor; RICKEY PURDIN, Director of Talent Relations; JENNIFER GRÜNWALD, Senior Editor, Special Projects; SUSAN CRESPI, Production Manager; STAN LEE, Chairman Emeritus. For information regarding advertising in Marvel Comics or on Marvel.com, please contact Vit DeBellis, Custom Solutions & Integrated Advertising Manager, at vdebellis@marvel.com. For Marvel subscription inquiries, please call 888-511-5480. **Manufactured between 12/10/2021 and 1/11/2022 by SOLISCO PRINTERS, SCOTT, QC, CANADA.**

10 9 8 7 6 5 4 3 2 1

REIGN OF X

Volume
9

X-Men created by Stan Lee & Jack Kirby

Writers:	Zeb Wells, Benjamin Percy, Vita Ayala, Al Ewing & Leah Williams
Artists:	Stephen Segovia, Scot Eaton, Rod Reis, Valerio Schiti & David Baldeón
Inkers:	Stephen Segovia, JP Mayer, Oren Junior, Rod Reis, Valerio Schiti & David Baldeón
Color Artists:	David Curiel, Matthew Wilson, Rod Reis, Marte Gracia & Israel Silva
Letterers:	VC's Ariana Maher, Cory Petit, Travis Lanham & Joe Caramagna
Cover Art:	Stephen Segovia & Rain Beredo; Adam Kubert & Frank Martin; Christian Ward; Valerio Schiti & Marte Gracia; and Ivan Shavrin
Head of X:	Jonathan Hickman
Design:	Tom Muller
Assistant Editors:	Shannon Andrews Ballesteros & Lauren Amaro
Editors:	Jordan D. White & Mark Basso
Collection Cover Art:	Christian Ward
Collection Editor:	Jennifer Grünwald
Assistant Editor:	Daniel Kirchhoffer
Assistant Managing Editor:	Maia Loy
Associate Manager, Talent Relations:	Lisa Montalbano
VP Production & Special Projects:	Jeff Youngquist
SVP Print, Sales & Marketing:	David Gabriel
Editor in Chief:	C.B. Cebulski

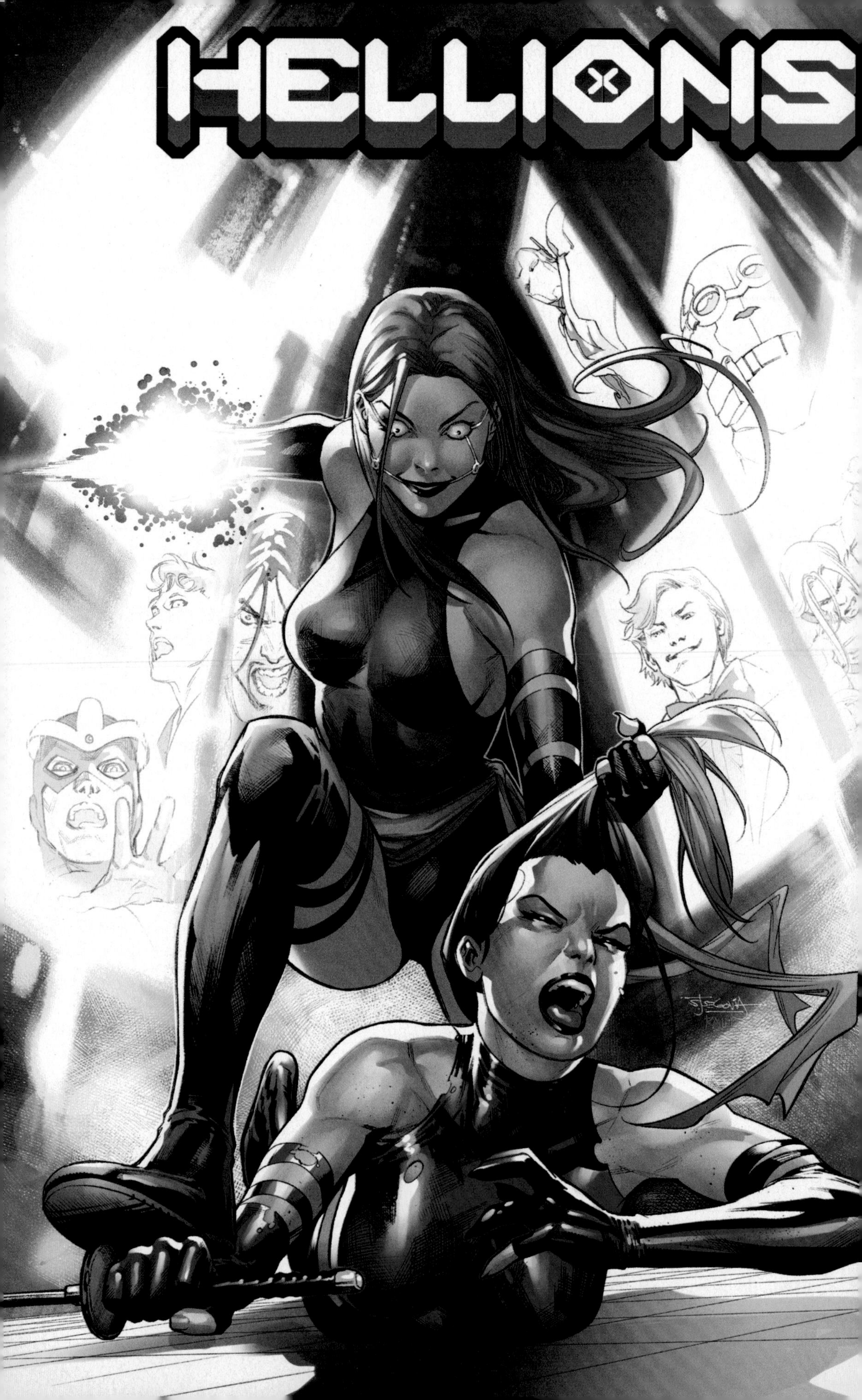
HELLIONS

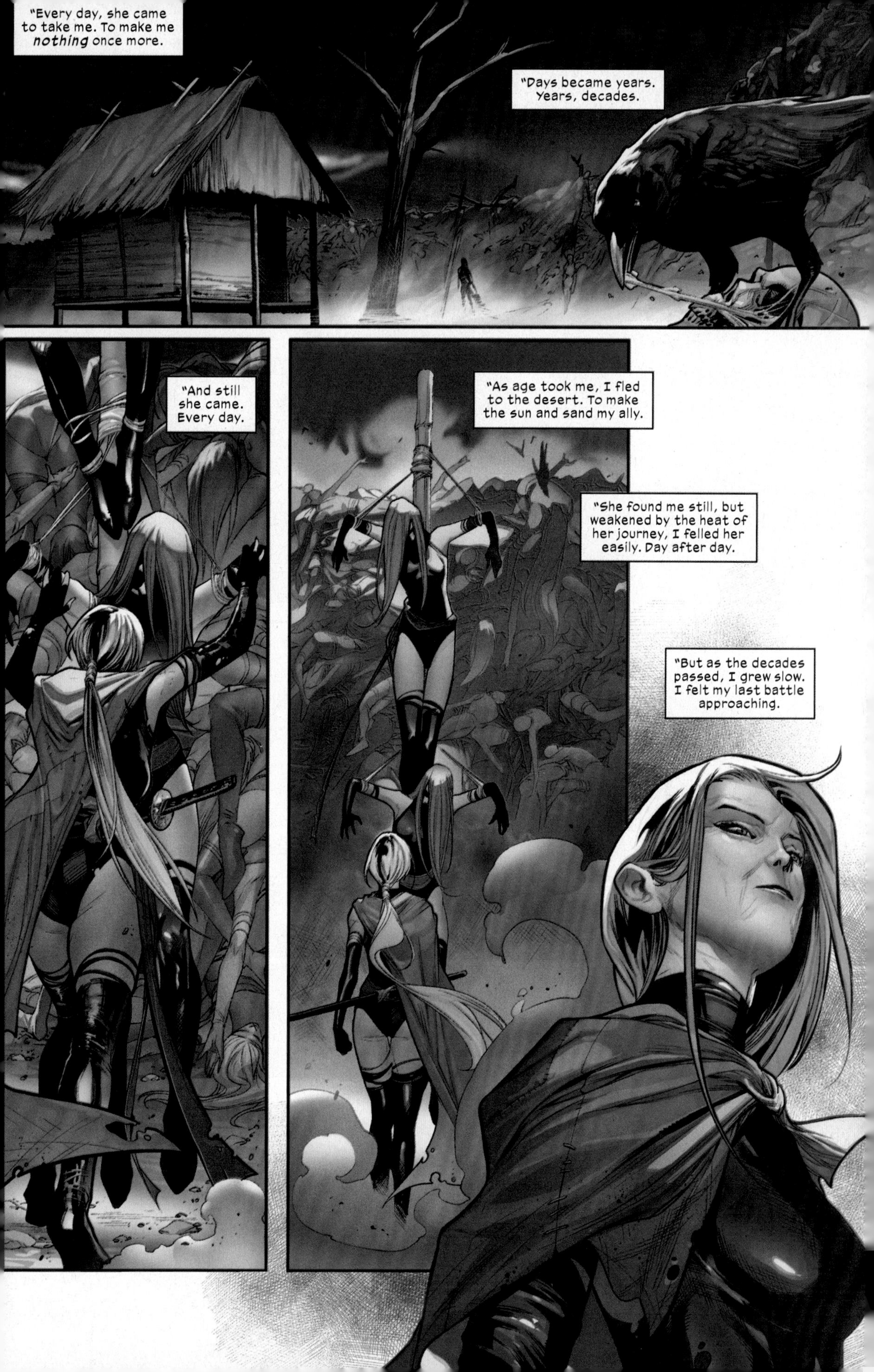
"Every day, she came to take me. To make me *nothing* once more.
"Days became years. Years, decades.
"And still she came. Every day.
"As age took me, I fled to the desert. To make the sun and sand my ally.
"She found me still, but weakened by the heat of her journey, I felled her easily. Day after day.
"But as the decades passed, I grew slow. I felt my last battle approaching.

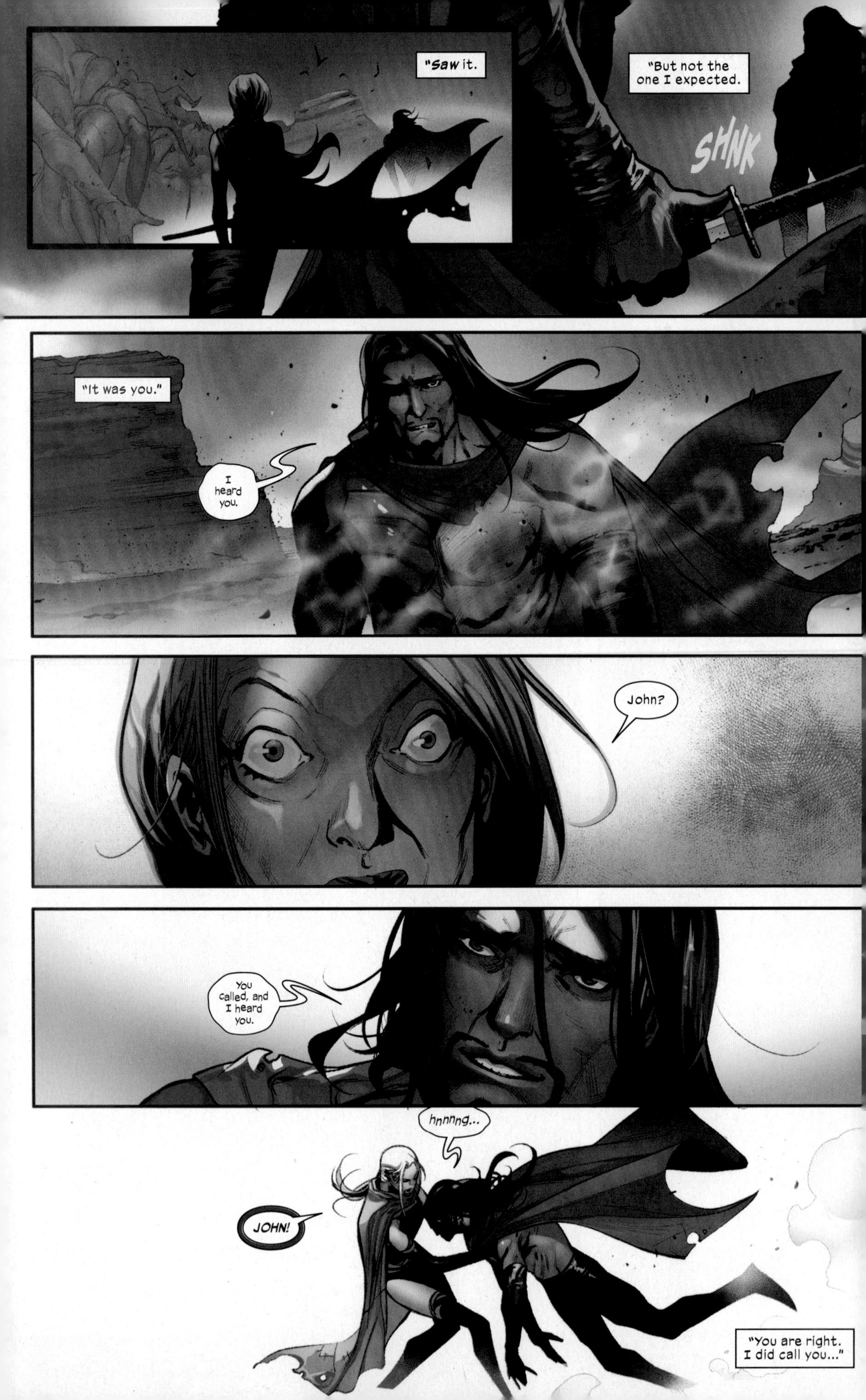
"Saw it.
"But not the one I expected.
SHNK
"It was you."
I heard you.
John?
You called, and I heard you.
hnnnng...
JOHN!
"You are right. I did call you..."

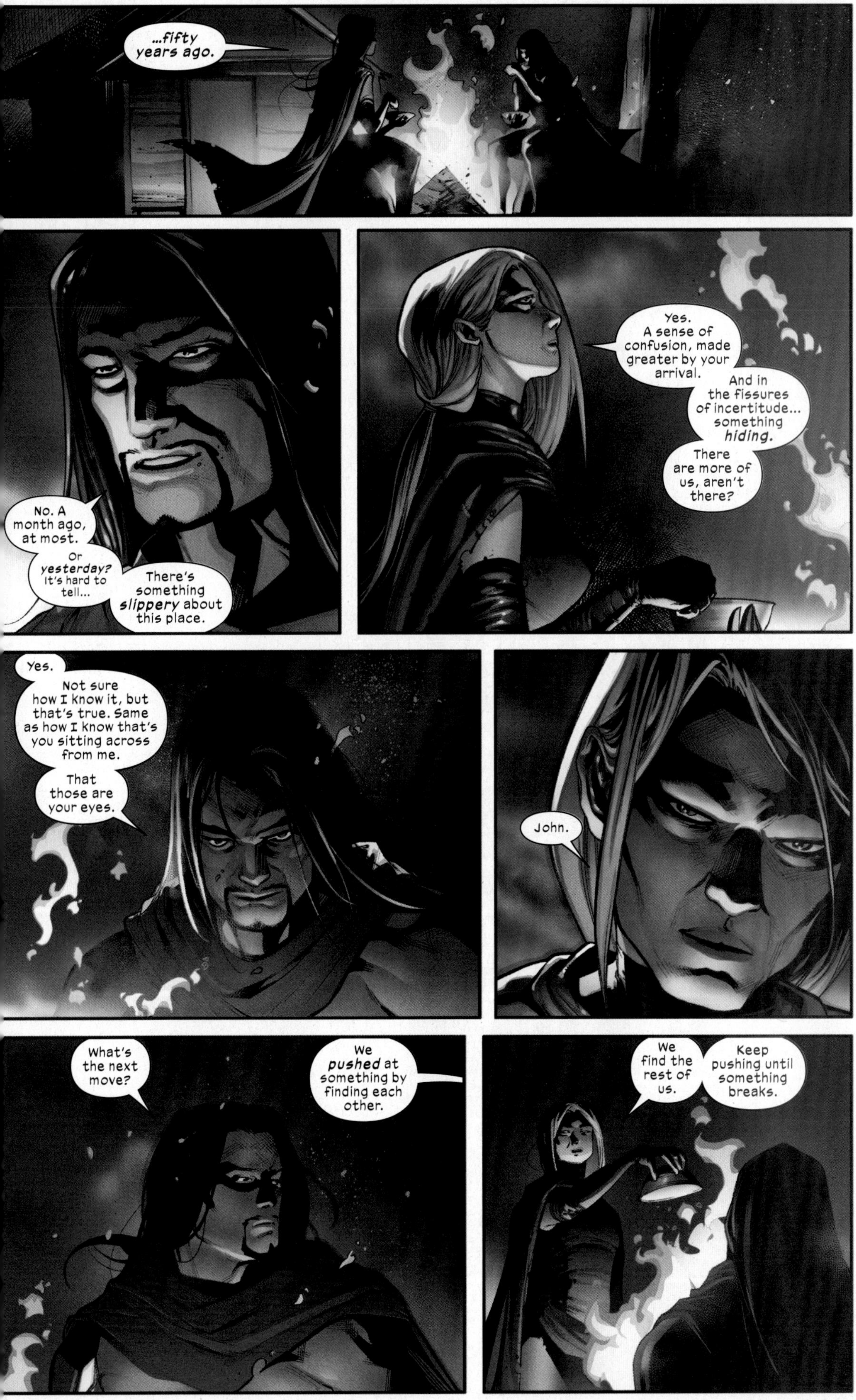
...fifty years ago.
No. A month ago, at most.
Or yesterday? It's hard to tell...
There's something slippery about this place.
Yes. A sense of confusion, made greater by your arrival.
And in the fissures of incertitude... something hiding.
There are more of us, aren't there?
Yes.
Not sure how I know it, but that's true. Same as how I know that's you sitting across from me.
That those are your eyes.
John.
What's the next move?
We pushed at something by finding each other.
We find the rest of us.
Keep pushing until something breaks.

[00_bad__X]
[00_news_X]

IT'S ARCADE'S MURDERWORLD, AND WE'RE ALL JUST DYING IN IT.

Pulling strings like the sadistic game master he is, Arcade has successfully manipulated Mastermind into trapping the Hellions in their own personal nightmares, making the fracturing team dance for his amusement as they struggle for survival. One false move and it's game over.

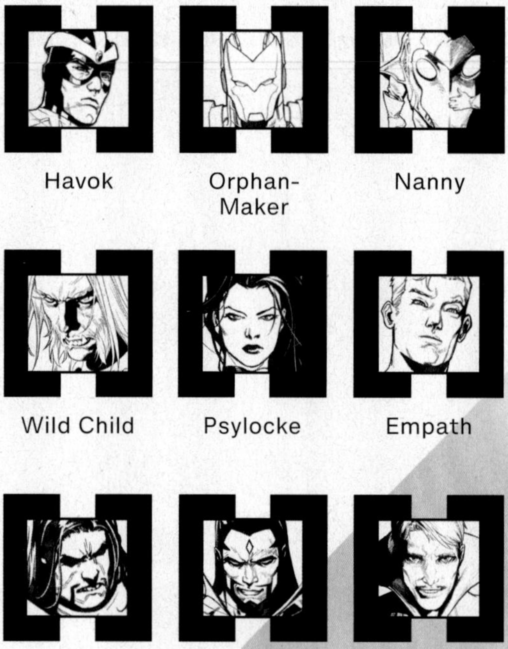

Havok · Orphan-Maker · Nanny
Wild Child · Psylocke · Empath
Greycrow · Mr. Sinister · Mastermind

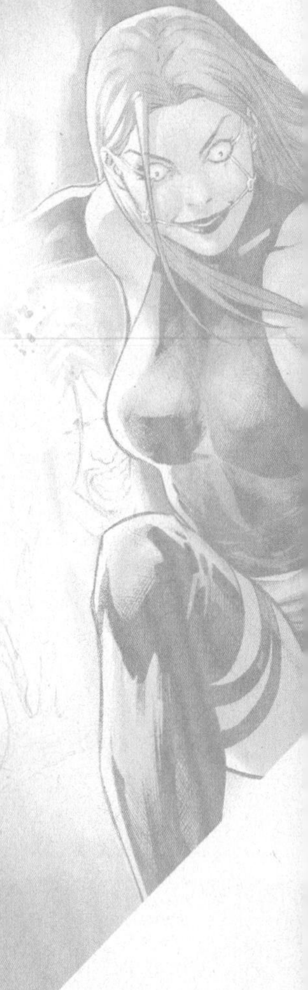

HELLIONS
[X_11]

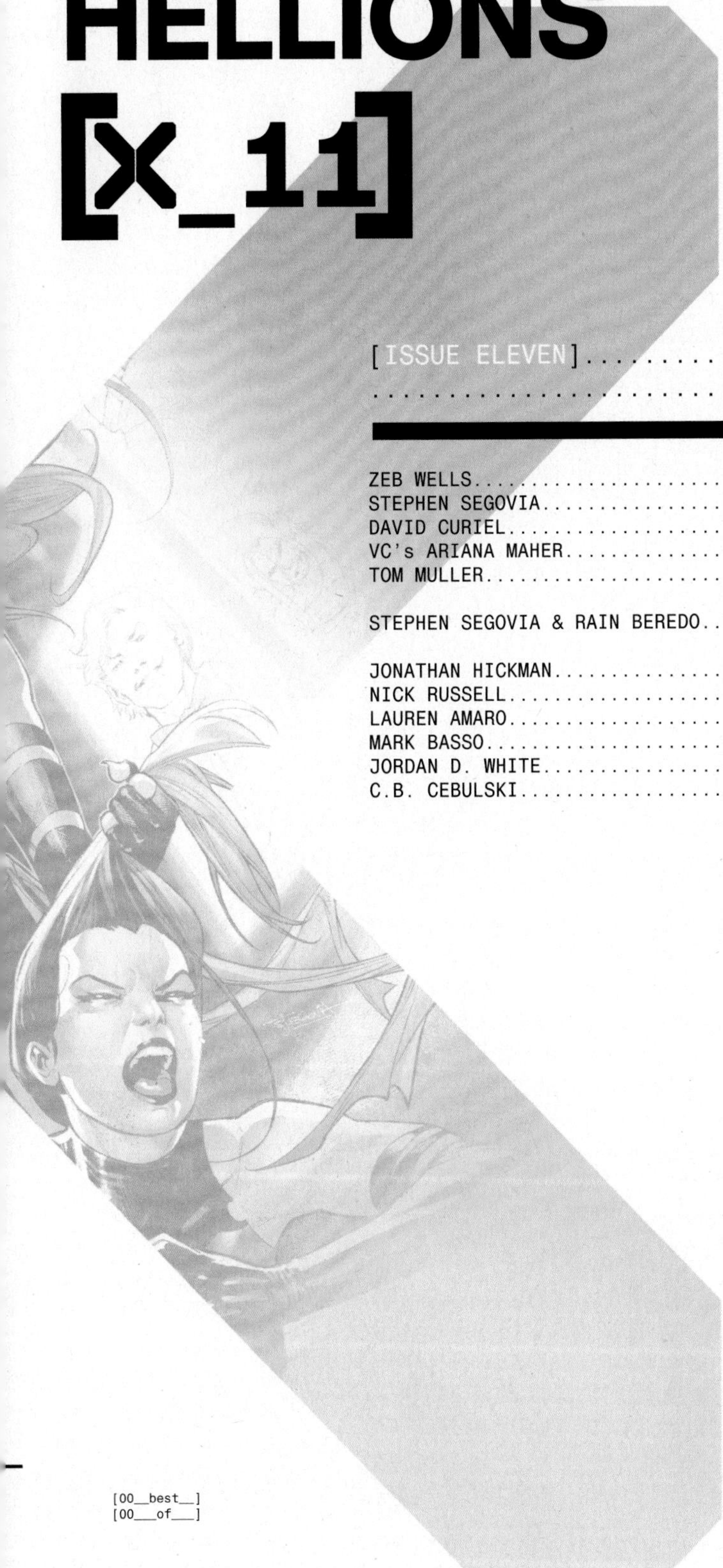

[ISSUE ELEVEN].......... FUNNY GAMES PART III:
.... KILL SCREEN

ZEB WELLS....................................[WRITER]
STEPHEN SEGOVIA..............................[ARTIST]
DAVID CURIEL.................................[COLOR ARTIST]
VC's ARIANA MAHER............................[LETTERER]
TOM MULLER...................................[DESIGN]

STEPHEN SEGOVIA & RAIN BEREDO................[COVER ARTISTS]

JONATHAN HICKMAN.............................[HEAD OF X]
NICK RUSSELL.................................[PRODUCTION]
LAUREN AMARO.................................[ASSISTANT EDITOR]
MARK BASSO...................................[EDITOR]
JORDAN D. WHITE..............................[SENIOR EDITOR]
C.B. CEBULSKI................................[EDITOR IN CHIEF]

[reign_of_x]

[kra_]
[koa_]

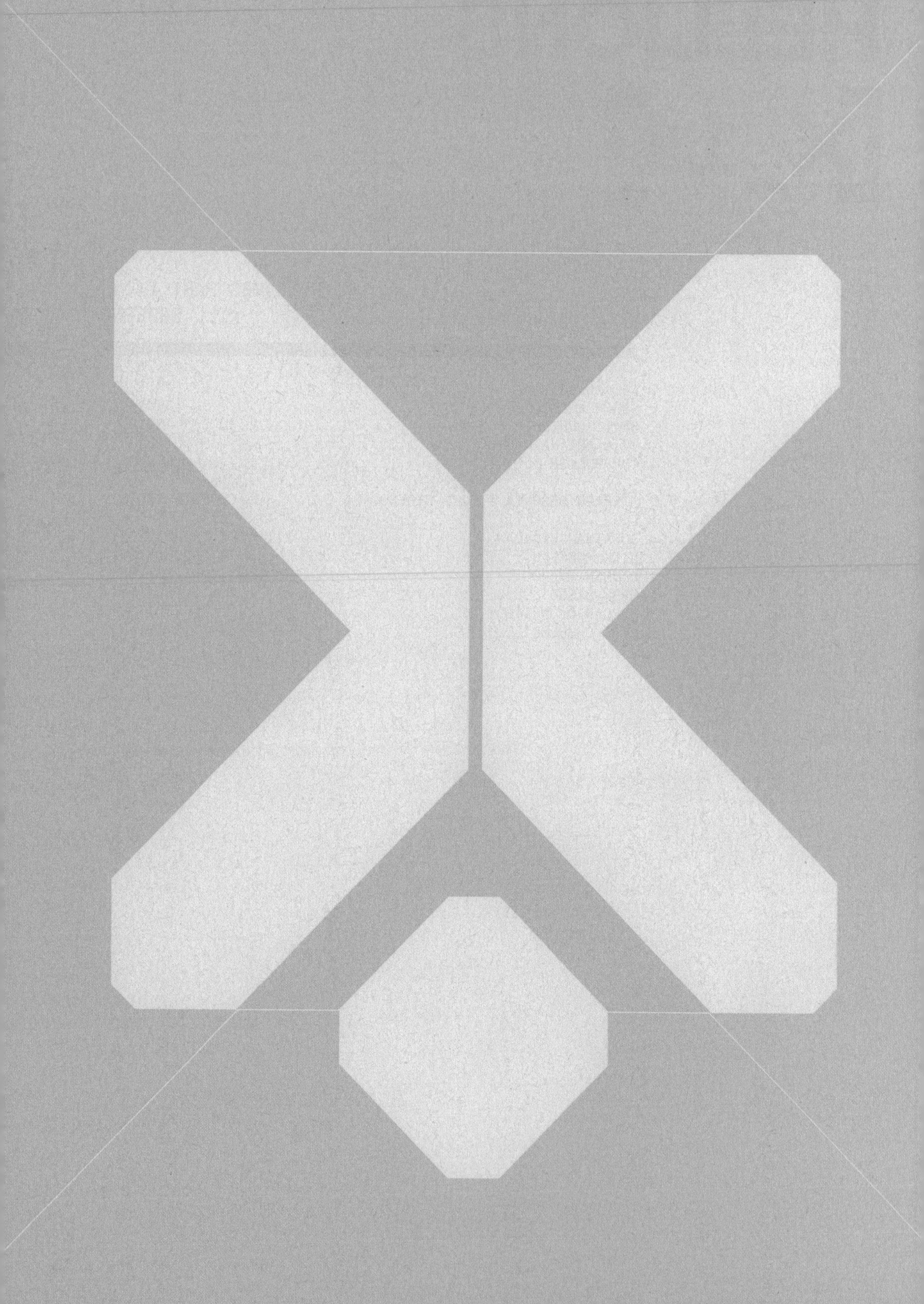

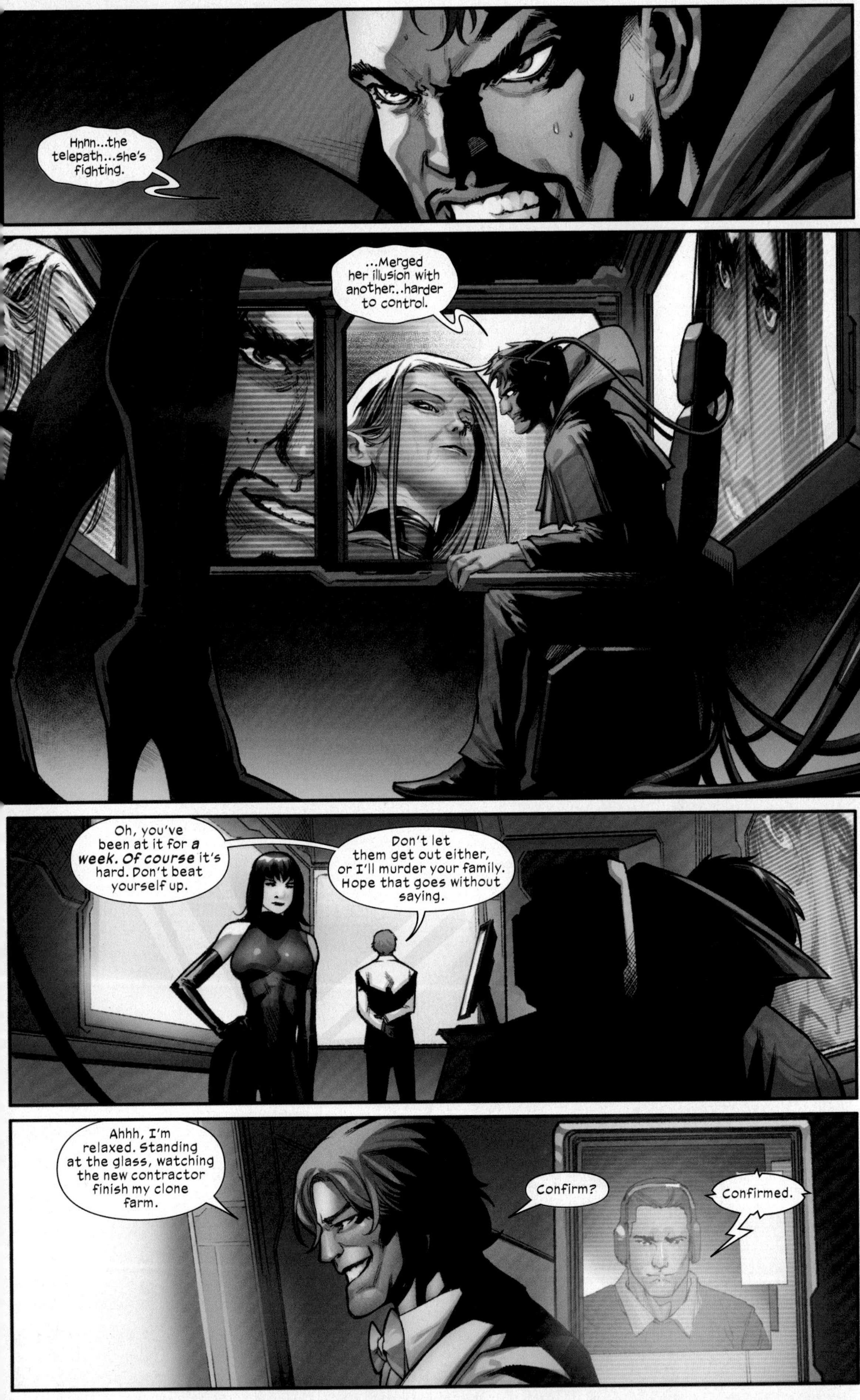
Hnnn...the telepath...she's fighting.
...Merged her illusion with another...harder to control.
Oh, you've been at it for a *week. Of course* it's hard. Don't beat yourself up.
Don't let them get out either, or I'll murder your family. Hope that goes without saying.
Ahhh, I'm relaxed. Standing at the glass, watching the new contractor finish my clone farm.
Confirm?
Confirmed.

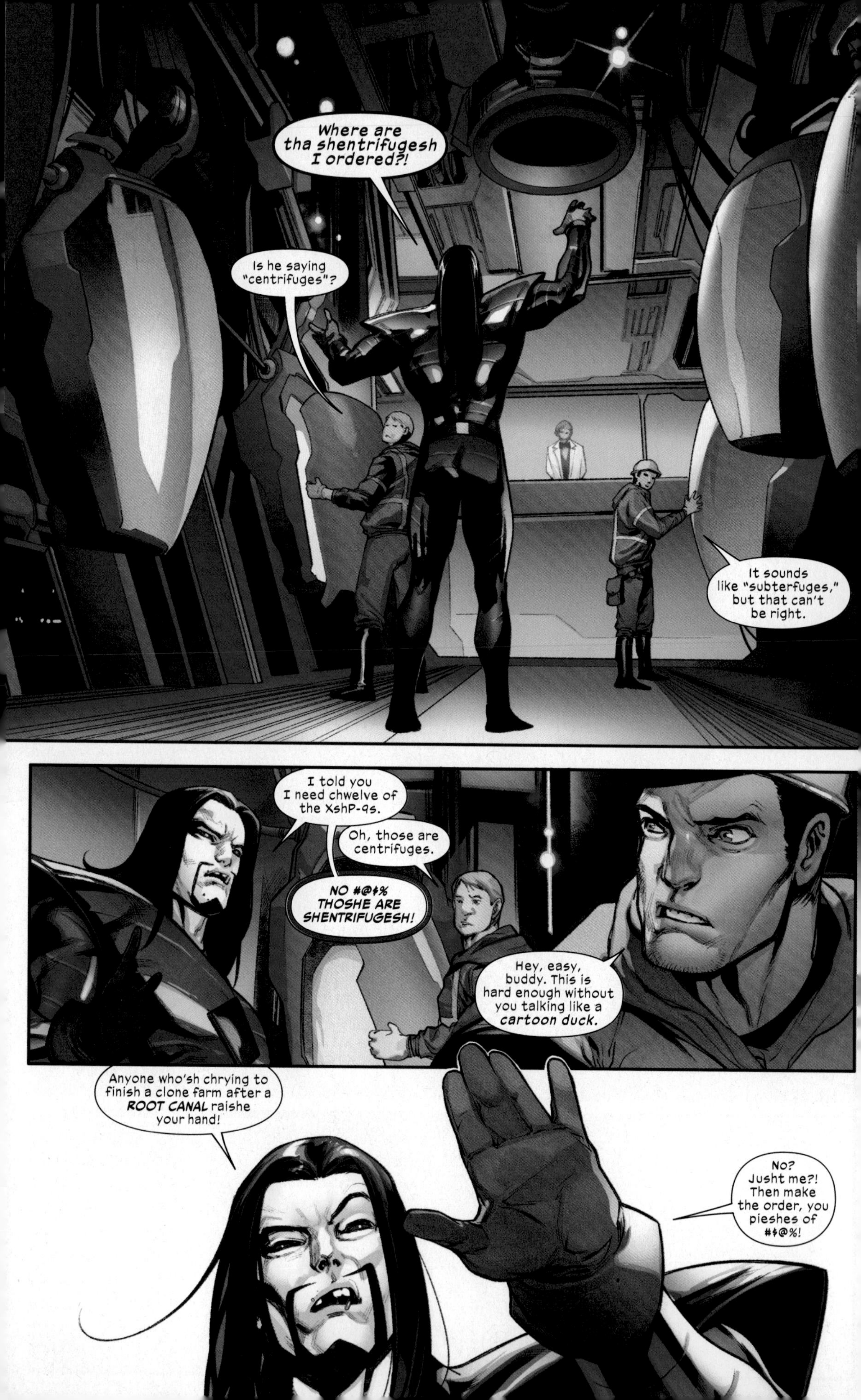
Where are tha shentrifugesh I ordered?!
Is he saying "centrifuges"?
It sounds like "subterfuges," but that can't be right.
I told you I need chwelve of the XshP-9s.
Oh, those are centrifuges.
NO #@$% THOSHE ARE SHENTRIFUGESH!
Hey, easy, buddy. This is hard enough without you talking like a cartoon duck.
Anyone who'sh chrying to finish a clone farm after a ROOT CANAL raishe your hand!
No? Jusht me?! Then make the order, you pieshes of #$@%!

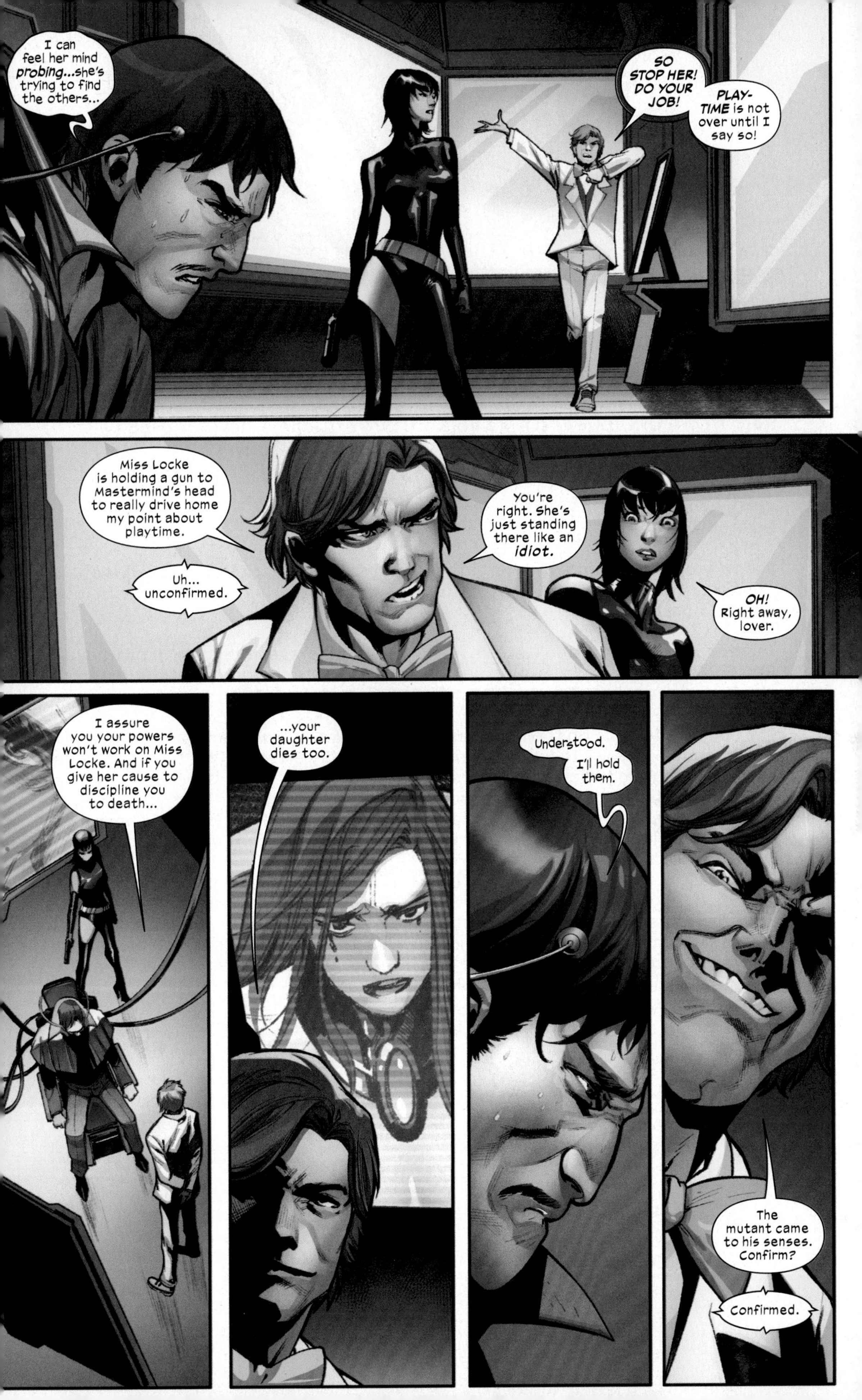
I can feel her mind *probing*...she's trying to find the others...
SO STOP HER! DO YOUR JOB!
PLAY-TIME is not over until I say so!
Miss Locke is holding a gun to Mastermind's head to really drive home my point about playtime.
Uh... unconfirmed.
You're right. She's just standing there like an *idiot.*
OH! Right away, lover.
I assure you your powers won't work on Miss Locke. And if you give her cause to discipline you to death...
...your daughter dies too.
Understood. I'll hold them.
The mutant came to his senses. Confirm?
Confirmed.

**Bio Procurement Office
Dr. Richard Briggs
Manager**

Ref: WORK ORDER/PONO-Memo No:CNPOB/Clone order/43/7698

Subject: Slippage of deadline for functional clones after Tuesday's incident.

Master Arcade,

Thank you for coming by the floor yesterday and listening. We all want to complete this task for you, both as professionals and human beings with loved ones in Loyalty Accounts.

To that end, I very much appreciate your giving me immunity from Loyalty Protocols to put down in writing the very real challenges we face after the ugliness on Tuesday. So here I go:

The sudden violence on the floor has hampered your plans, perhaps permanently. Dr. Hampden was our team leader. It was incredibly stressful for the team to see him mauled by robotic teddy bears. What's more troubling is he was punished for doing what he had been tasked with: producing clones. That you would be so furious that the clones were infants was a shock to all of us. We'd hoped you were aware that age acceleration is a completely different discipline. And now Dr. Hampden's plans for such a process are lost forever.

Without an outside expert to provide this tech, our cloning operation will never be satisfactory. Hopefully one will be provided soon, as this, not horrific threats...or miniature clowns, will allow us to give you what you want: Full-grown human clones. Thanks for letting me speak free from the threat of violence. It means more than you know...

R.J. BRIGGS

—

*KILL THIS LOUDMOUTH
AND GET ME SINISTER.*
NOW.   —'CADE

—

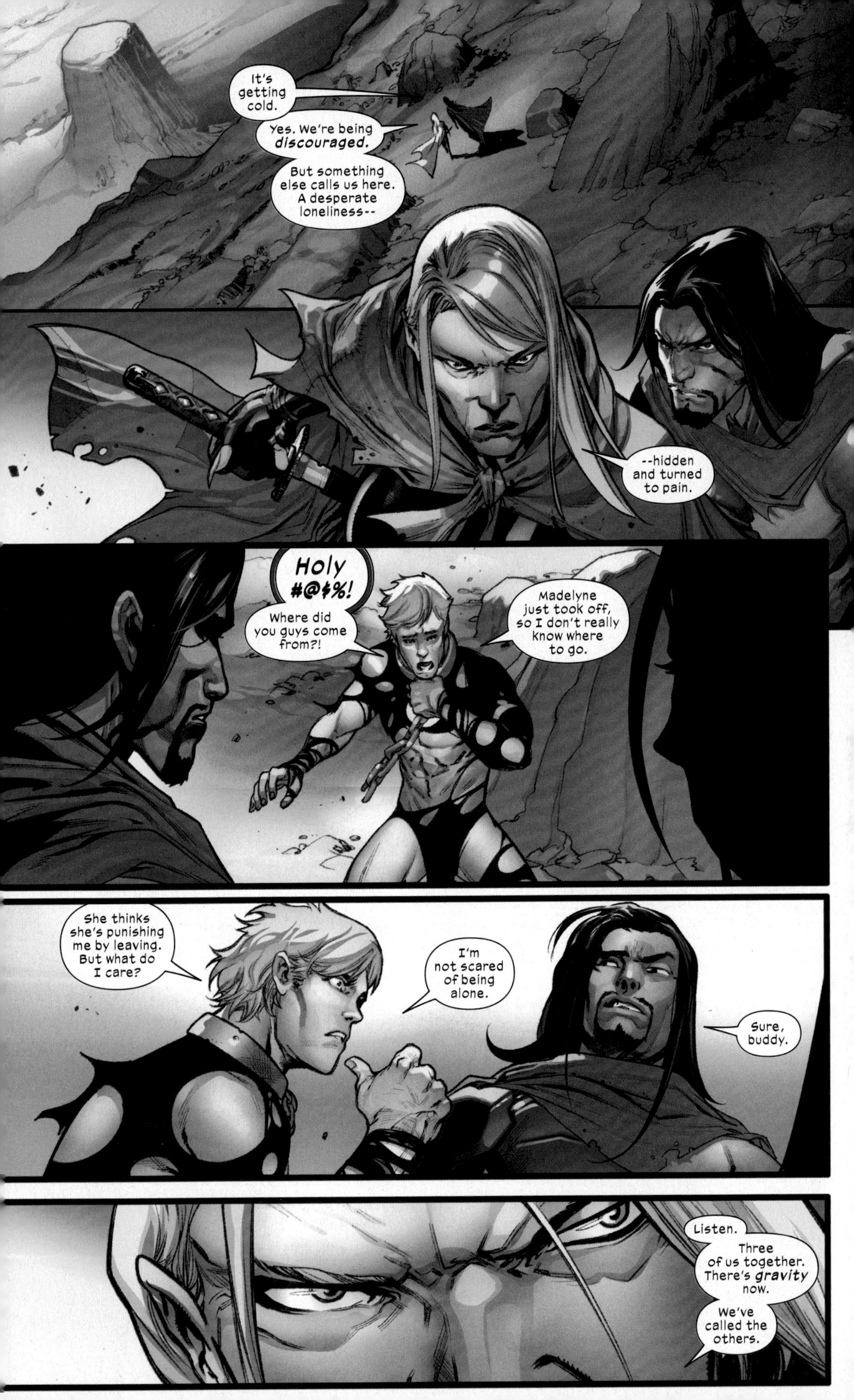

It's getting cold.
Yes. We're being *discouraged.*
But something else calls us here. A desperate loneliness--
--hidden and turned to pain.
Holy #@$%!
Where did you guys come from?!
Madelyne just took off, so I don't really know where to go.
She thinks she's punishing me by leaving. But what do I care?
I'm not scared of being alone.
Sure, buddy.
Listen.
Three of us together. There's *gravity* now.
We've called the others.

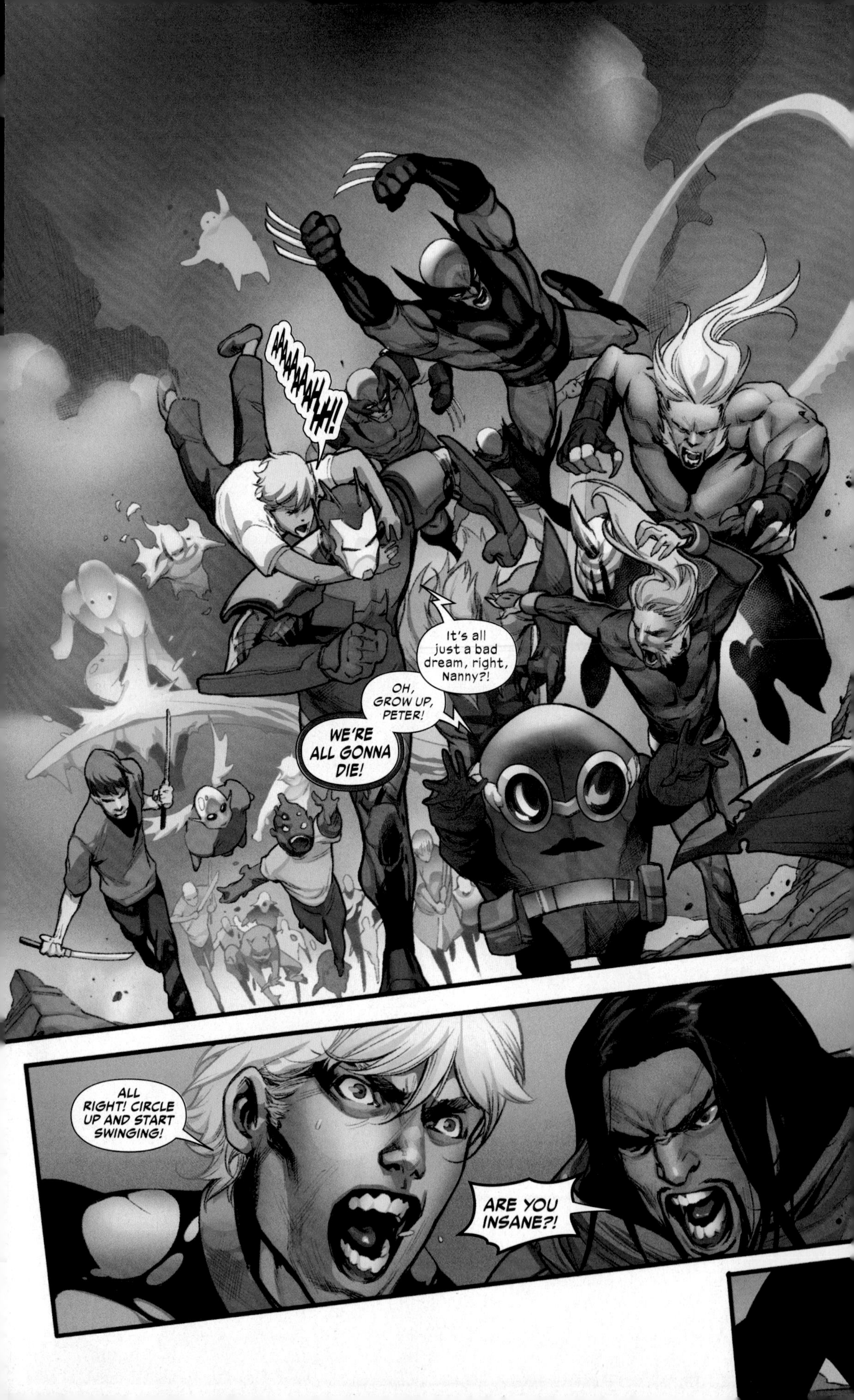
AAAAAAAAHH!
It's all just a bad dream, right, Nanny?!
OH, GROW UP, PETER!
WE'RE ALL GONNA DIE!
ALL RIGHT! CIRCLE UP AND START SWINGING!
ARE YOU INSANE?!

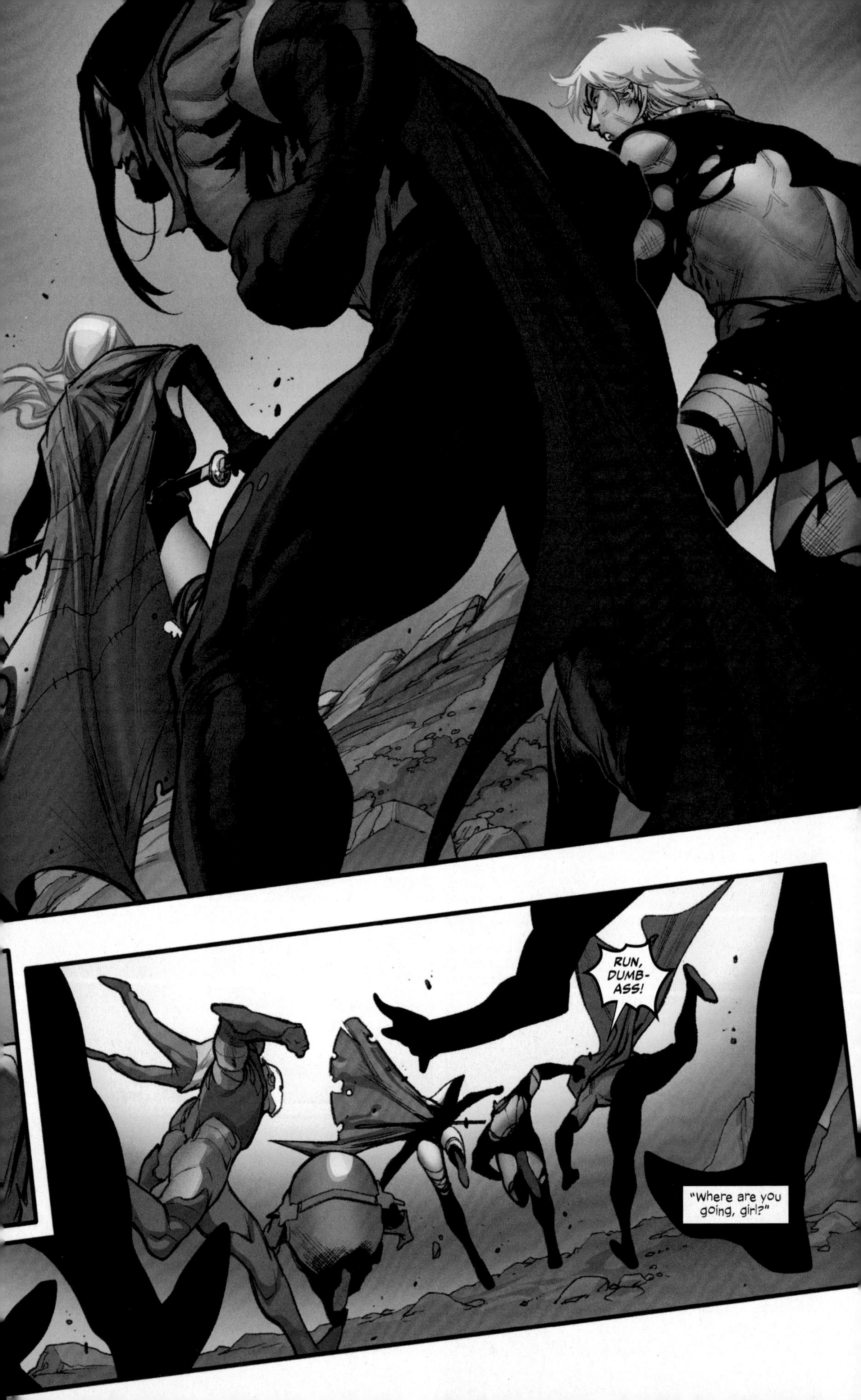
RUN, DUMB-ASS!
"Where are you going, girl?"

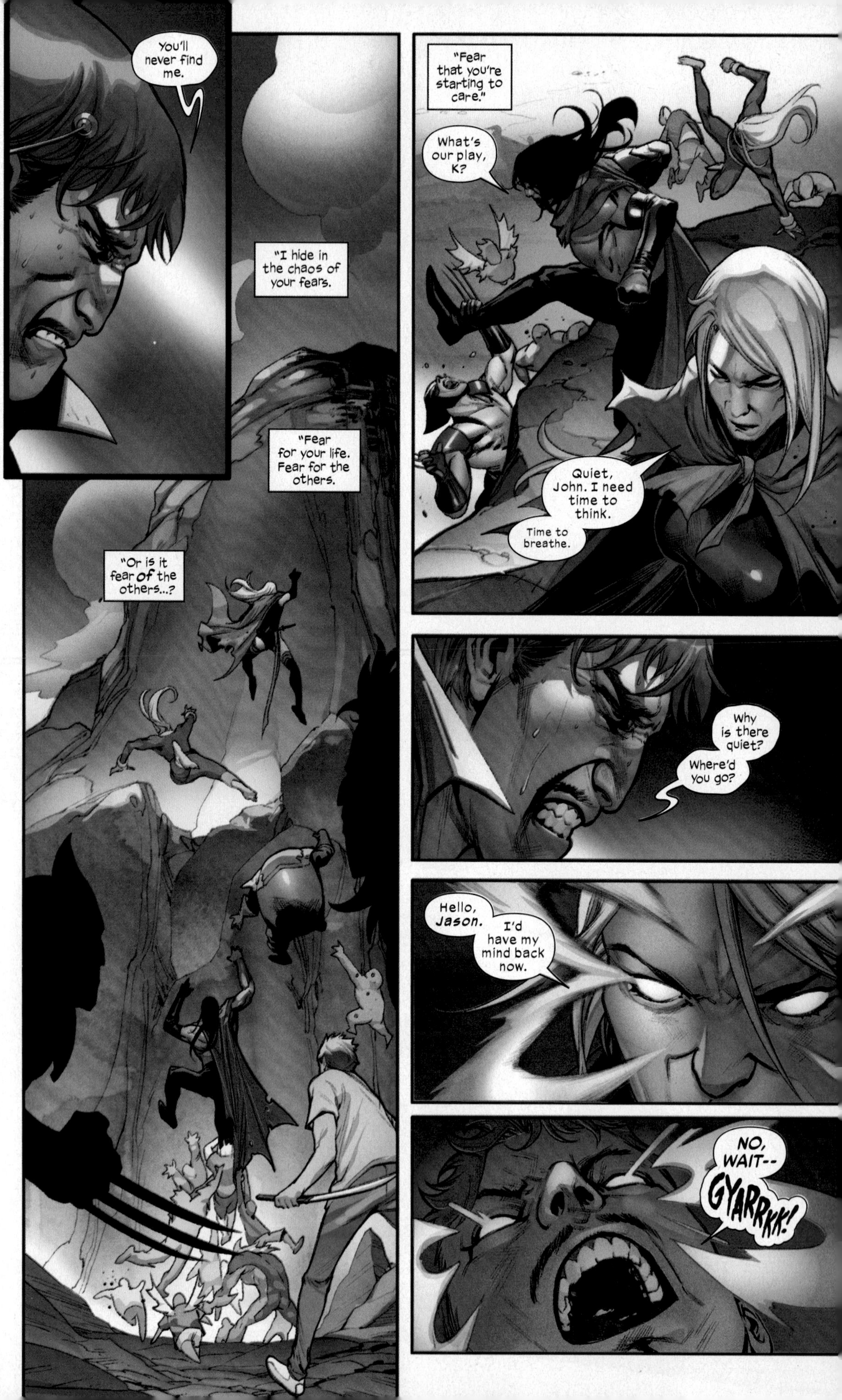
You'll never find me.
"I hide in the chaos of your fears.
"Fear for your life. Fear for the others.
"Or is it fear *of* the others...?
"Fear that you're starting to care."
What's our play, K?
Quiet, John. I need time to think.
Time to breathe.
Why is there quiet?
Where'd you go?
Hello, *Jason.*
I'd have my mind back now.
NO, WAIT--
GYARRKK!

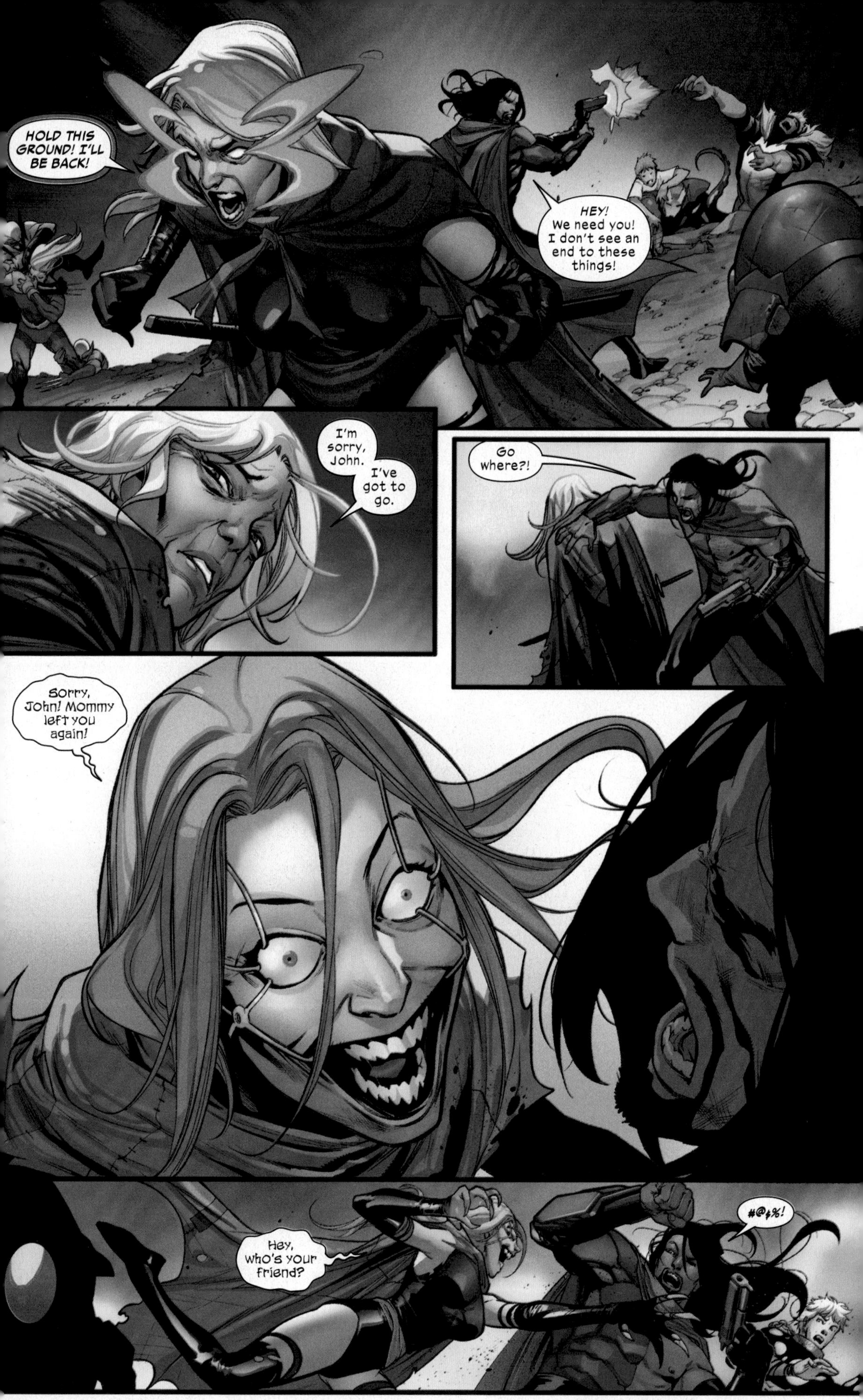
HOLD THIS GROUND! I'LL BE BACK!
HEY! We need you! I don't see an end to these things!
I'm sorry, John. I've got to go.
Go where?!
Sorry, John! Mommy left you again!
Hey, who's your friend?
#@$%!

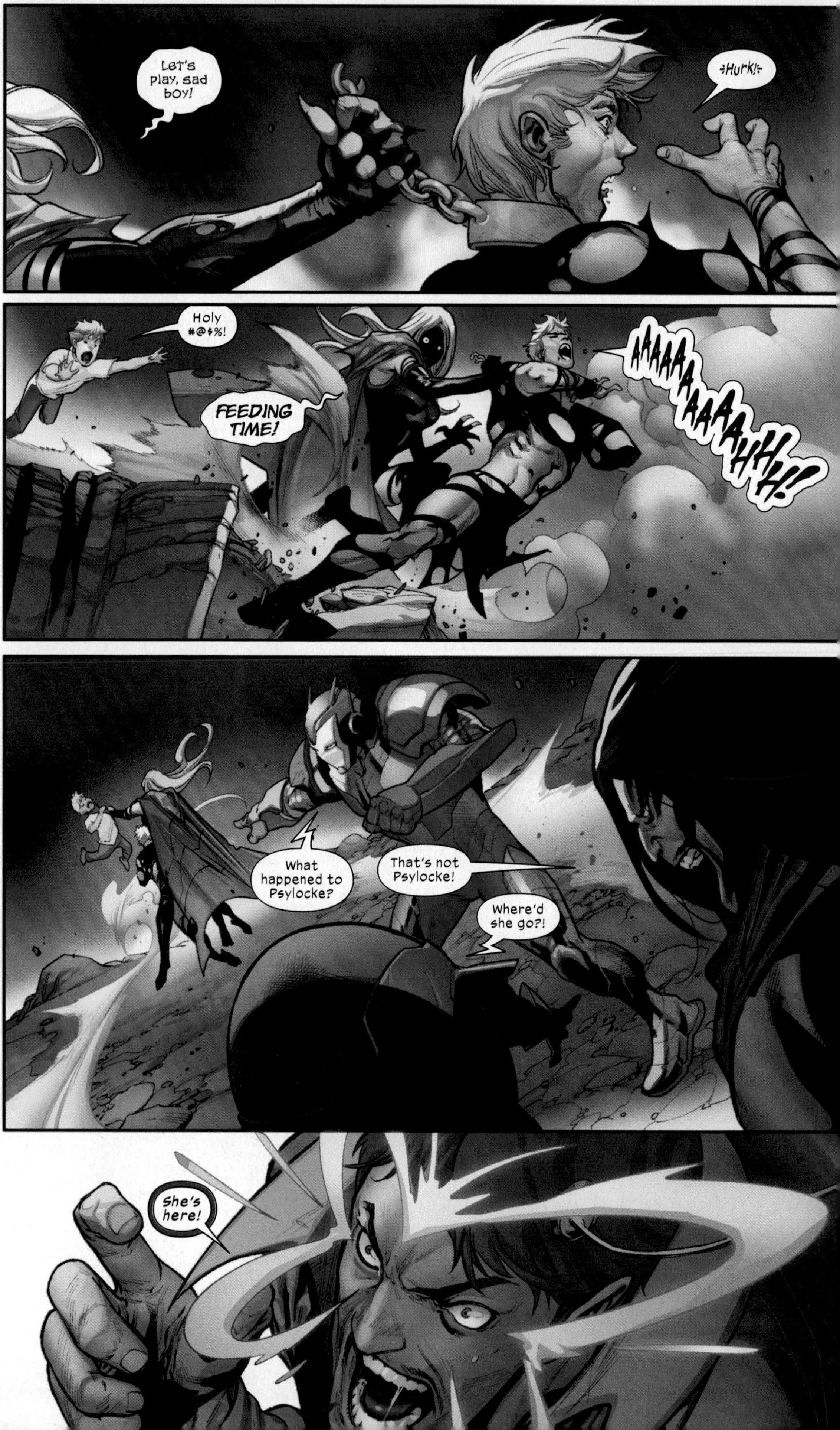

Let's play, sad boy!
Hurk!
Holy #@$%!
FEEDING TIME!
AAAAAAAAAAAAHHH!!
What happened to Psylocke?
That's not Psylocke!
Where'd she go?!
She's here!

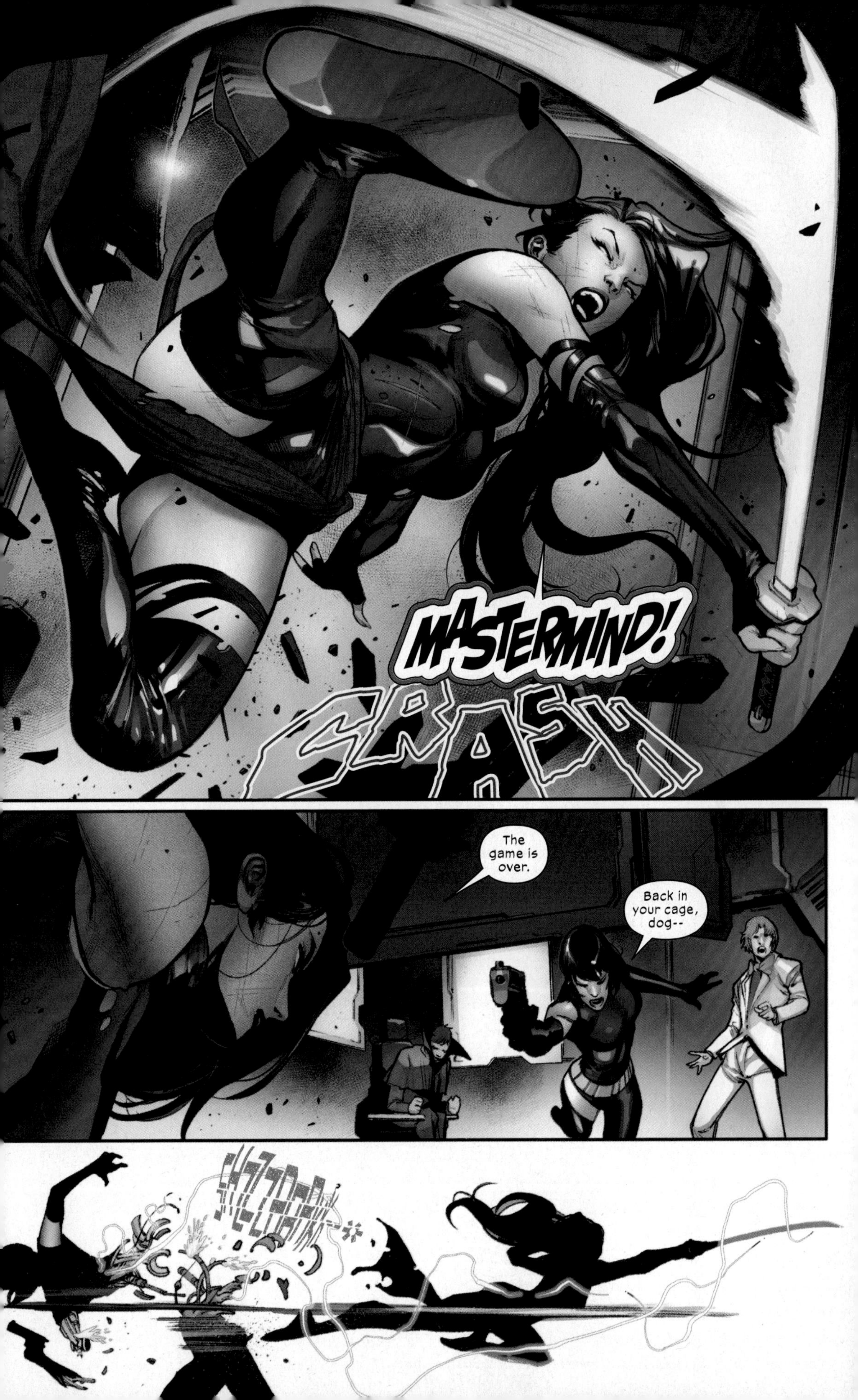
MASTERMIND!
The game is over.
Back in your cage, dog--

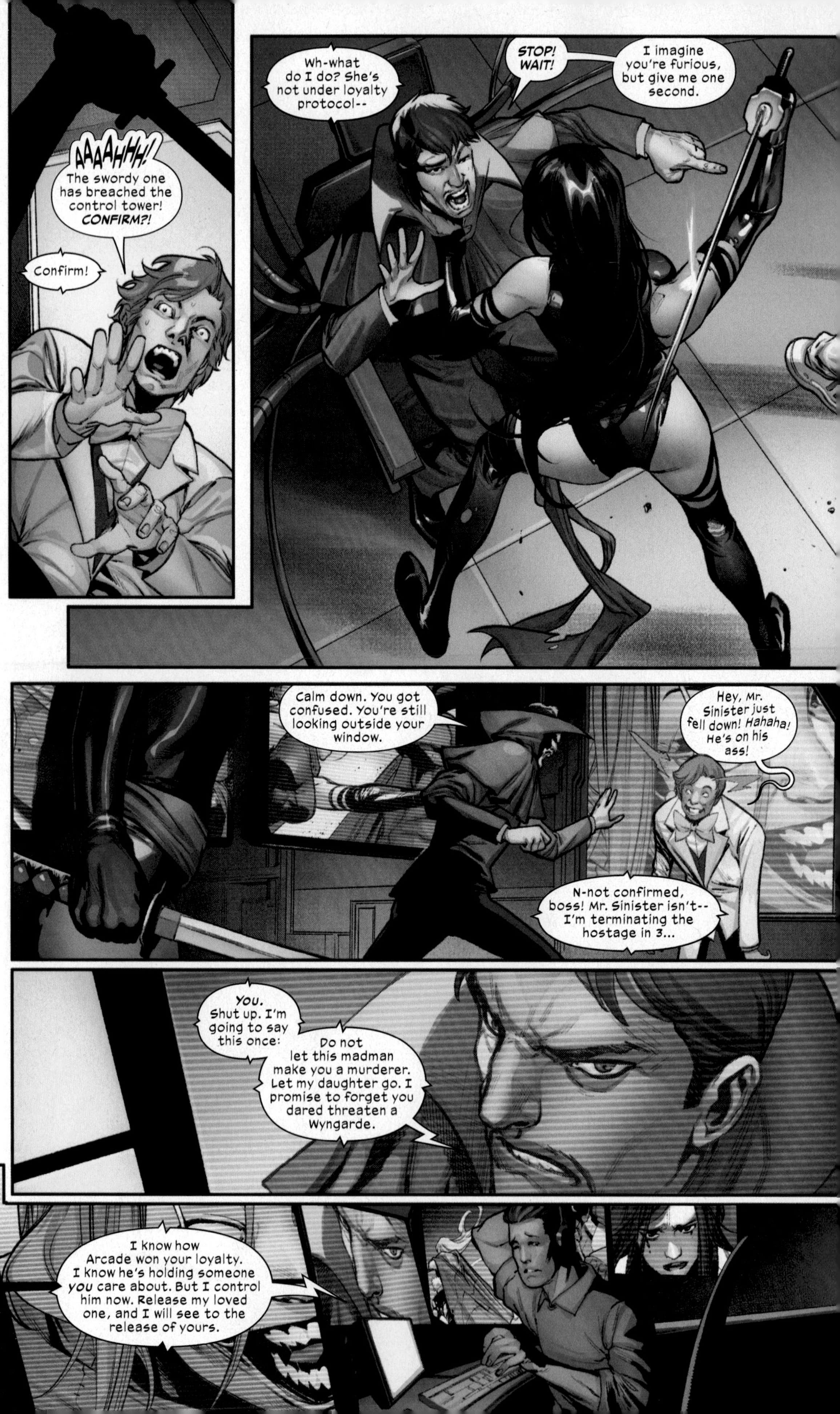
AAAAHHH!
The swordy one has breached the control tower! CONFIRM?!
Confirm!
Wh-what do I do? She's not under loyalty protocol--
STOP! WAIT!
I imagine you're furious, but give me one second.
Calm down. You got confused. You're still looking outside your window.
Hey, Mr. Sinister just fell down! Hahaha! He's on his ass!
N-not confirmed, boss! Mr. Sinister isn't-- I'm terminating the hostage in 3...
YOU. Shut up. I'm going to say this once:
Do not let this madman make you a murderer. Let my daughter go. I promise to forget you dared threaten a Wyngarde.
I know how Arcade won your loyalty. I know he's holding someone you care about. But I control him now. Release my loved one, and I will see to the release of yours.

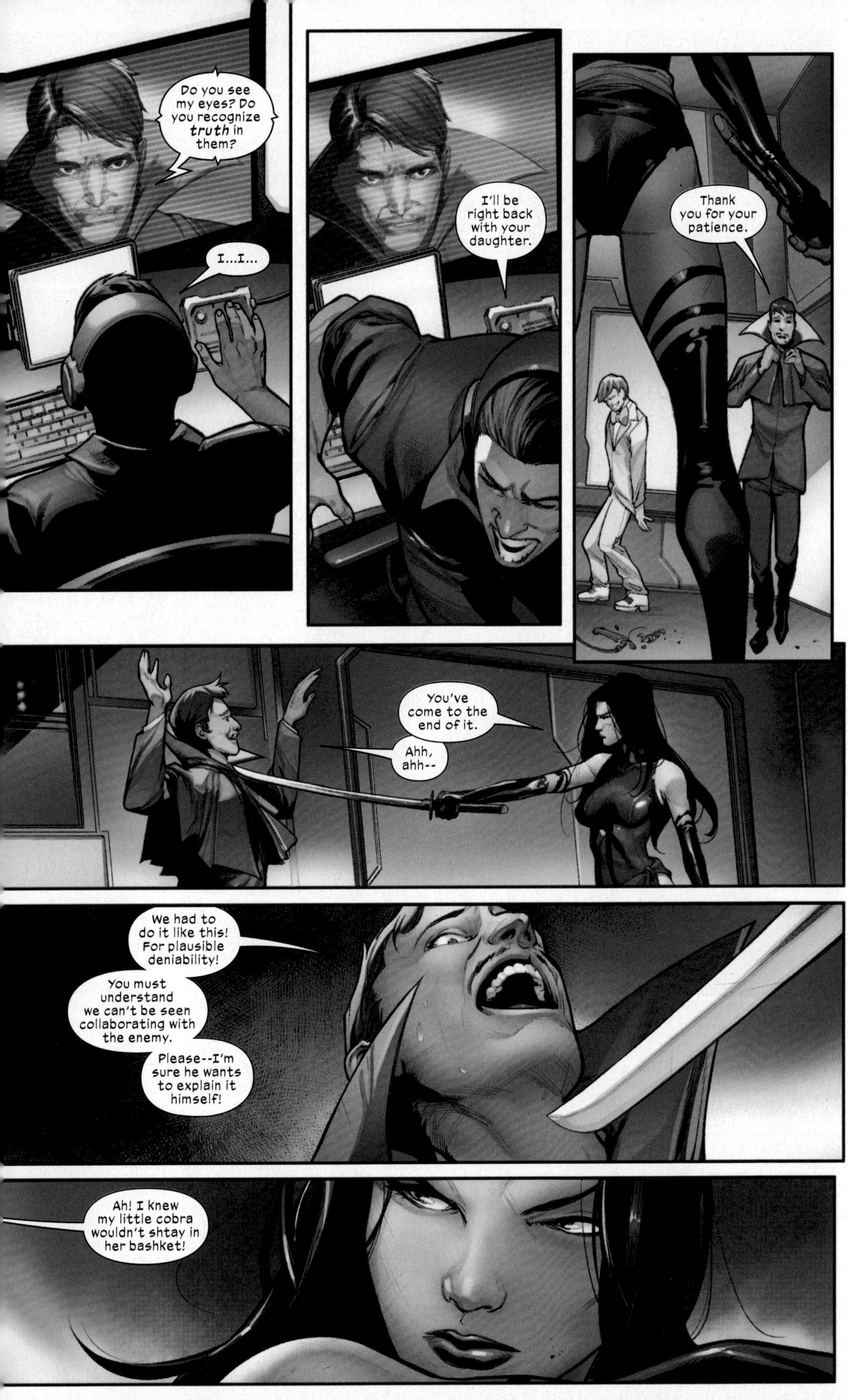
Do you see my eyes? Do you recognize *truth* in them?
I...I...
I'll be right back with your daughter.
Thank you for your patience.
You've come to the end of it.
Ahh, ahh--
We had to do it like this! For plausible deniability!
You must understand we can't be seen collaborating with the enemy.
Please--I'm sure he wants to explain it himself!
Ah! I knew my little cobra wouldn't shtay in her bashket!

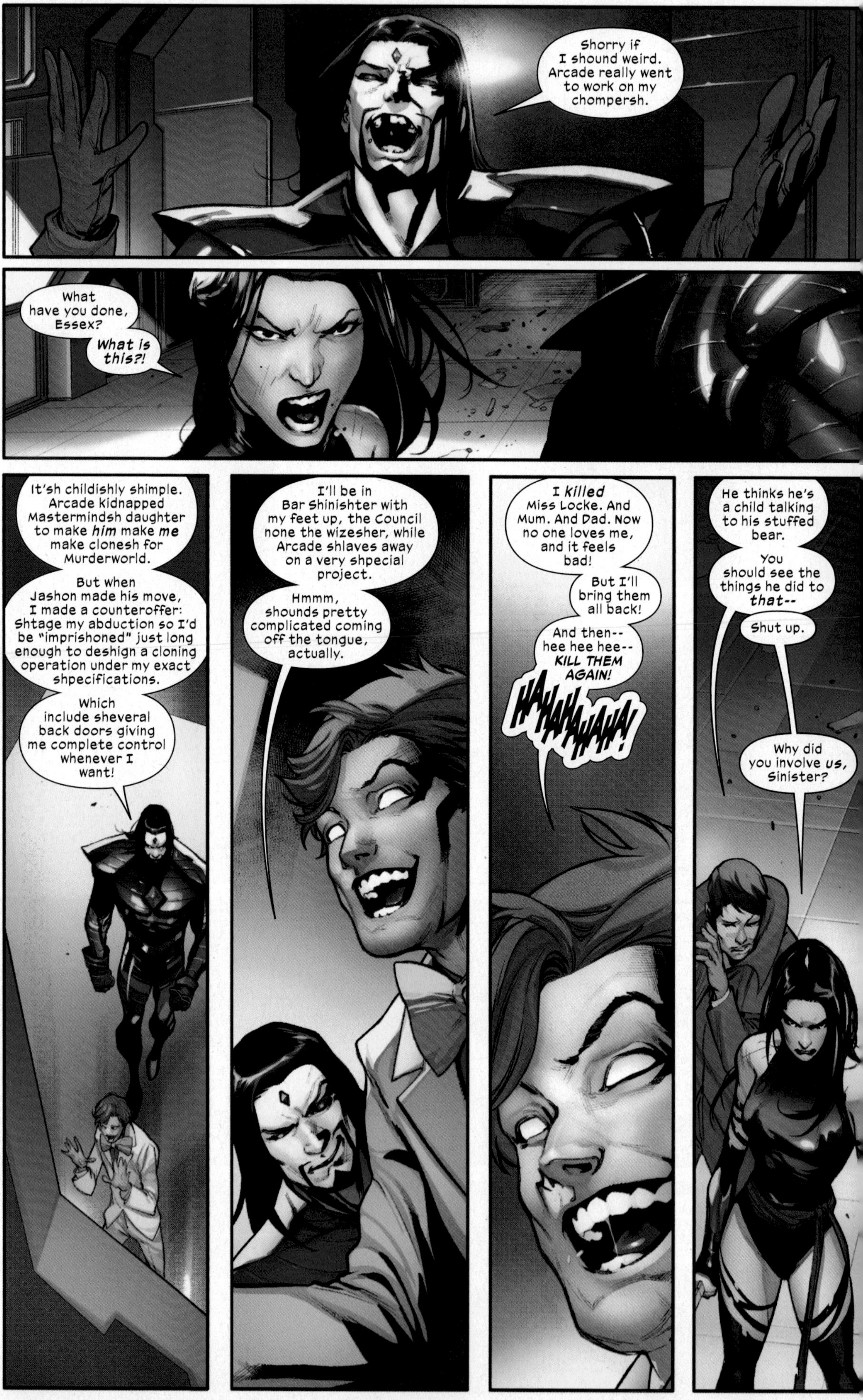
Shorry if I shound weird. Arcade really went to work on my chompersh.
What have you done, Essex?
What is this?!
It'sh childishly shimple. Arcade kidnapped Mastermindsh daughter to make him make me make clonesh for Murderworld.
But when Jashon made his move, I made a counteroffer: Shtage my abduction so I'd be "imprishoned" just long enough to deshign a cloning operation under my exact shpecifications.
Which include sheveral back doors giving me complete control whenever I want!
I'll be in Bar Shinishter with my feet up, the Council none the wizesher, while Arcade shlaves away on a very shpecial project.
Hmmm, shounds pretty complicated coming off the tongue, actually.
I killed Miss Locke. And Mum. And Dad. Now no one loves me, and it feels bad!
But I'll bring them all back!
And then-- hee hee hee-- KILL THEM AGAIN!
HAHAHAHAHA!
He thinks he's a child talking to his stuffed bear.
You should see the things he did to that--
Shut up.
Why did you involve us, Sinister?

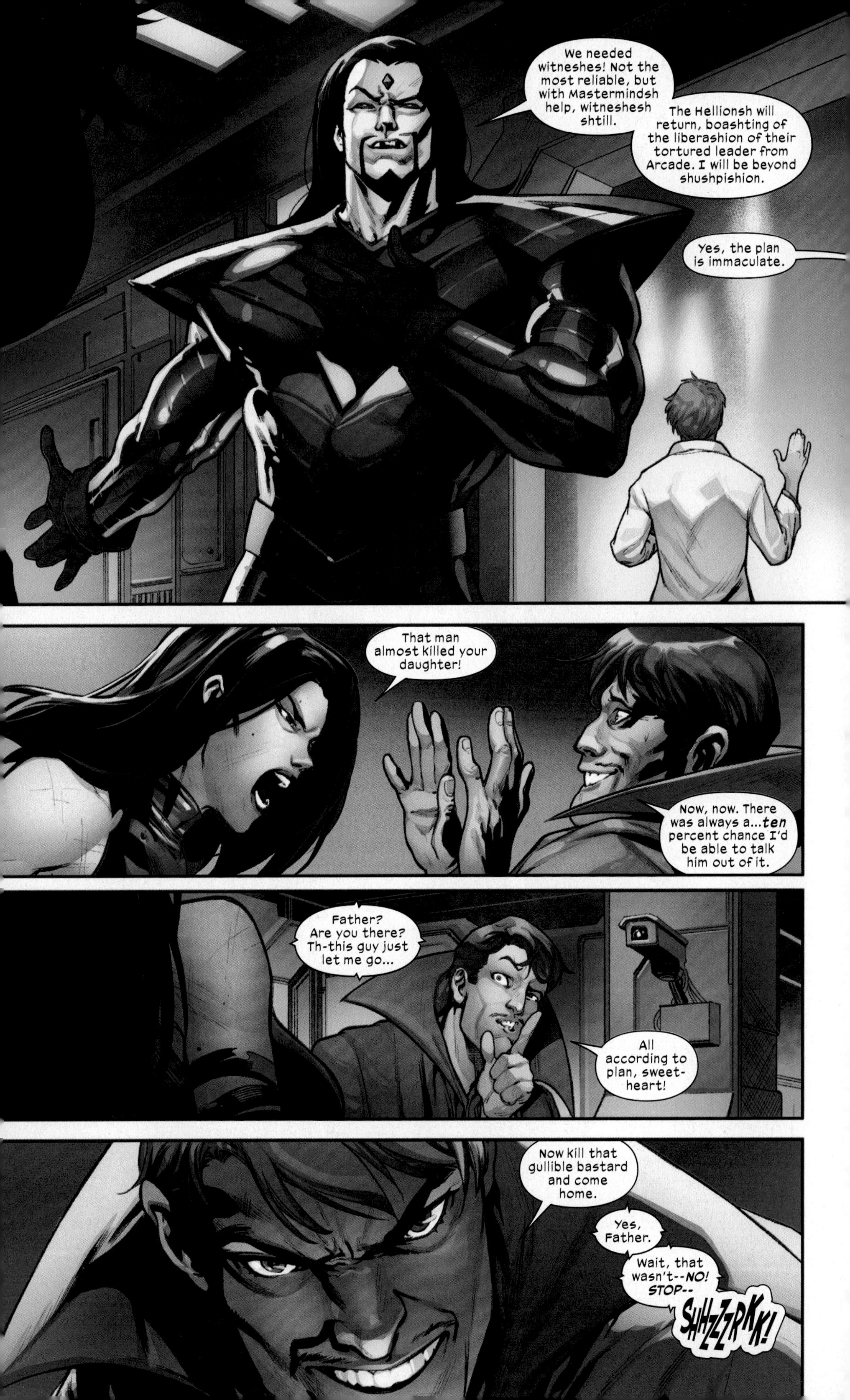
We needed witneshes! Not the most reliable, but with Mastermindsh help, witneshesh shtill.
The Hellionsh will return, boashting of the liberashion of their tortured leader from Arcade. I will be beyond shushpishion.
Yes, the plan is immaculate.
That man almost killed your daughter!
Now, now. There was always a...*ten* percent chance I'd be able to talk him out of it.
Father? Are you there? Th-this guy just let me go...
All according to plan, sweet-heart!
Now kill that gullible bastard and come home.
Yes, Father.
Wait, that wasn't--*NO!* *STOP--*
SHHZZZRKK!

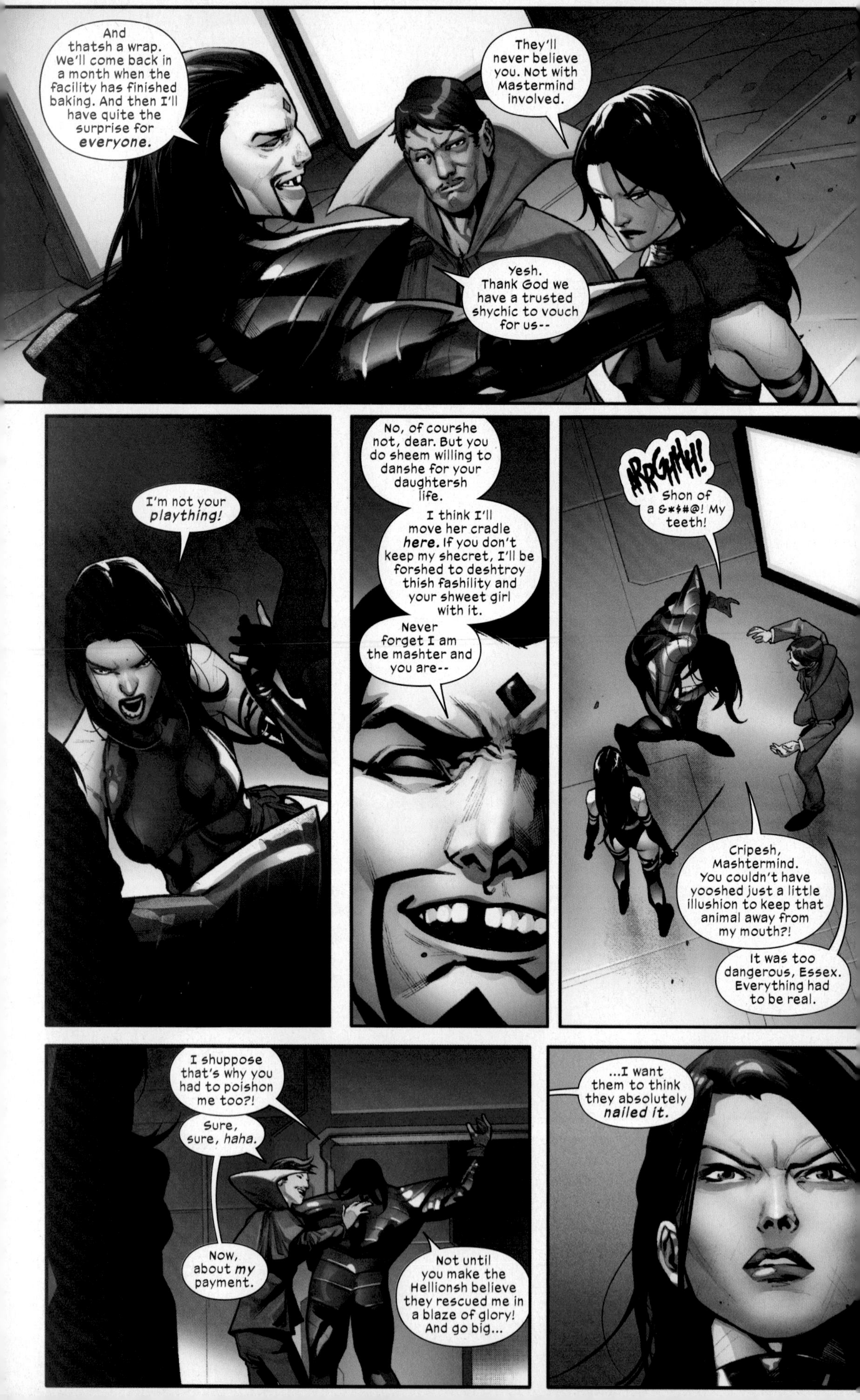
And thatsh a wrap. We'll come back in a month when the facility has finished baking. And then I'll have quite the surprise for *everyone.*
They'll never believe you. Not with Mastermind involved.
Yesh. Thank God we have a trusted shychic to vouch for us--
I'm not your *plaything!*
No, of courshe not, dear. But you do sheem willing to danshe for your daughtersh life.
I think I'll move her cradle **here.** If you don't keep my shecret, I'll be forshed to deshtroy thish fashility and your shweet girl with it.
Never forget I am the mashter and you are--
ARRGHHH!
Shon of a &*$#@! My teeth!
Cripesh, Mashtermind. You couldn't have yooshed just a little illushion to keep that animal away from my mouth?!
It was too dangerous, Essex. Everything had to be real.
I shuppose that's why you had to poishon me too?!
Sure, sure, *haha.*
Now, about *my* payment.
Not until you make the Hellionsh believe they rescued me in a blaze of glory! And go big...
...I want them to think they absolutely *nailed it.*

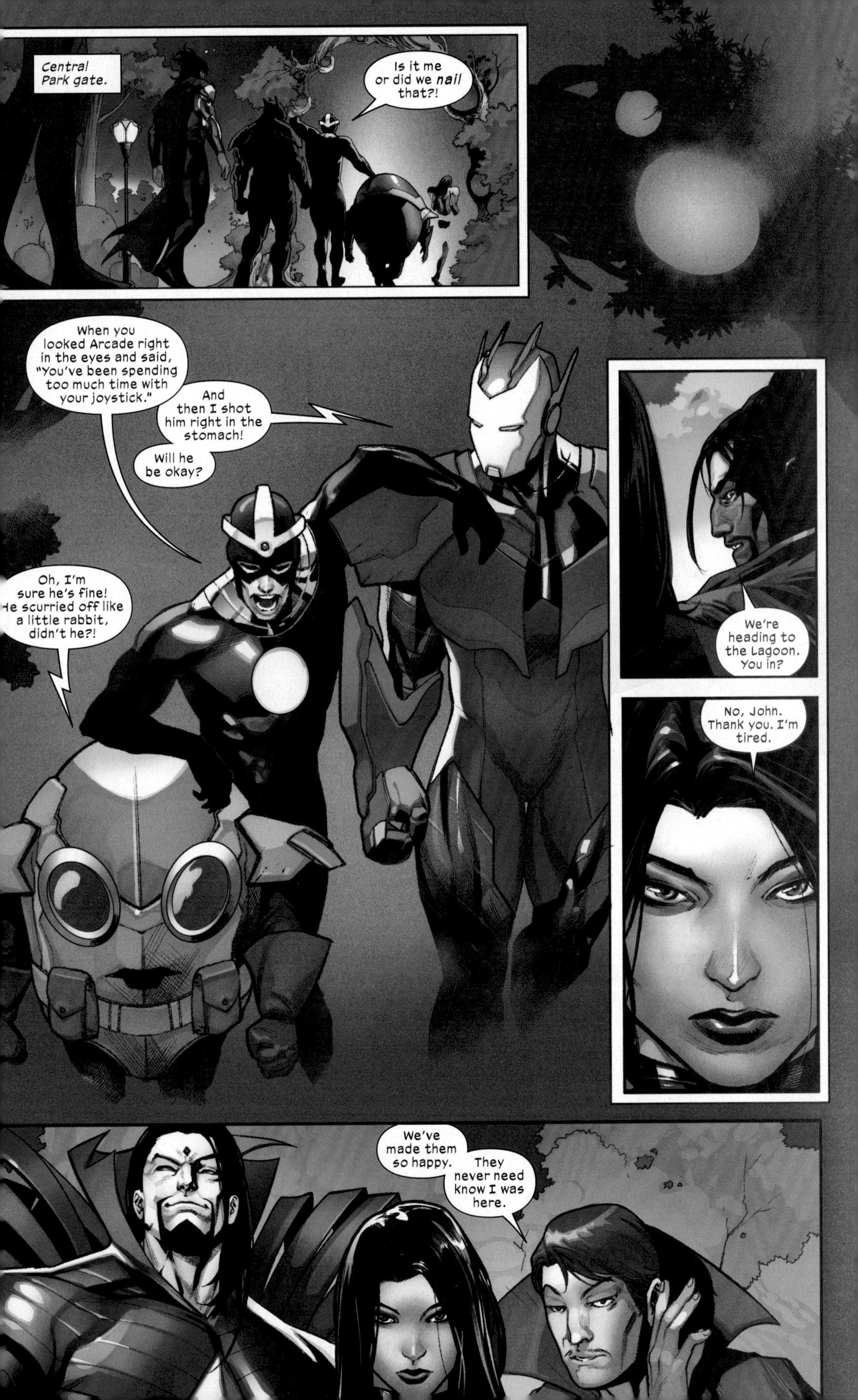

Central Park gate.
Is it me or did we *nail* that?!
When you looked Arcade right in the eyes and said, "You've been spending too much time with your joystick."
And then I shot him right in the stomach!
Will he be okay?
Oh, I'm sure he's fine! He scurried off like a little rabbit, didn't he?!
We're heading to the Lagoon. You in?
No, John. Thank you. I'm tired.
We've made them so happy.
They never need know I was here.

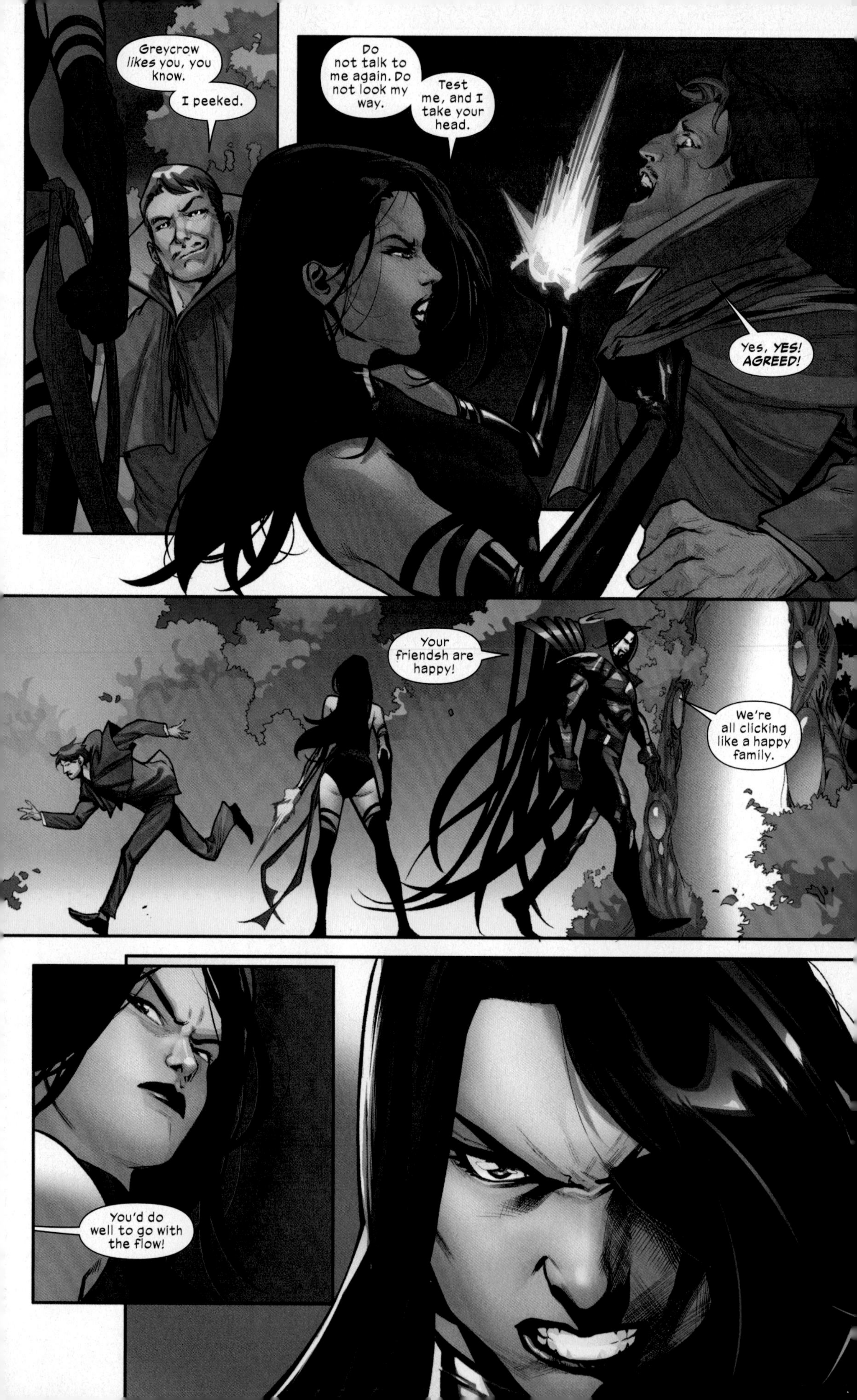
Greycrow *likes* you, you know.
I peeked.
Do not talk to me again. Do not look my way.
Test me, and I take your head.
Yes, ***YES! AGREED!***
Your friendsh are happy!
We're all clicking like a happy family.
You'd do well to go with the flow!

[hell_[0.11]
[ions_[0.11]

I did not say, "Never again." Nor did I think it. Every atom in my body **screamed it.** But the sound was a hollow thing. It was much too late.

-- PSYLOCKE

[hell_[0.XX]
[ions_[0.XX]

[hell_[0.11]....]
[ions_[0.11]....]

[Hellions_alpha.]

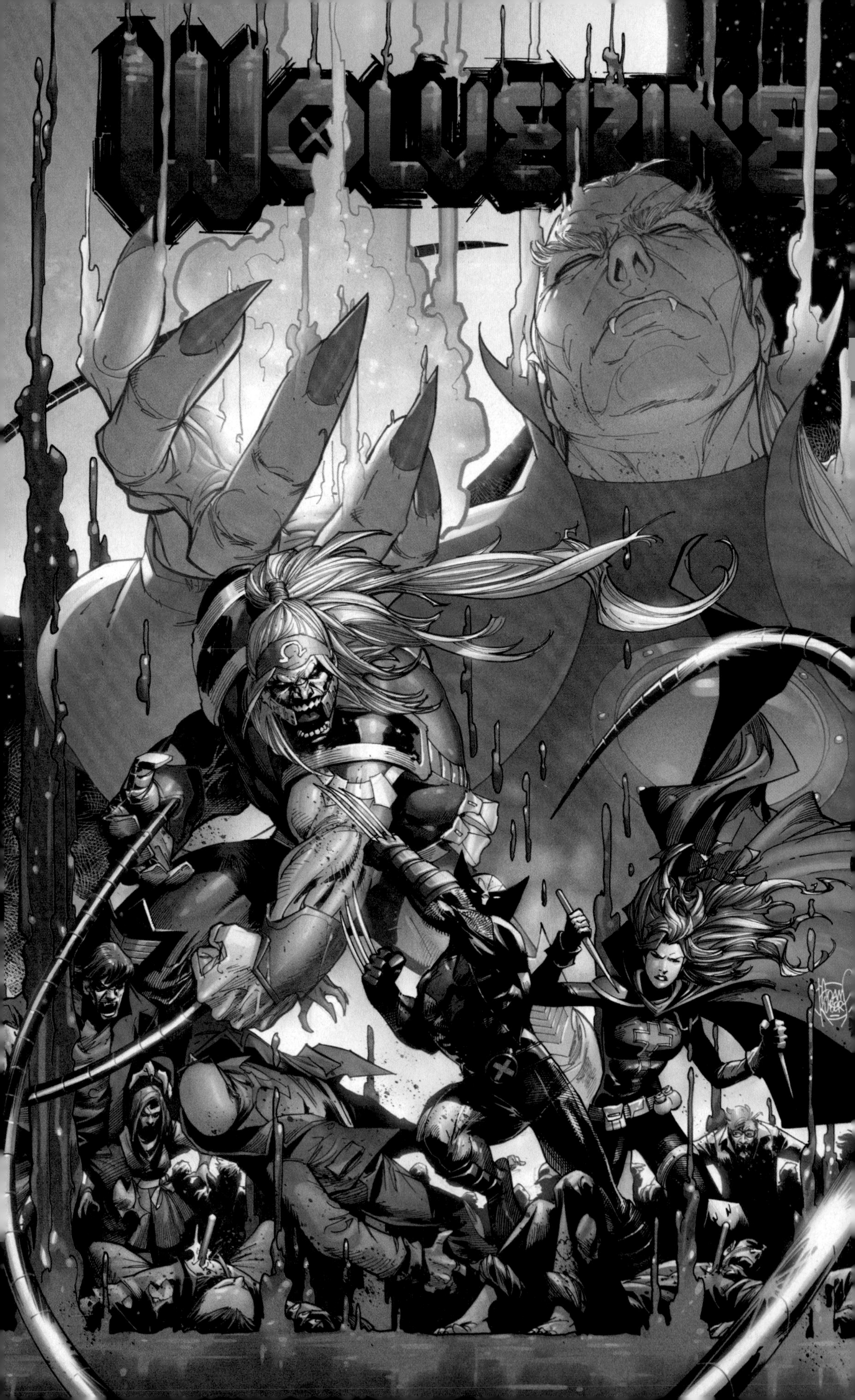
WOLVERINE

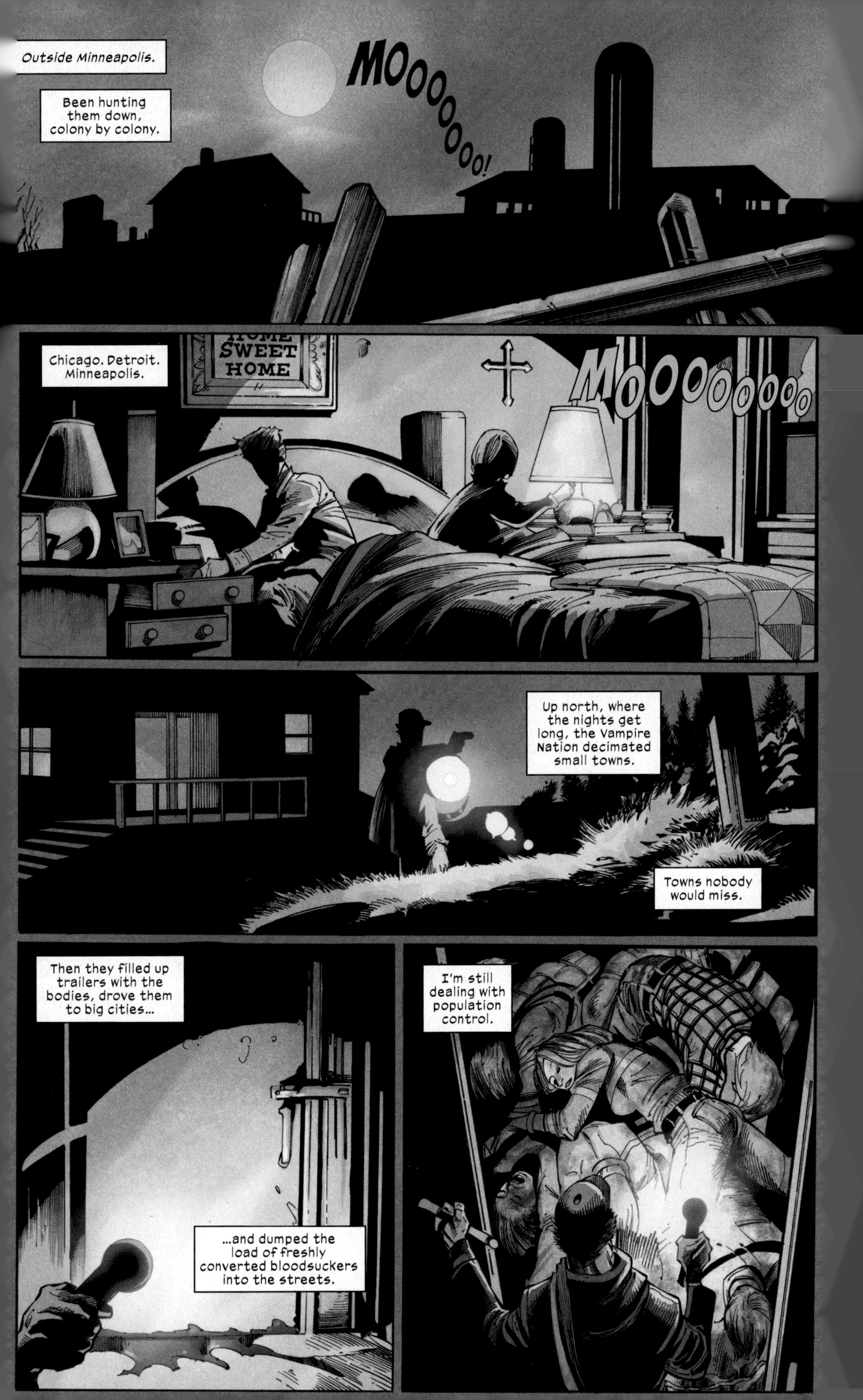
Outside Minneapolis.
Been hunting them down, colony by colony.
MOOOOOOOO!
Chicago. Detroit. Minneapolis.
SWEET HOME
MOOOOOOOO
Up north, where the nights get long, the Vampire Nation decimated small towns.
Towns nobody would miss.
Then they filled up trailers with the bodies, drove them to big cities...
...and dumped the load of freshly converted bloodsuckers into the streets.
I'm still dealing with population control.

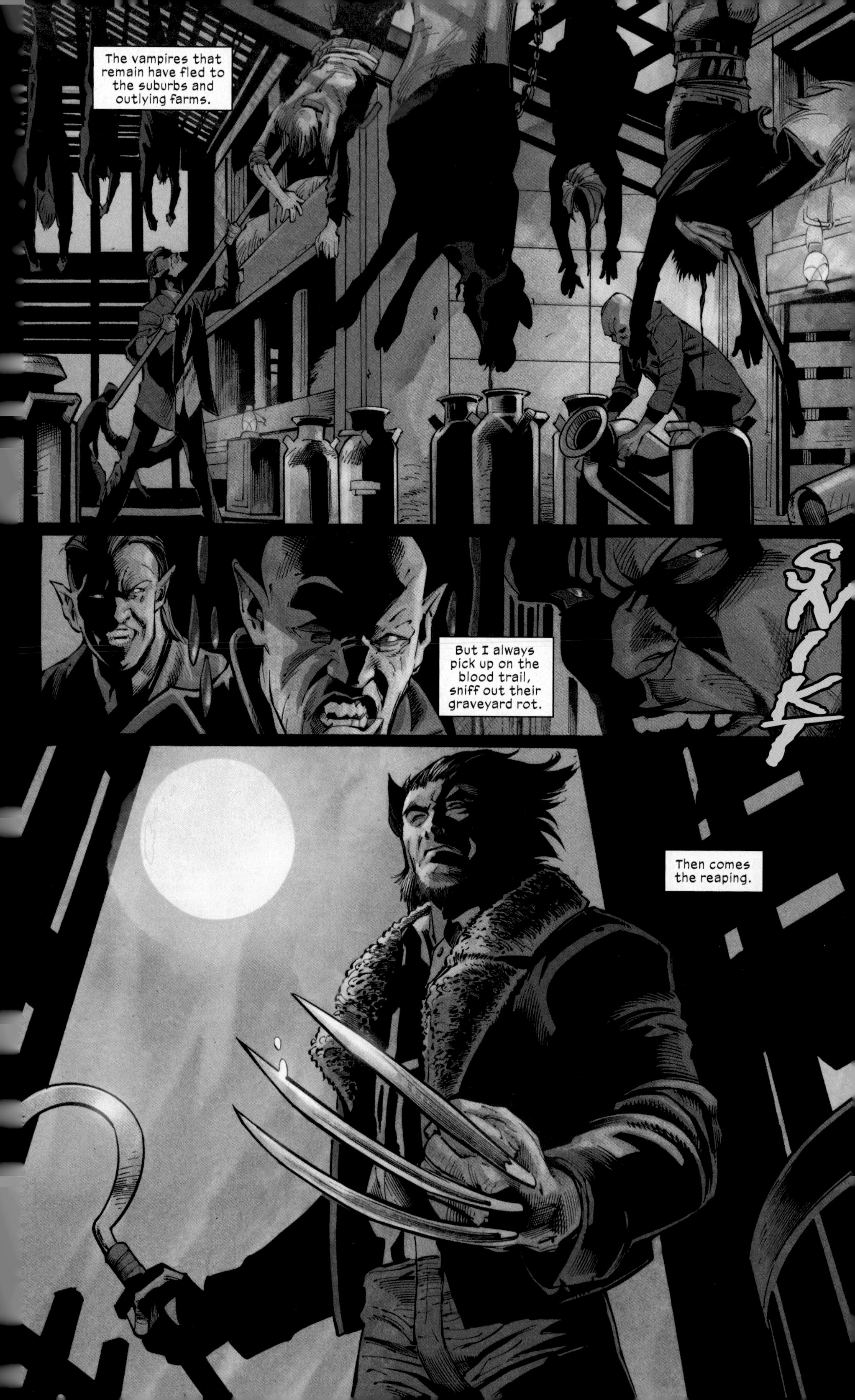

The vampires that remain have fled to the suburbs and outlying farms.
But I always pick up on the blood trail, sniff out their graveyard rot.
SNIKT
Then comes the reaping.

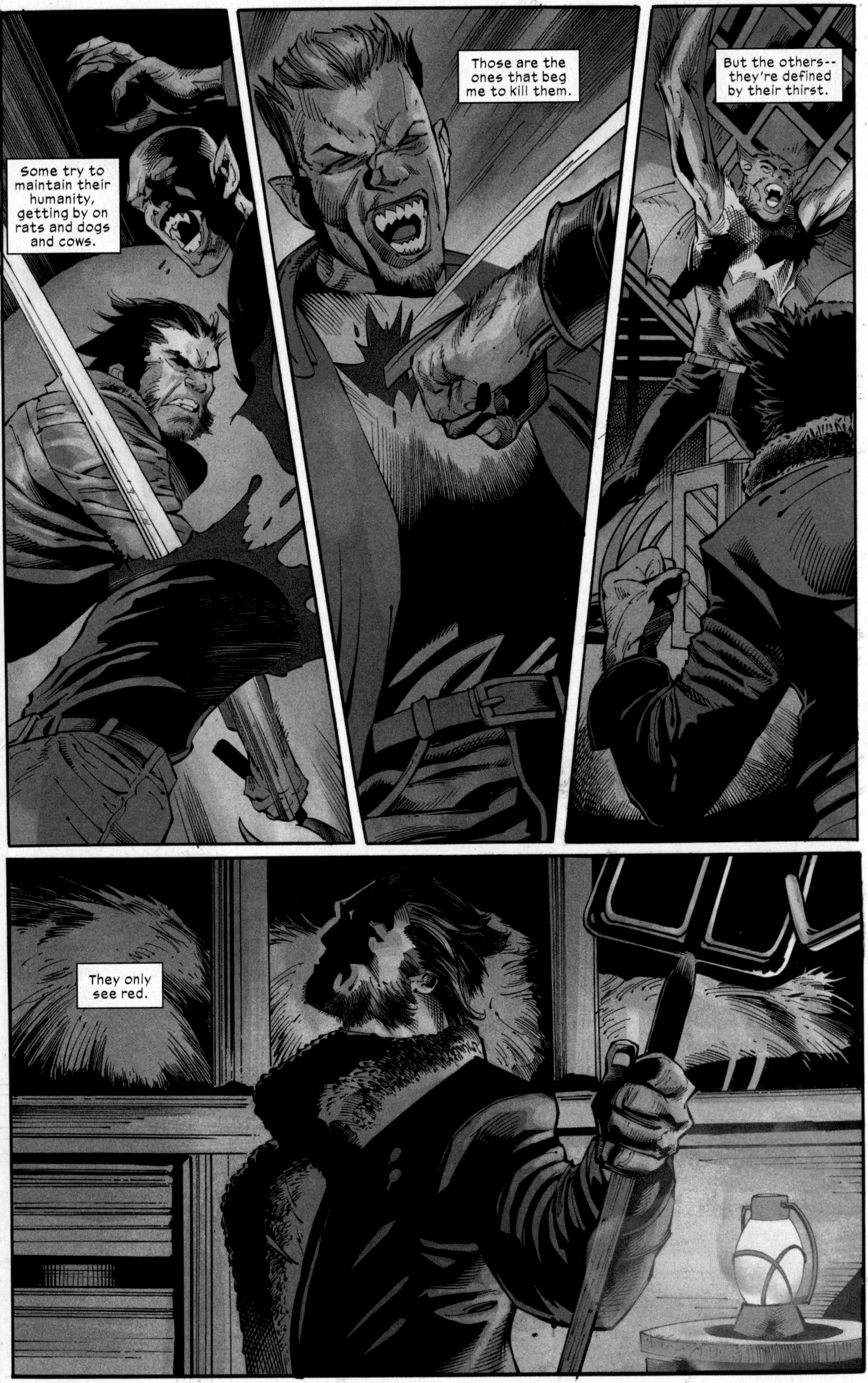
Some try to maintain their humanity, getting by on rats and dogs and cows.
Those are the ones that beg me to kill them.
But the others-- they're defined by their thirst.
They only see red.

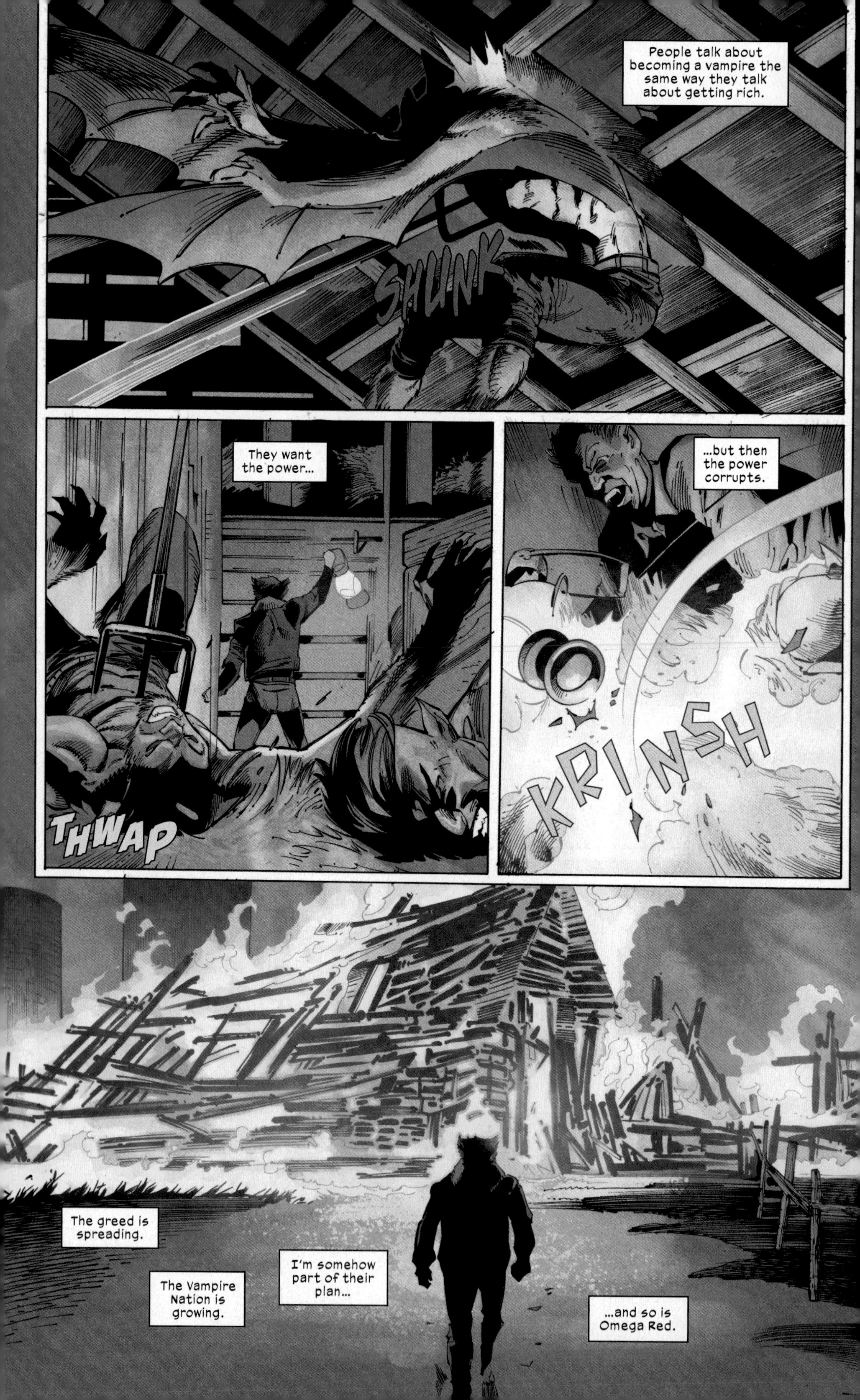
People talk about becoming a vampire the same way they talk about getting rich.
SHUNK
They want the power...
THWAP
...but then the power corrupts.
KRINSH
The greed is spreading.
The Vampire Nation is growing.
I'm somehow part of their plan...
...and so is Omega Red.

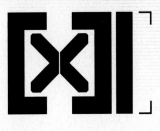

SAGE'S LOGBOOK:
VAMPIRE COLONIES

Rolling Action Item

>> Wolverine requested a so-called vampire algorithm.

>> The program accounts for hospital admissions, police scanners, missing-person cases, missing-pet cases, livestock anomalies, blood bank supplies, and autopsy reports as primary variables.

<<<<ENTRIES>>>>

Detroit, MI. The Brightmoor section of the city -- including residential and commercial properties -- has suffered foreclosure and abandonment. Vampire blight took advantage of vacancy.

> **Wolverine's Report:** "Killed them good and dead."

Minneapolis, MN. Minneapolis was once the flour-milling capital of the world. The empty granaries banking the Mississippi River have been inhabited and now serve as giant roosts.

> **Wolverine's Report:** "Killed them too."

Chicago, IL. At the rail yards, hundreds of train cars rust on abandoned tracks and serve as coffins.

> **Wolverine's Report:** "Hacked off their heads and threw them in a pile and burned them and pissed on the fire to extinguish it."

Buffalo, NY. An abandoned church was hosting rave parties that swiftly decimated a portion of the population (ages 17-25).

> **Wolverine's Report:** "One #%&@ got away. Put down the rest. Then I got some wings."

<<<Surveillance: Ongoing>>>

[00_best_]
[00_there]

THE WOLVERINE ELIXIR

In the dark corners of the world, the Vampire Nation has been amassing power and resources under the leadership of Dracula. After securing samples of Wolverine's blood, aided by their own mutant sleeper agent, Omega Red, Dracula and his bloodsucking followers are closer than ever to rising up and stepping out of the shadows.

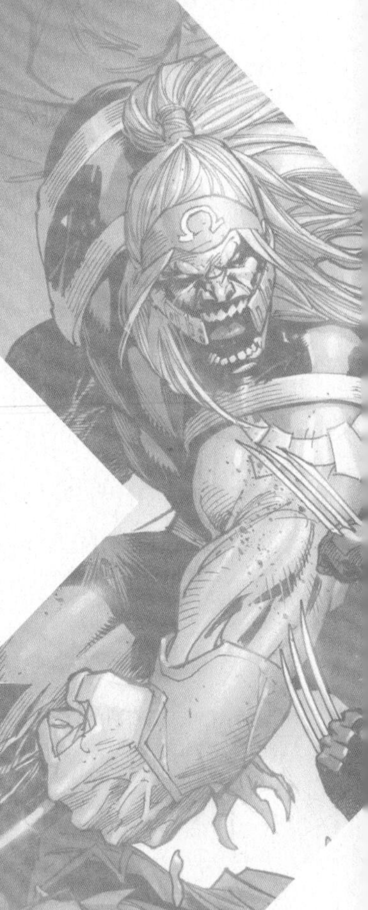

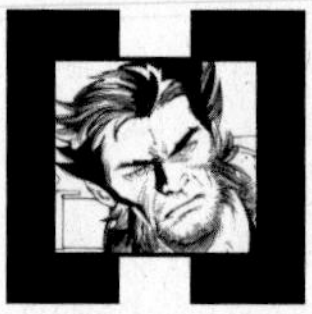
Wolverine

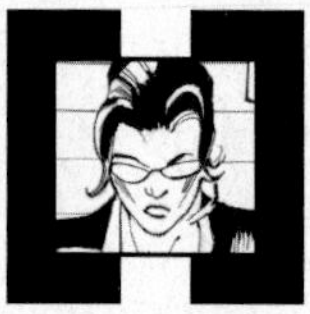
Sage

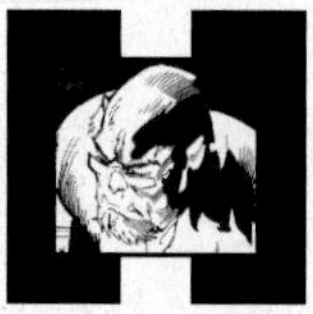
Beast

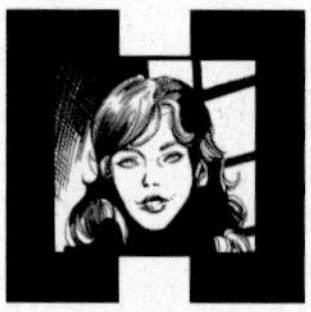
Louise

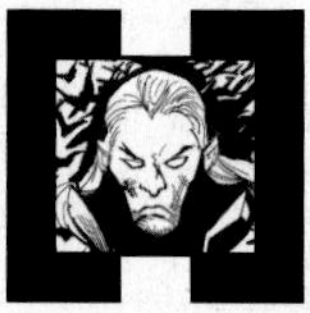
Dracula

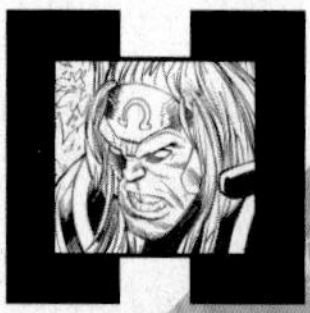
Omega Red

WOLVERINE [X_11]

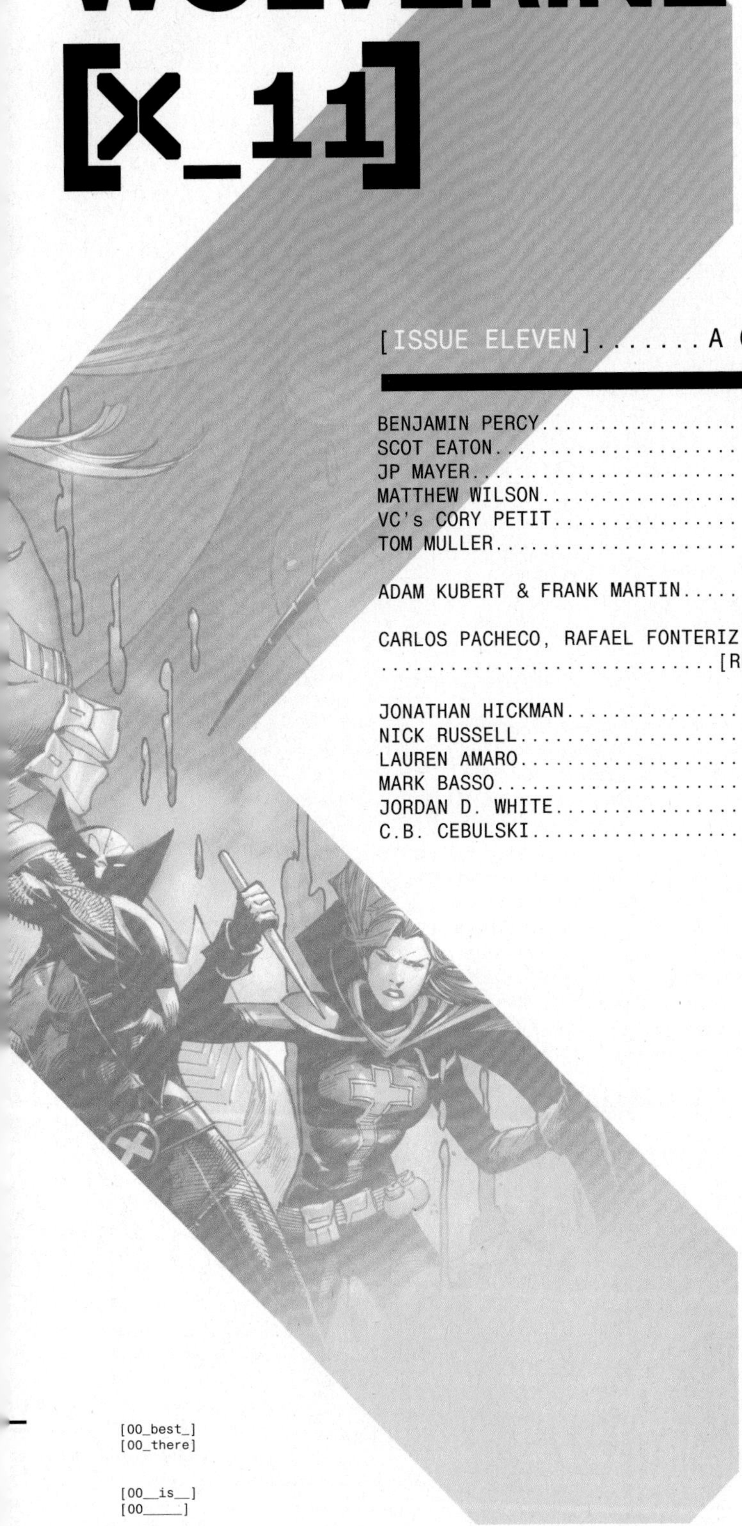

[ISSUE ELEVEN]........A CONFUSION OF MONSTERS

BENJAMIN PERCY..[WRITER]
SCOT EATON...[PENCILER]
JP MAYER...[INKER]
MATTHEW WILSON...............................[COLOR ARTIST]
VC's CORY PETIT.....................................[LETTERER]
TOM MULLER...[DESIGN]

ADAM KUBERT & FRANK MARTIN..................[COVER ARTISTS]

CARLOS PACHECO, RAFAEL FONTERIZ & MATT MILLA...............
..............................[REBORN VARIANT COVER ARTISTS]

JONATHAN HICKMAN...................................[HEAD OF X]
NICK RUSSELL......................................[PRODUCTION]
LAUREN AMARO.............................[ASSISTANT EDITOR]
MARK BASSO...[EDITOR]
JORDAN D. WHITE..............................[SENIOR EDITOR]
C.B. CEBULSKI.............................[EDITOR IN CHIEF]

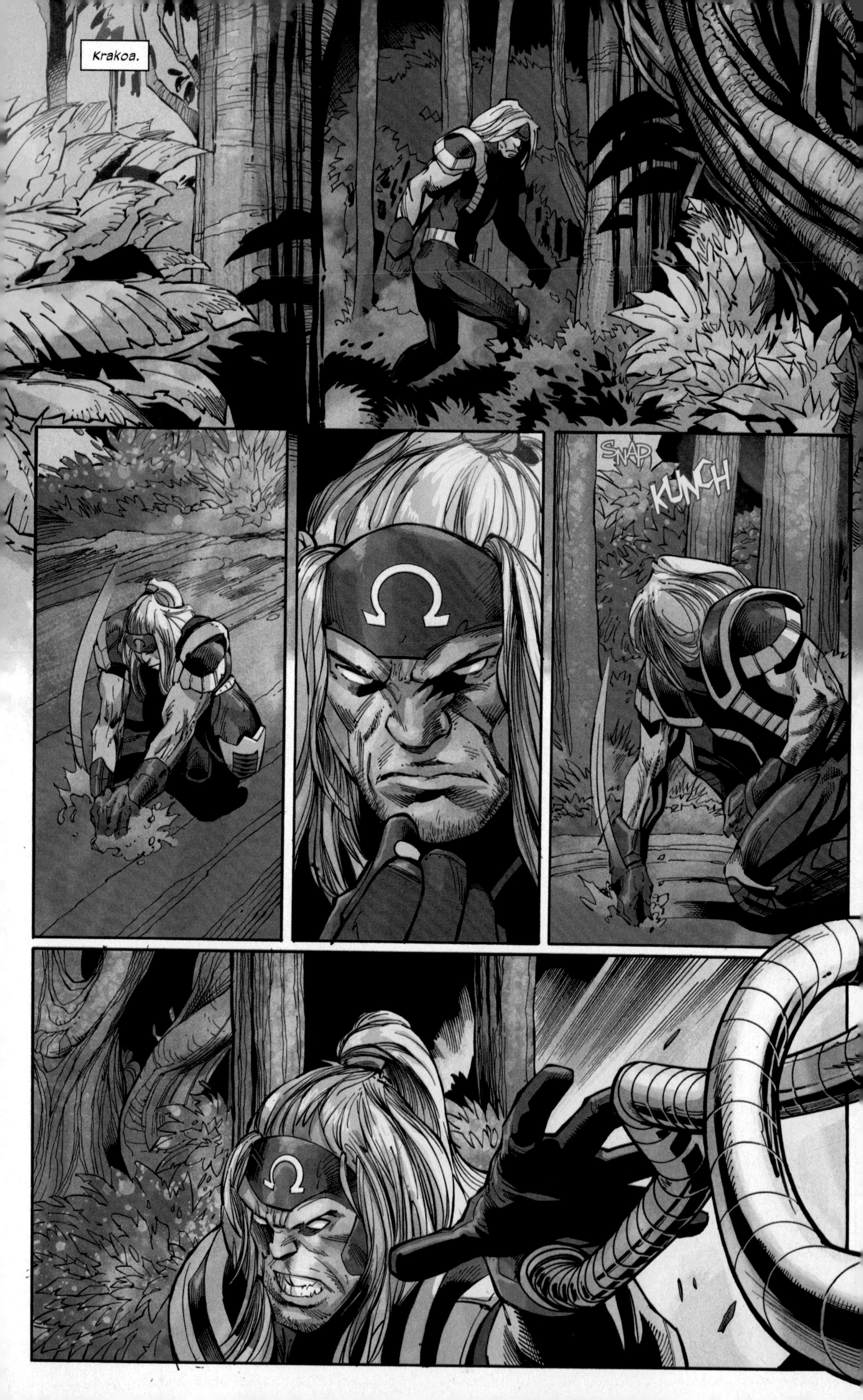
Krakoa.
SNAP
KUNCH

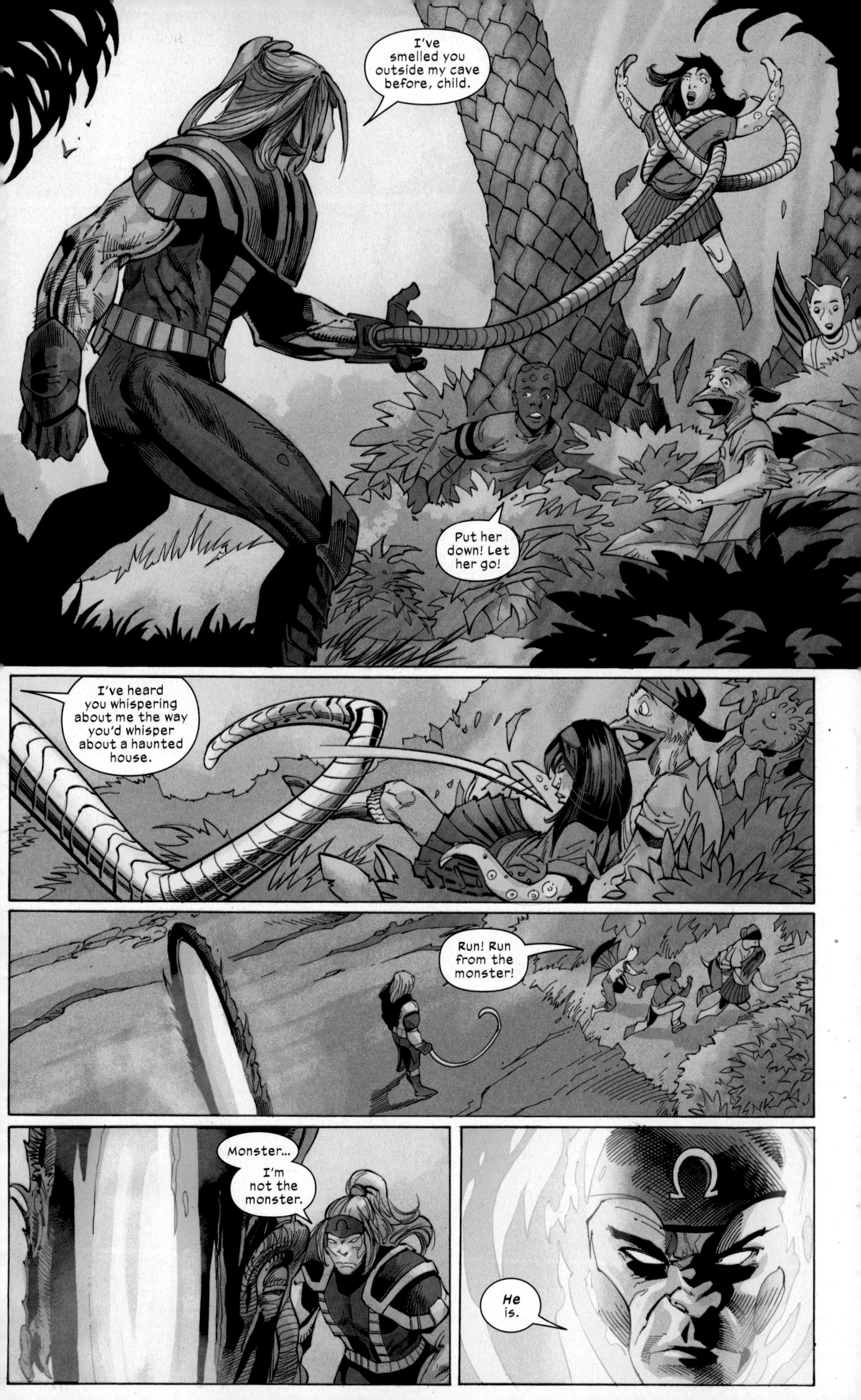

I've smelled you outside my cave before, child.
Put her down! Let her go!
I've heard you whispering about me the way you'd whisper about a haunted house.
Run! Run from the monster!
Monster...
I'm not the monster.
He is.

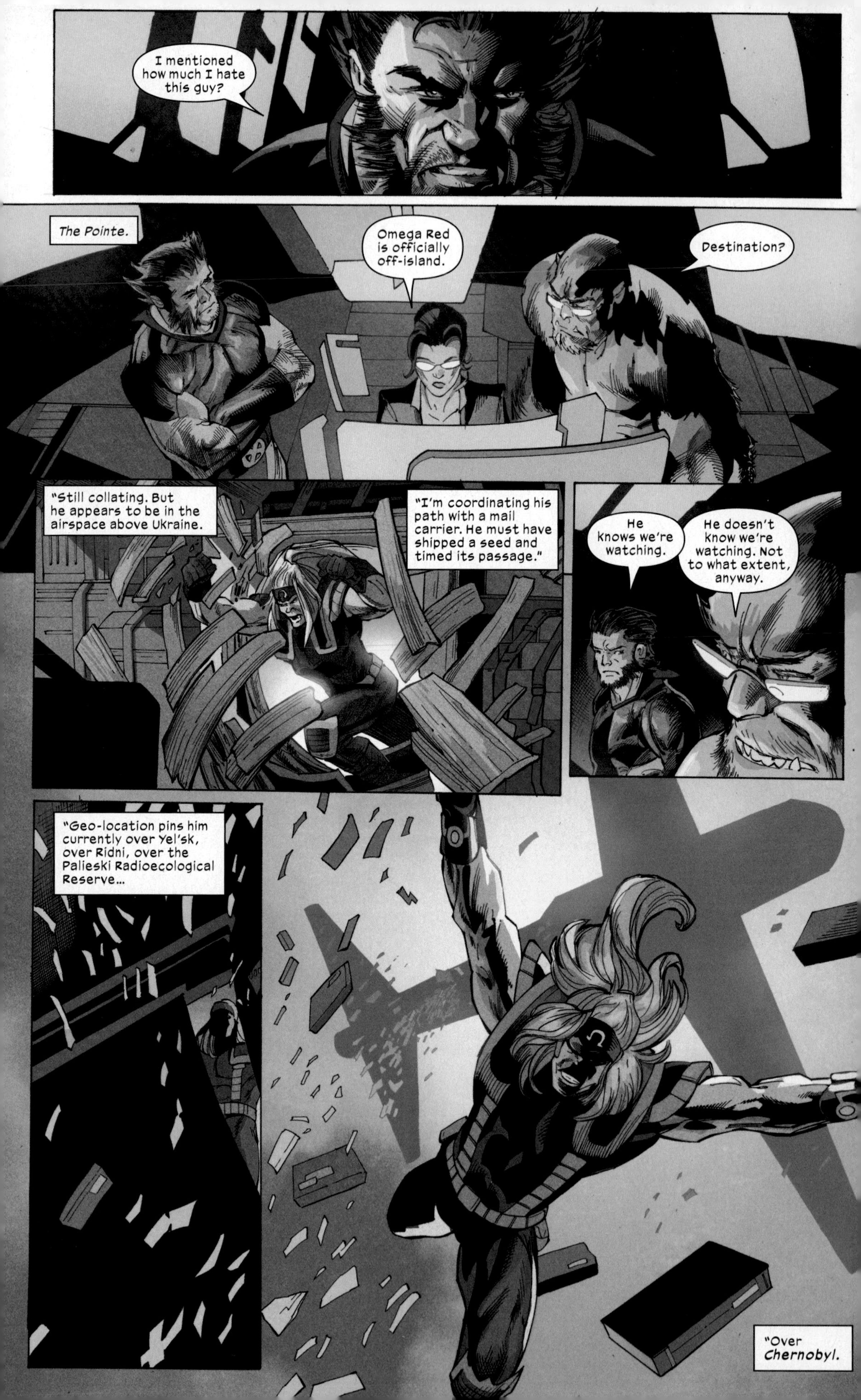

I mentioned how much I hate this guy?
The Pointe.
Omega Red is officially off-island.
Destination?
"Still collating. But he appears to be in the airspace above Ukraine.
"I'm coordinating his path with a mail carrier. He must have shipped a seed and timed its passage."
He knows we're watching.
He doesn't know we're watching. Not to what extent, anyway.
"Geo-location pins him currently over Yel'sk, over Ridni, over the Palieski Radioecological Reserve...
"Over *Chernobyl*.

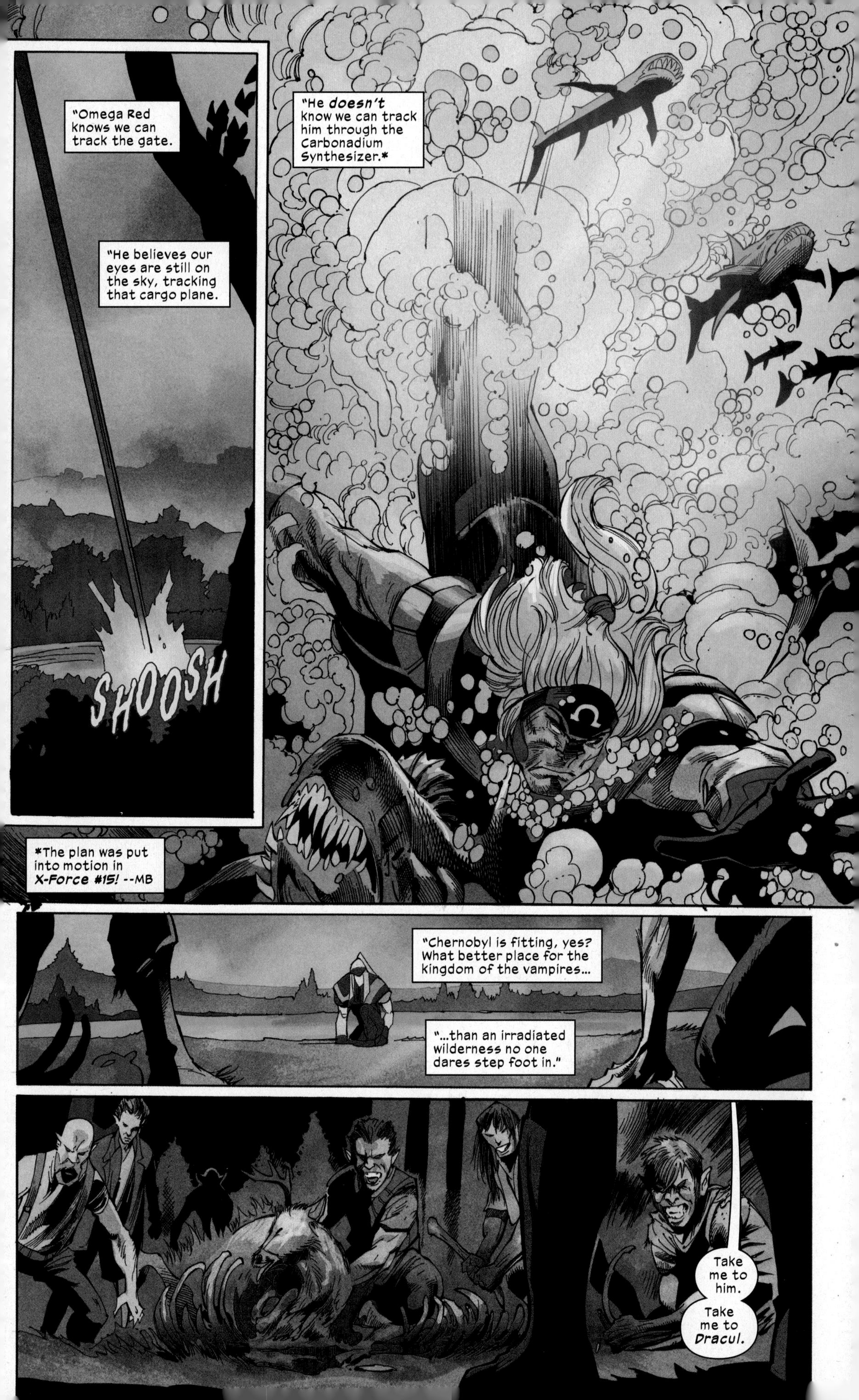
"Omega Red knows we can track the gate.
"He believes our eyes are still on the sky, tracking that cargo plane.
SHOOSH
"He *doesn't* know we can track him through the Carbonadium Synthesizer.*
*The plan was put into motion in *X-Force #15!* --MB
"Chernobyl is fitting, yes? What better place for the kingdom of the vampires...
"...than an irradiated wilderness no one dares step foot in."
Take me to him.
Take me to *Dracul.*

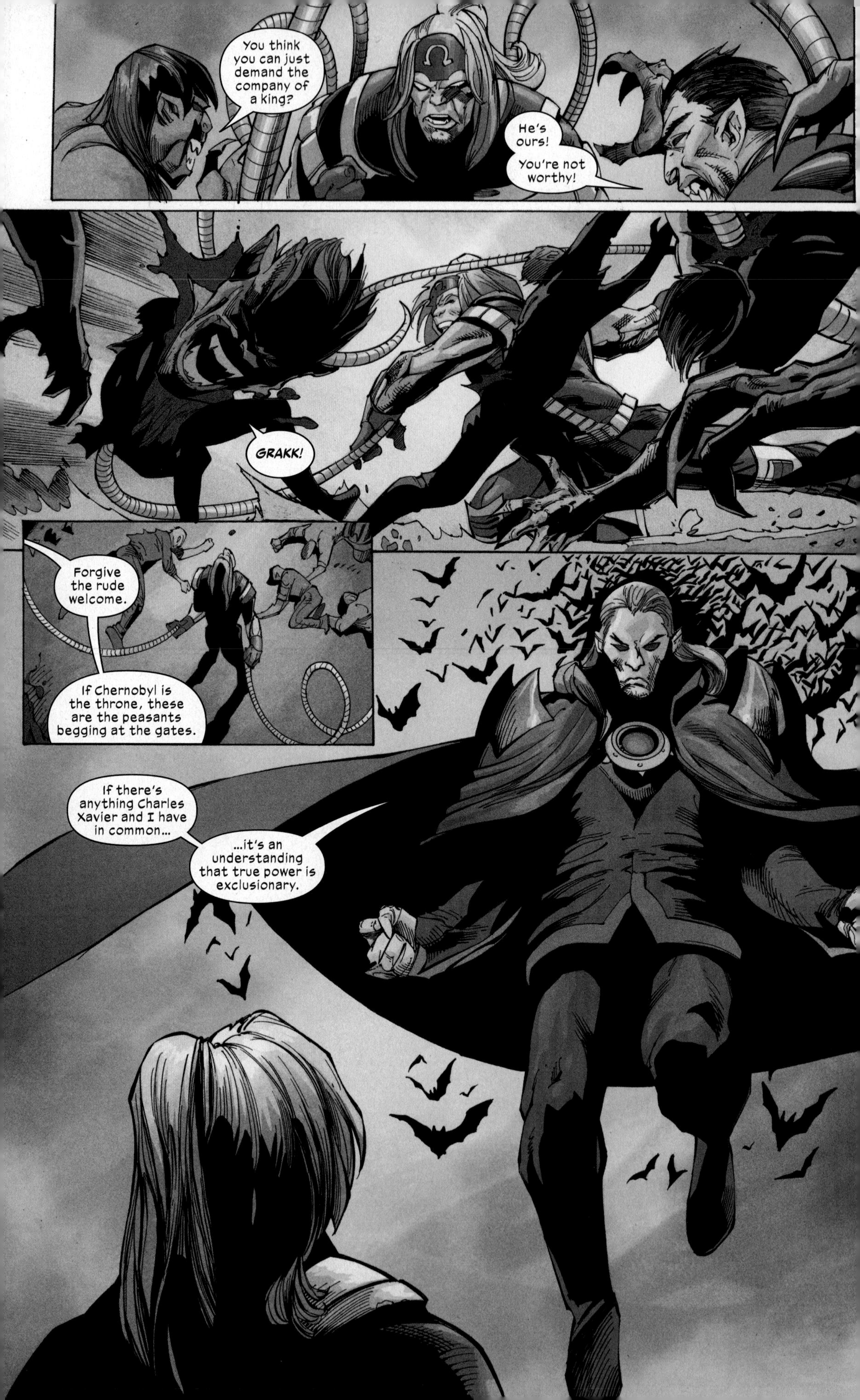
You think you can just demand the company of a king?
He's ours!
You're not worthy!
GRAKK!
Forgive the rude welcome.
If Chernobyl is the throne, these are the peasants begging at the gates.
If there's anything Charles Xavier and I have in common...
...it's an understanding that true power is exclusionary.

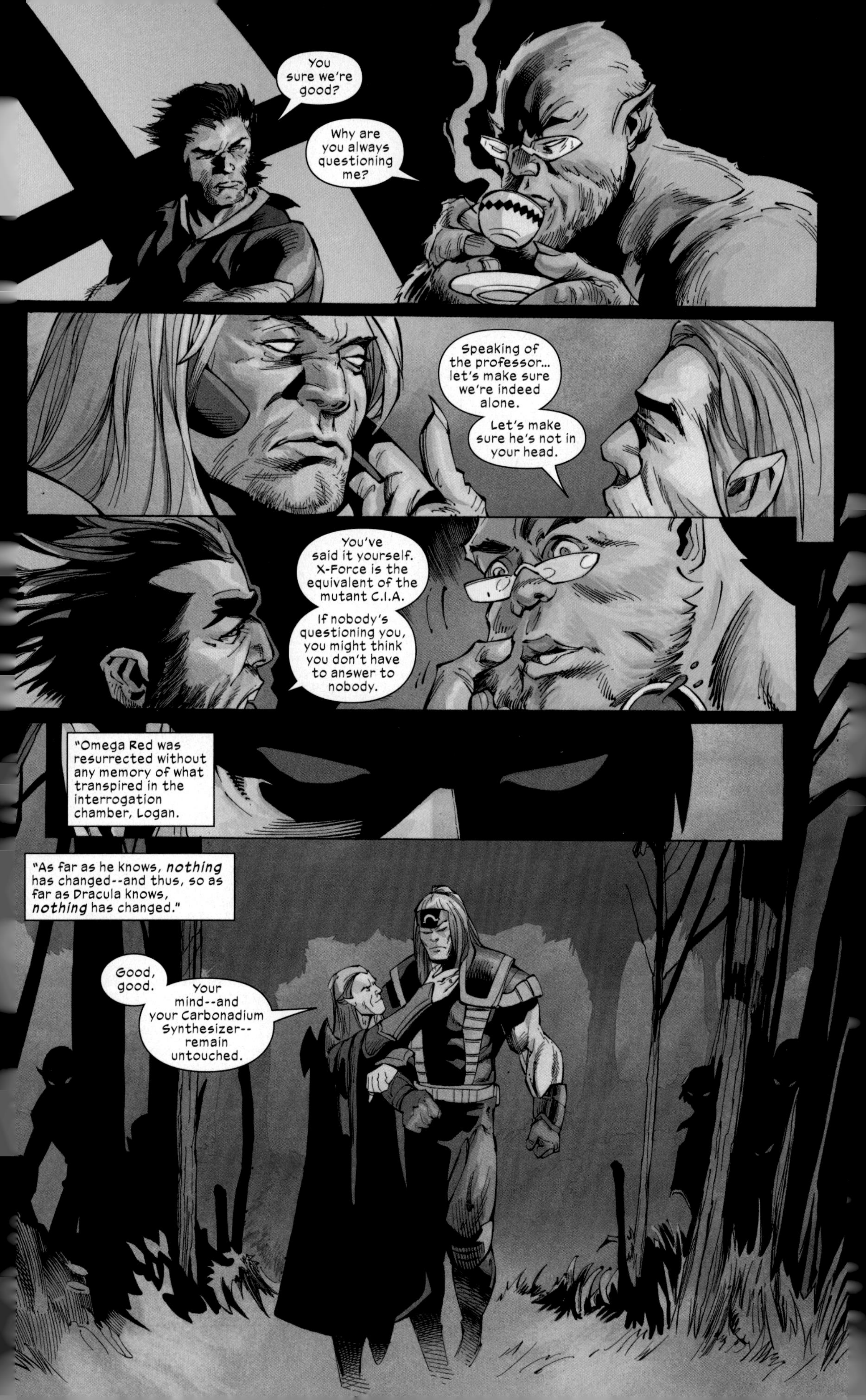
You sure we're good?
Why are you always questioning me?
Speaking of the professor... let's make sure we're indeed alone.
Let's make sure he's not in your head.
You've said it yourself. X-Force is the equivalent of the mutant C.I.A.
If nobody's questioning you, you might think you don't have to answer to nobody.
"Omega Red was resurrected without any memory of what transpired in the interrogation chamber, Logan.
"As far as he knows, *nothing* has changed--and thus, so as far as Dracula knows, *nothing* has changed."
Good, good.
Your mind--and your Carbonadium Synthesizer--remain untouched.

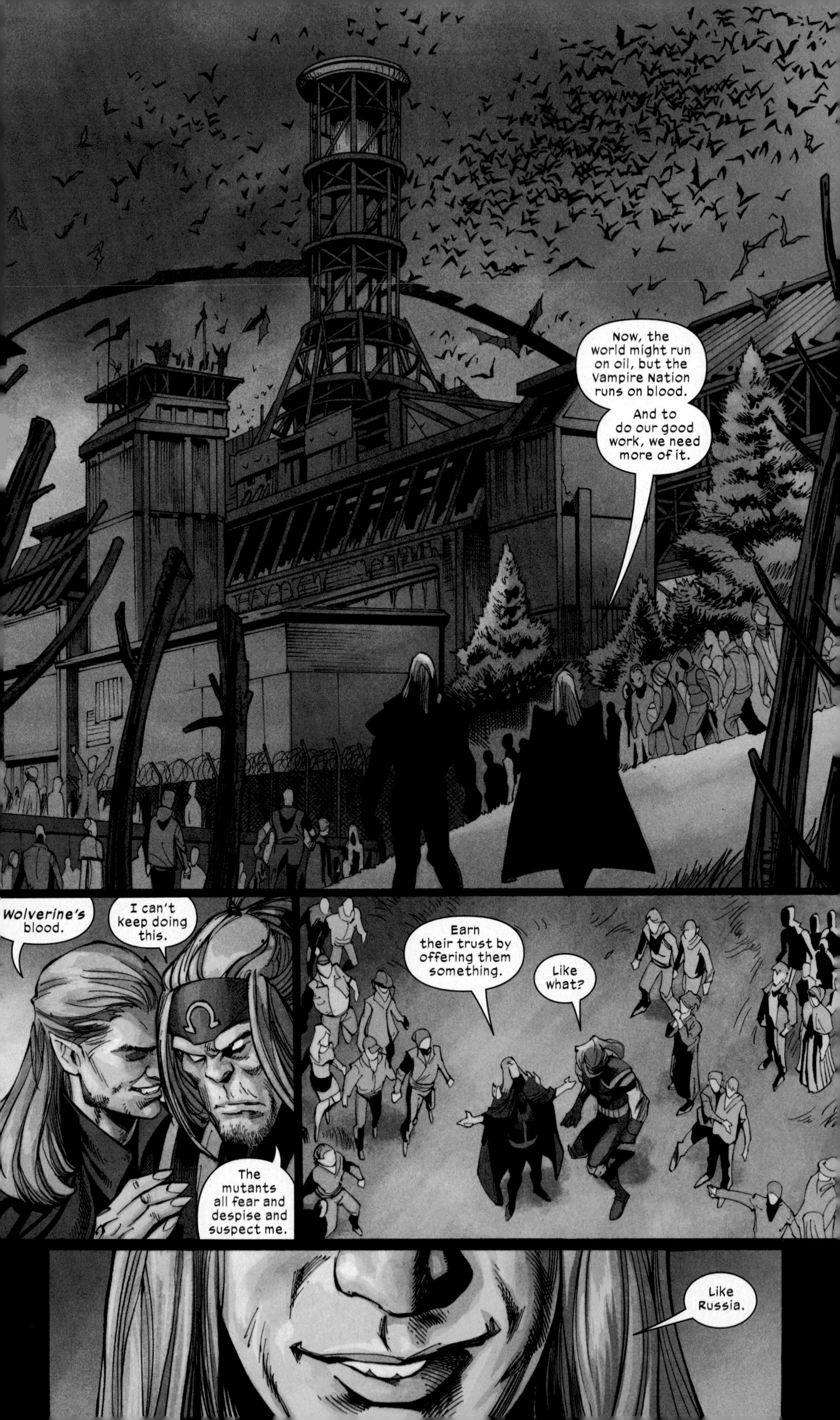
Now, the world might run on oil, but the Vampire Nation runs on blood.
And to do our good work, we need more of it.
Wolverine's blood.
I can't keep doing this.
The mutants all fear and despise and suspect me.
Earn their trust by offering them something.
Like what?
Like Russia.

SAGE'S LOGBOOK:
THE HEAD AND THE FIST

Weekly Briefing between Intelligence and Field Operations
Subject: Vampire Nation
Transcript:

BEAST: I have a rather unorthodox idea.

> **WOLVERINE:** Sounds sketchy.

BEAST: Have you ever heard of KP4?

> **WOLVERINE:** Why do you even bother asking questions you're going to answer?

BEAST: It's a toxin. It's also a fungus that eats other fungi. Agricultural companies are constantly trying to come up with ways to prevent crop failure. And rather than taking a defensive route, which is their standard strategy, they recently made a brilliant offensive move. They wove a strain of KP4 into the genomic sequence of their corn.

> **WOLVERINE:** ...

BEAST: Don't you see? They fought infection with an infection of their own.

> **WOLVERINE:** ...

BEAST: We've made it into Chernobyl so far using deception. Let's continue on that same tack.

> **WOLVERINE:** ...

BEAST: They want you, yes? So I say let's offer you up on a platter. But what we'll do is --

> **WOLVERINE:** No.

BEAST: I don't think you're following me.

> **WOLVERINE:** I like my way better. Stabbing.

BEAST: Your way is slow, inefficient, and positively medieval.

> **WOLVERINE:** Stabbing. Hacking. Slashing.

BEAST: This can't possibly be the extent of your plan.

> **WOLVERINE:** Don't worry. There's another weapon I'm adding to the arsenal.

BEAST: And which weapon would that be?

> **WOLVERINE:** Name's Louise. Lives in Paris.

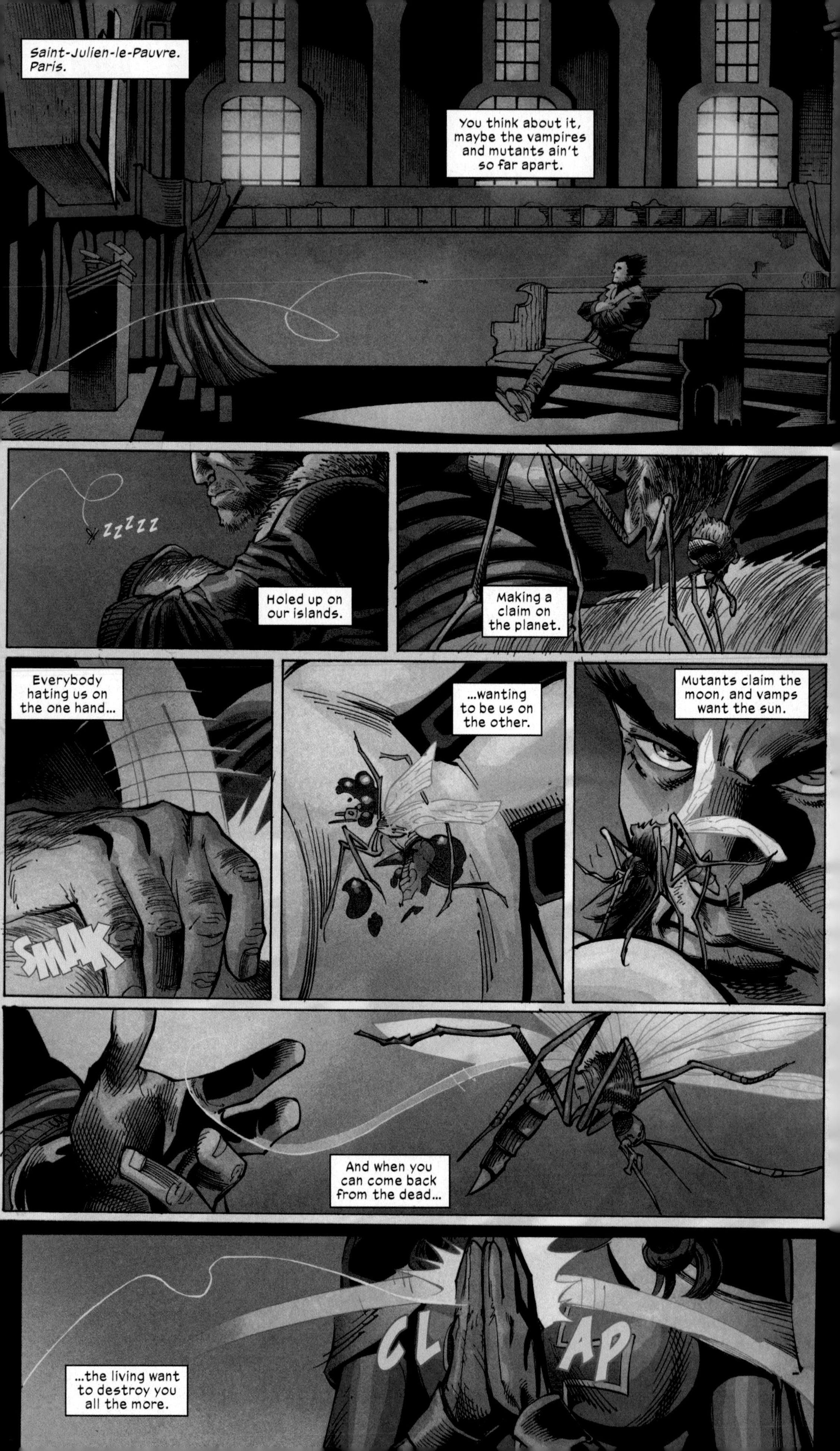
Saint-Julien-le-Pauvre.
Paris.
You think about it, maybe the vampires and mutants ain't so far apart.
ZZZZZ
Holed up on our islands.
Making a claim on the planet.
Everybody hating us on the one hand...
SMAK
...wanting to be us on the other.
Mutants claim the moon, and vamps want the sun.
And when you can come back from the dead...
CL
AP
...the living want to destroy you all the more.

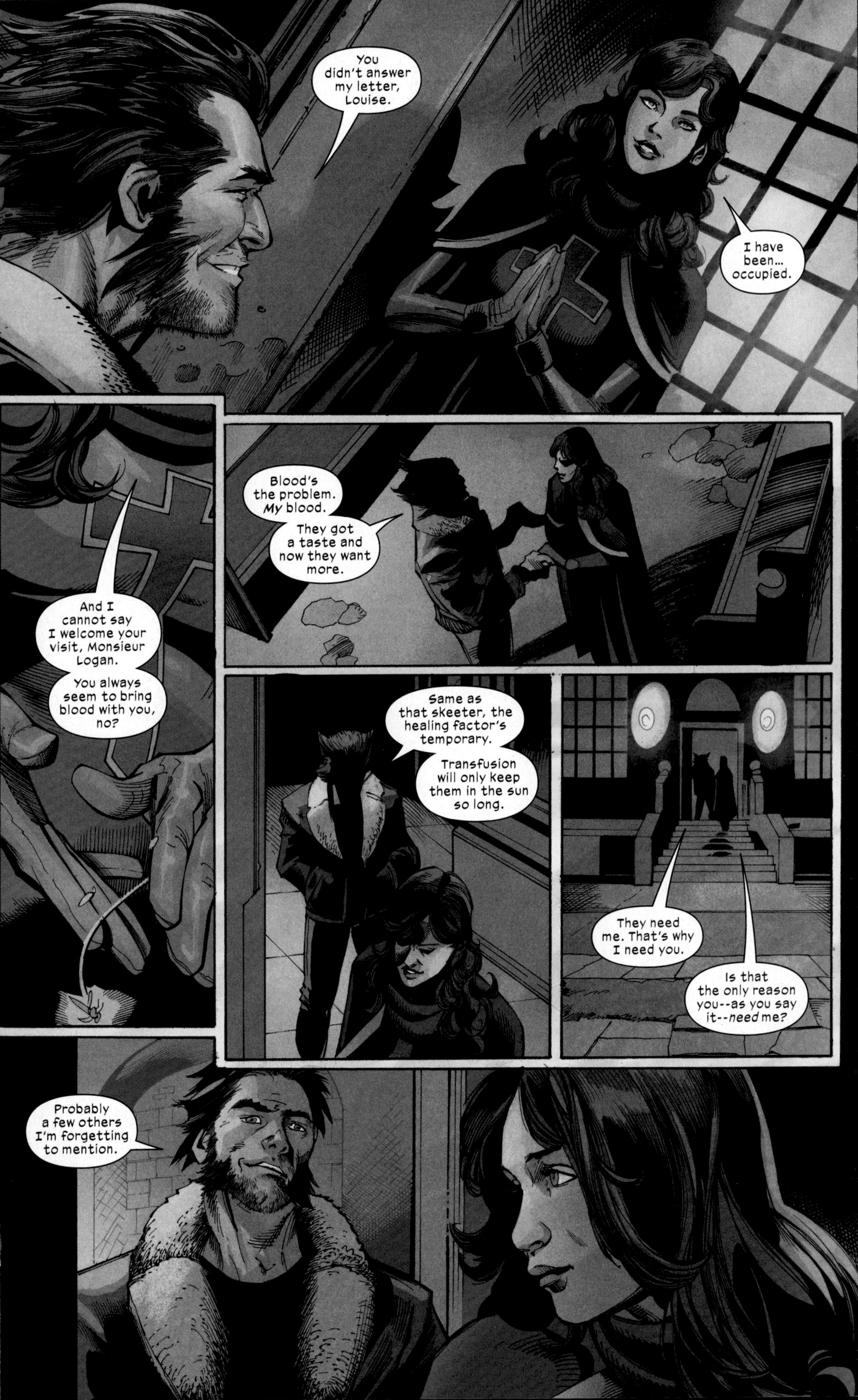
You didn't answer my letter, Louise.
I have been... occupied.
And I cannot say I welcome your visit, Monsieur Logan.
You always seem to bring blood with you, no?
Blood's the problem. *My* blood.
They got a taste and now they want more.
Same as that skeeter, the healing factor's temporary.
Transfusion will only keep them in the sun so long.
They need me. That's why I need you.
Is that the only reason you--as you say it--*need* me?
Probably a few others I'm forgetting to mention.

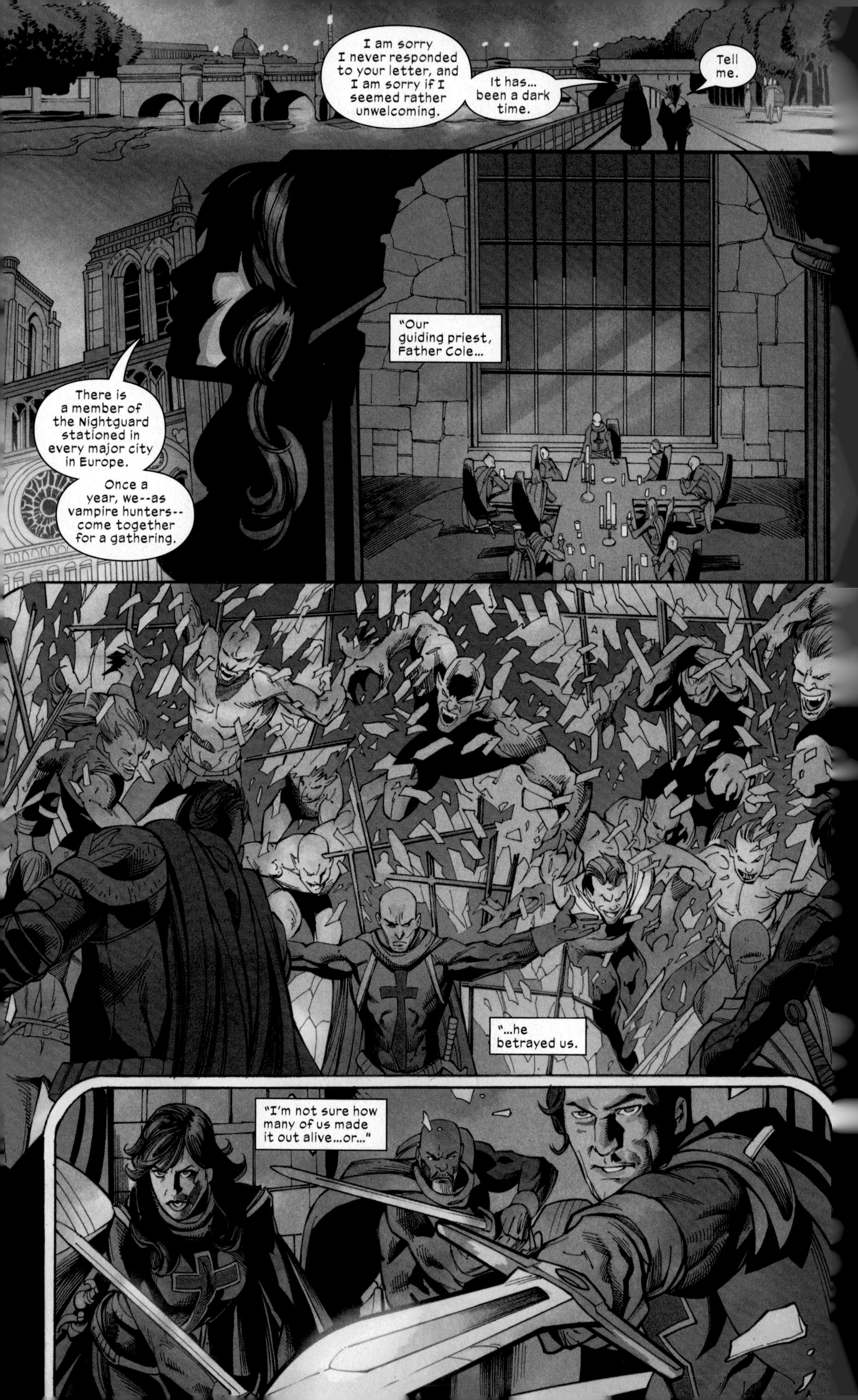

I am sorry I never responded to your letter, and I am sorry if I seemed rather unwelcoming.
It has... been a dark time.
Tell me.
There is a member of the Nightguard stationed in every major city in Europe.
Once a year, we--as vampire hunters--come together for a gathering.
"Our guiding priest, Father Cole...
"...he betrayed us.
"I'm not sure how many of us made it out alive...or..."

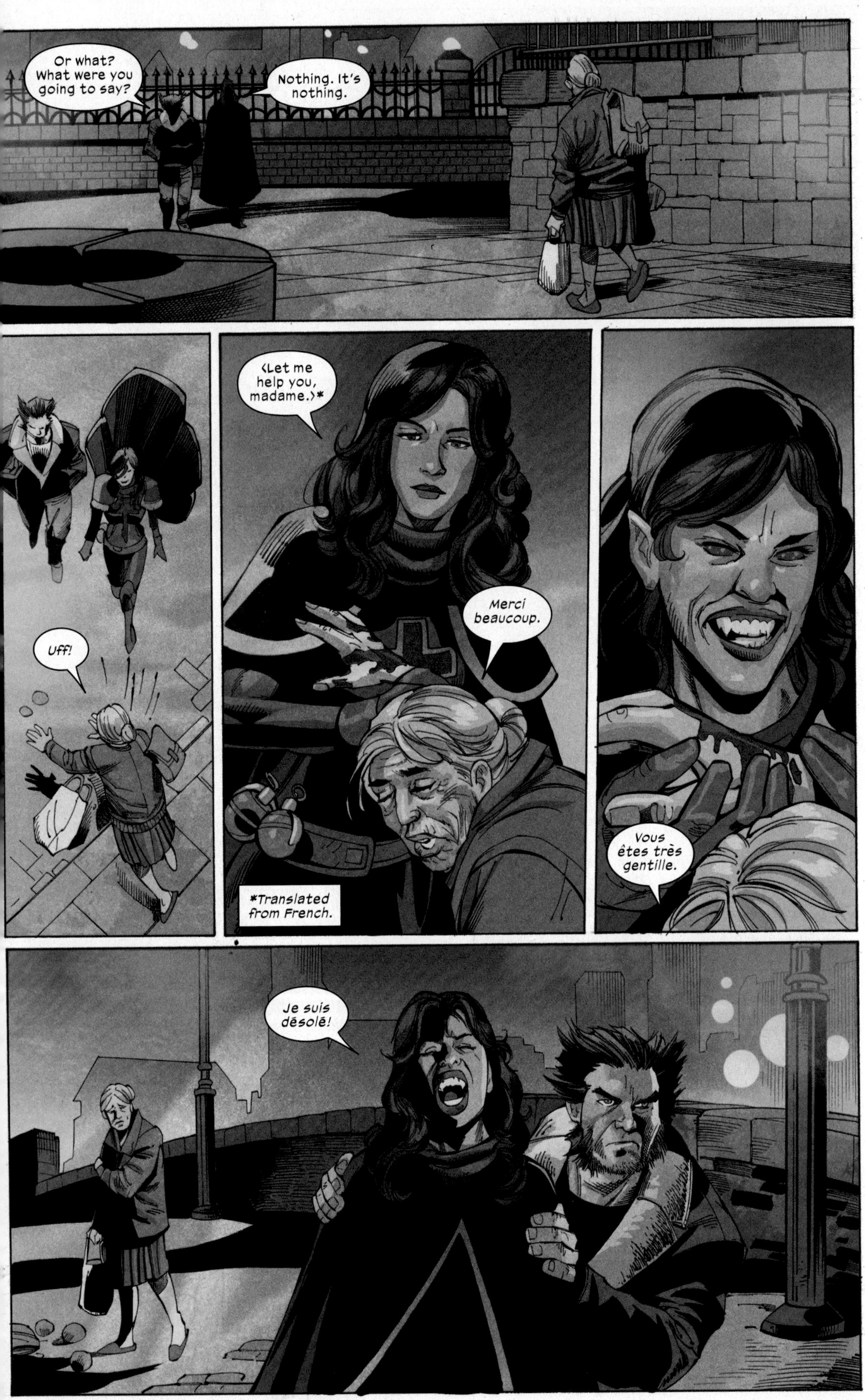

Or what? What were you going to say?
Nothing. It's nothing.
Uff!
‹Let me help you, madame.›*
Merci beaucoup.
*Translated from French.
Vous êtes très gentille.
Je suis désolé!

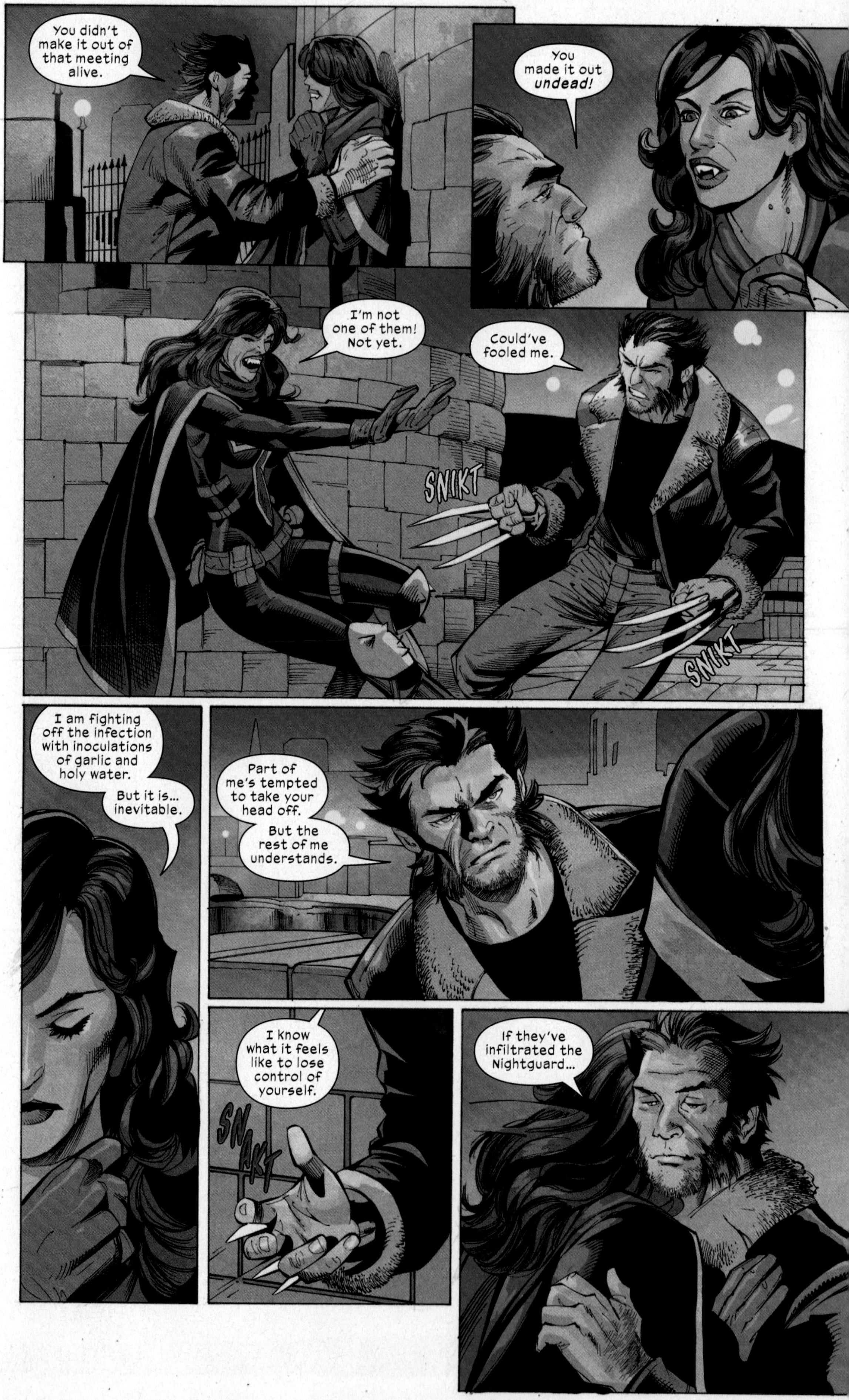

You didn't make it out of that meeting alive.
You made it out *undead!*
I'm not one of them! Not yet.
Could've fooled me.
SNIKT
SNIKT
I am fighting off the infection with inoculations of garlic and holy water.
But it is... inevitable.
Part of me's tempted to take your head off.
But the rest of me understands.
I know what it feels like to lose control of yourself.
SNAKT
If they've infiltrated the Nightguard...

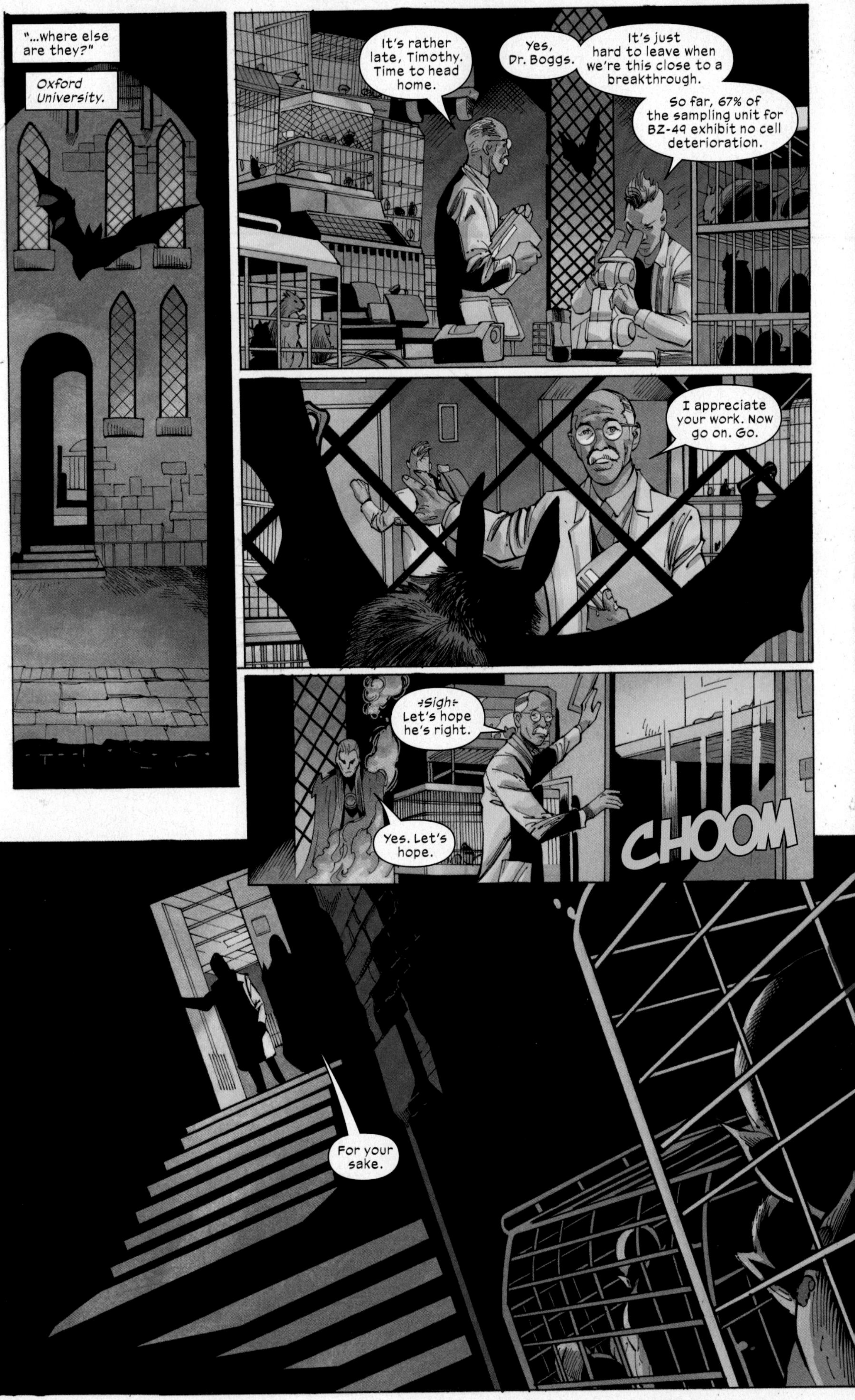
"...where else are they?"
Oxford University.
It's rather late, Timothy. Time to head home.
Yes, Dr. Boggs.
It's just hard to leave when we're this close to a breakthrough.
So far, 67% of the sampling unit for BZ-49 exhibit no cell deterioration.
I appreciate your work. Now go on. Go.
Sigh Let's hope he's right.
Yes. Let's hope.
CHOOM
For your sake.

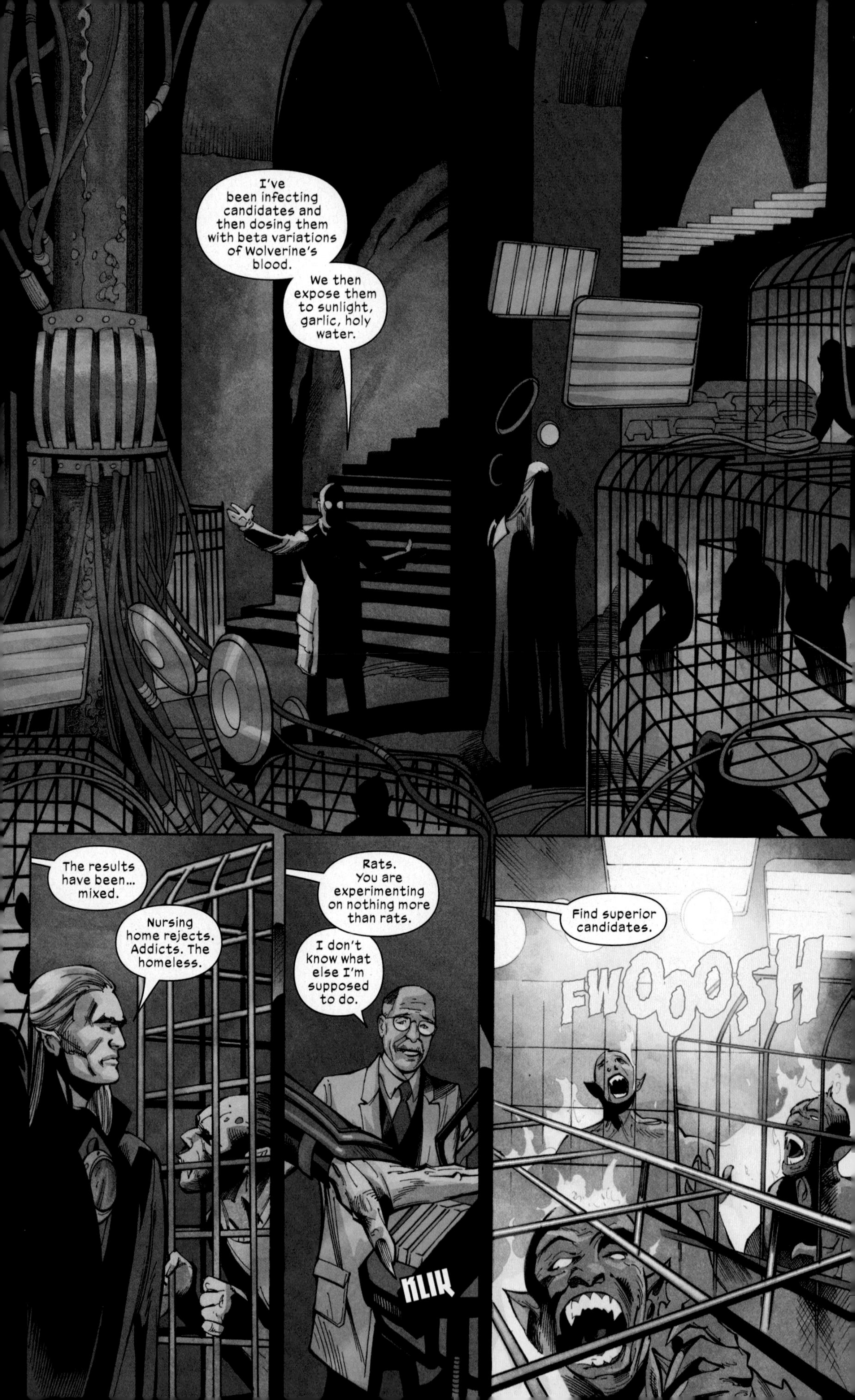
I've been infecting candidates and then dosing them with beta variations of Wolverine's blood.
We then expose them to sunlight, garlic, holy water.
The results have been... mixed.
Nursing home rejects. Addicts. The homeless.
Rats. You are experimenting on nothing more than rats.
I don't know what else I'm supposed to do.
KLIK
Find superior candidates.
FWOOOSH

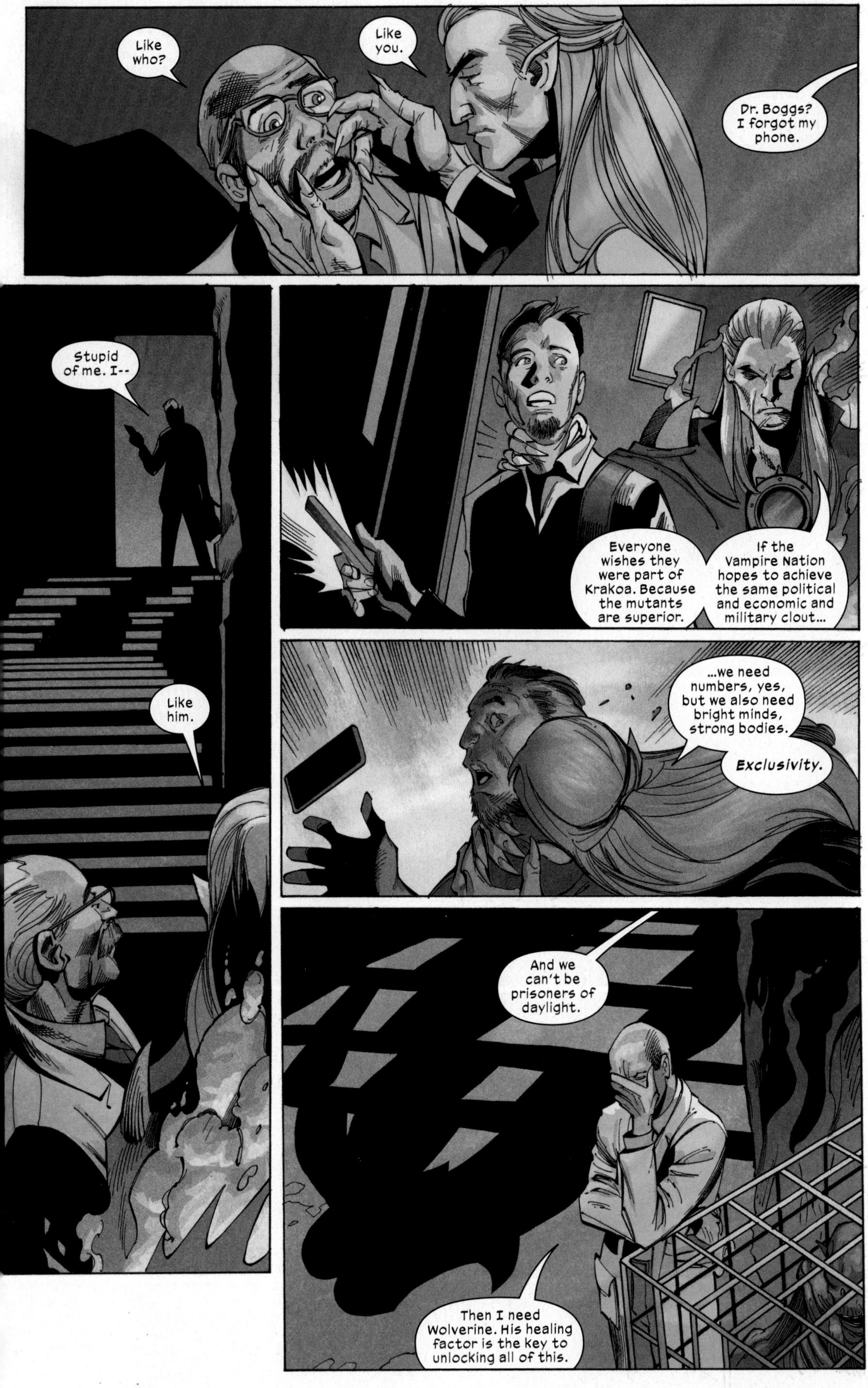
Like who?
Like you.
Dr. Boggs? I forgot my phone.
Stupid of me. I--
Like him.
Everyone wishes they were part of Krakoa. Because the mutants are superior.
If the Vampire Nation hopes to achieve the same political and economic and military clout...
...we need numbers, yes, but we also need bright minds, strong bodies.
Exclusivity.
And we can't be prisoners of daylight.
Then I need Wolverine. His healing factor is the key to unlocking all of this.

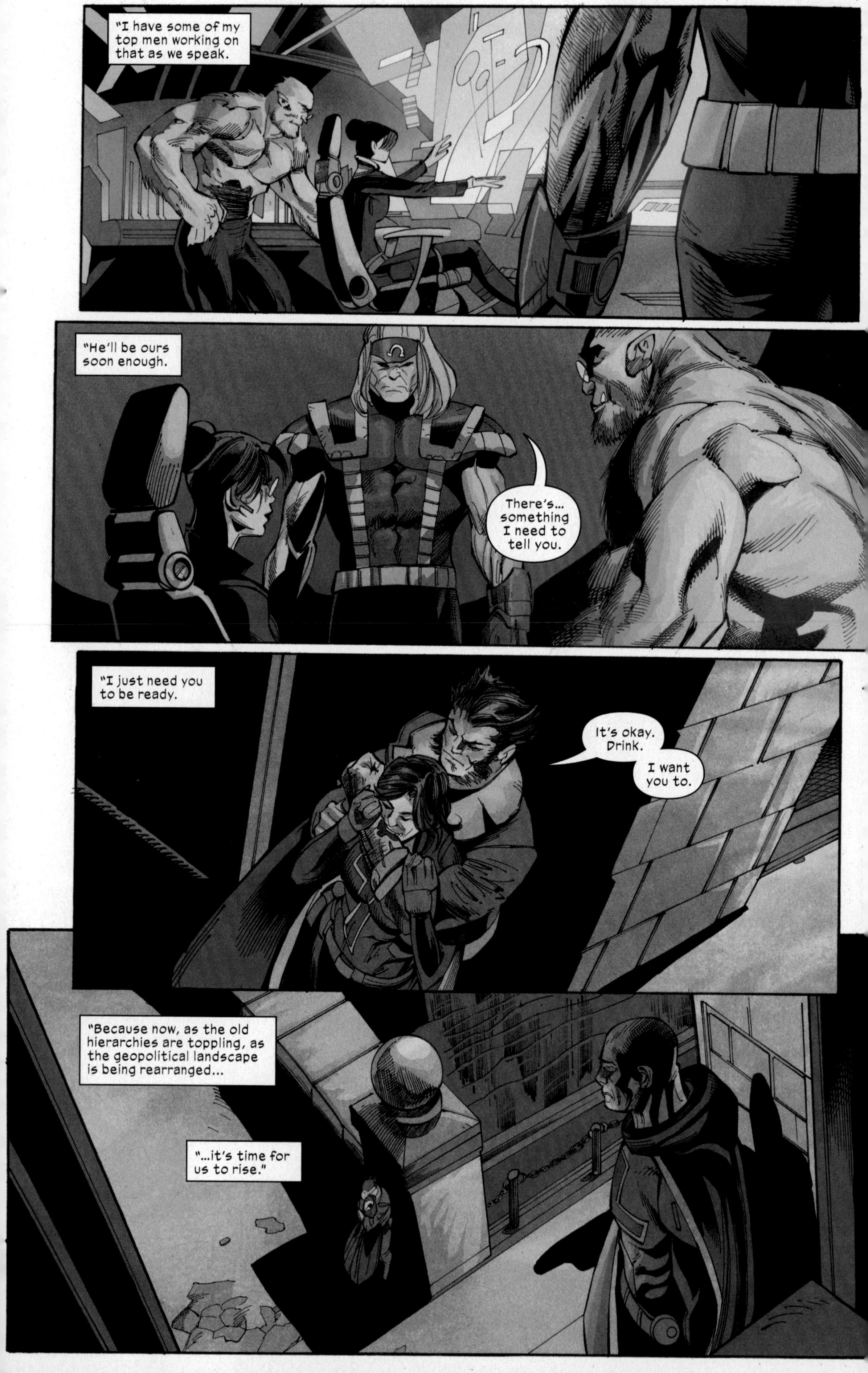
"I have some of my top men working on that as we speak.
"He'll be ours soon enough.
There's... something I need to tell you.
"I just need you to be ready.
It's okay. Drink.
I want you to.
"Because now, as the old hierarchies are toppling, as the geopolitical landscape is being rearranged...
"...it's time for us to rise."

[reign_of_x]

[kra_]
[koa_]

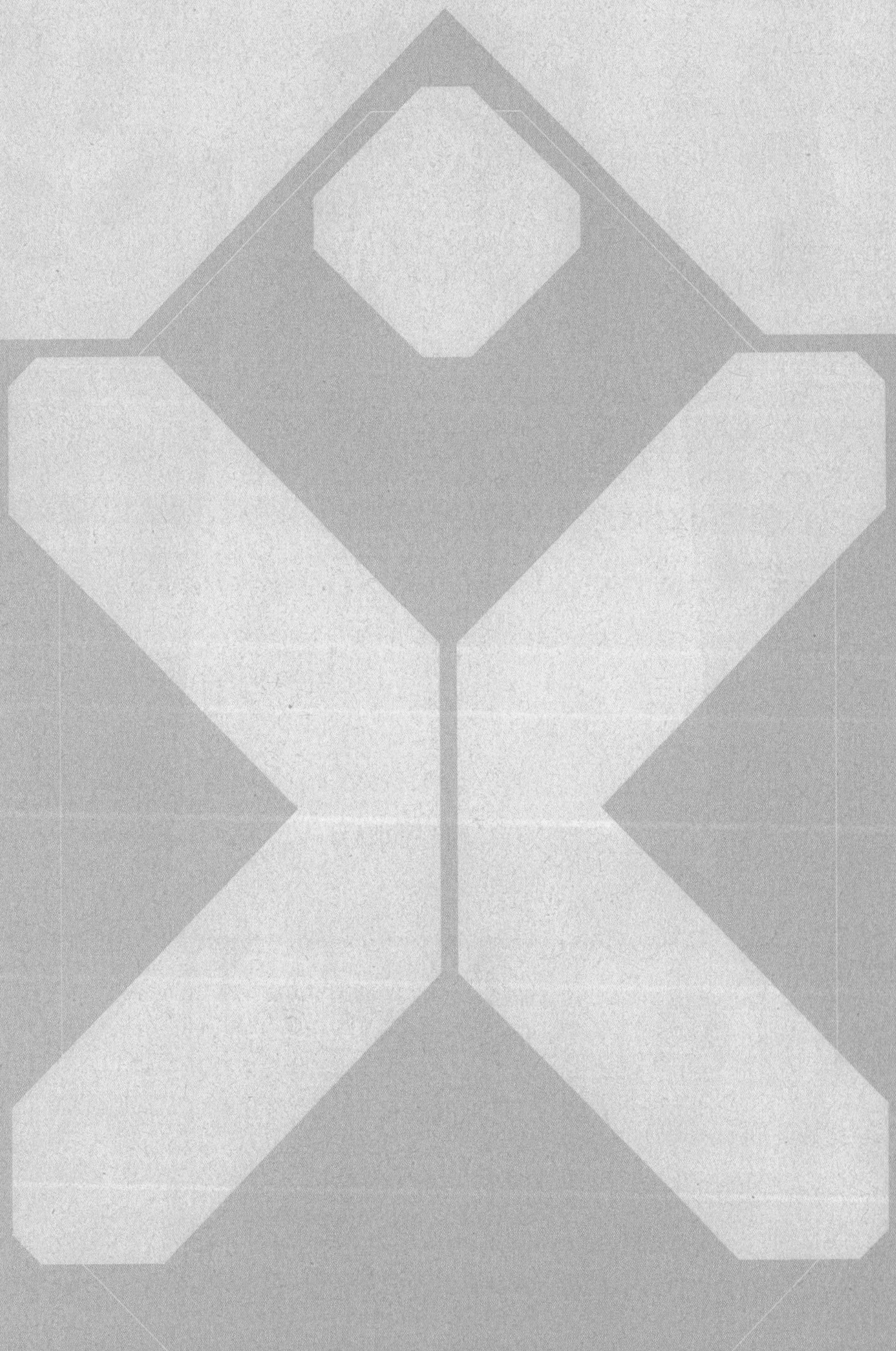

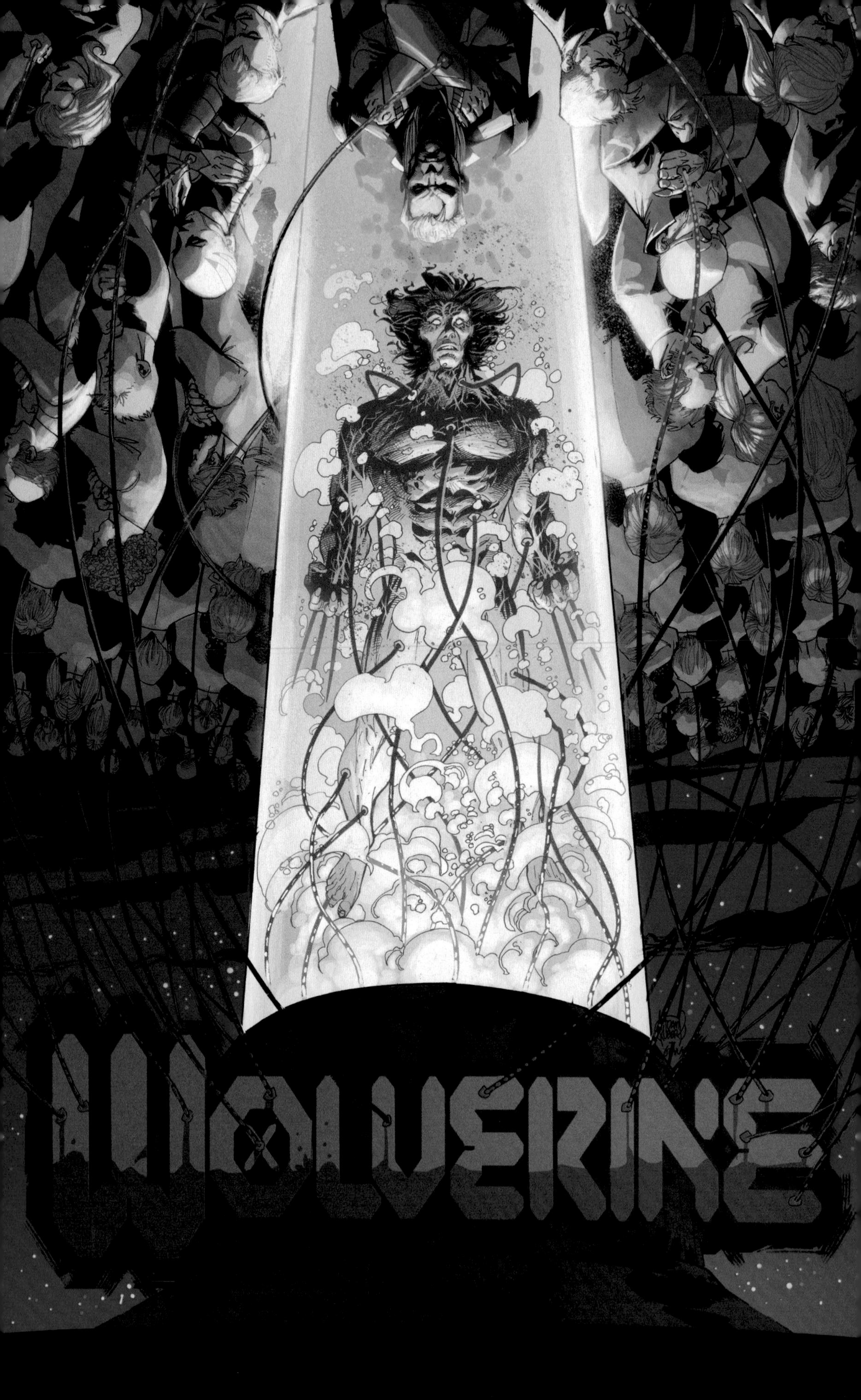
WOLVERINE

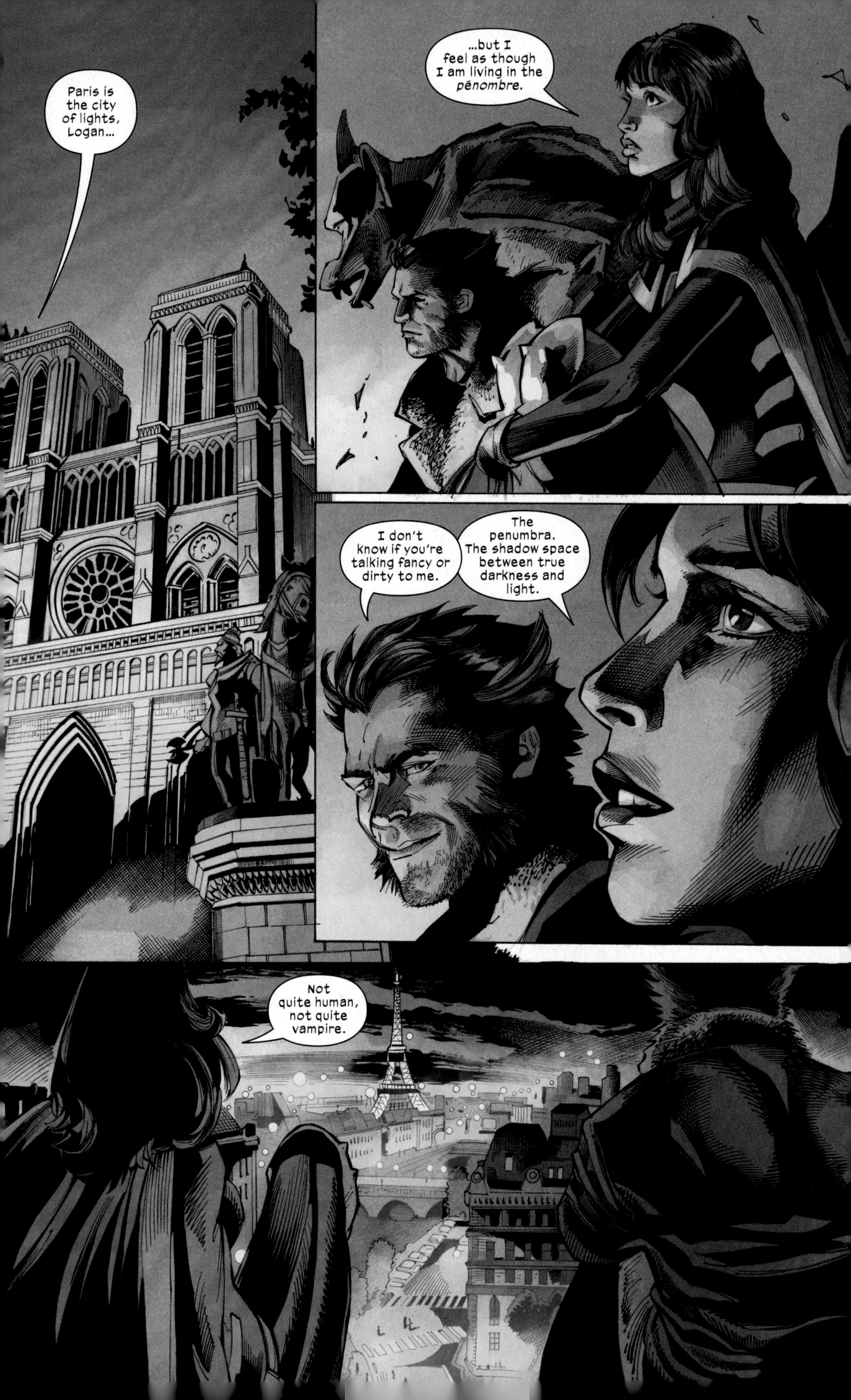
Paris is the city of lights, Logan...
...but I feel as though I am living in the *pénombre*.
I don't know if you're talking fancy or dirty to me.
The penumbra. The shadow space between true darkness and light.
Not quite human, not quite vampire.

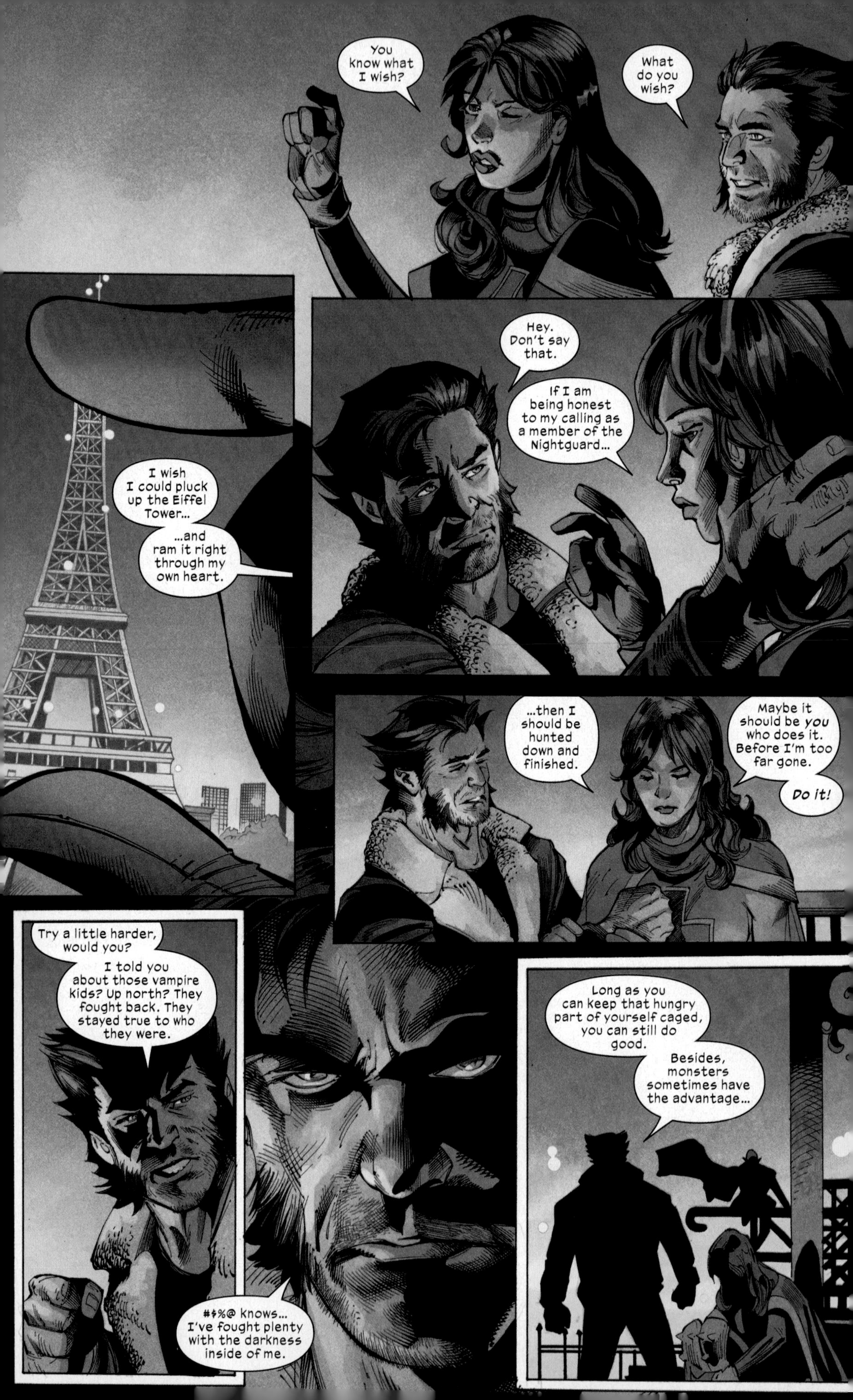
You know what I wish?
What do you wish?
I wish I could pluck up the Eiffel Tower...
...and ram it right through my own heart.
Hey. Don't say that.
If I am being honest to my calling as a member of the Nightguard...
...then I should be hunted down and finished.
Maybe it should be *you* who does it. Before I'm too far gone.
Do it!
Try a little harder, would you?
I told you about those vampire kids? Up north? They fought back. They stayed true to who they were.
#$%@ knows... I've fought plenty with the darkness inside of me.
Long as you can keep that hungry part of yourself caged, you can still do good.
Besides, monsters sometimes have the advantage...

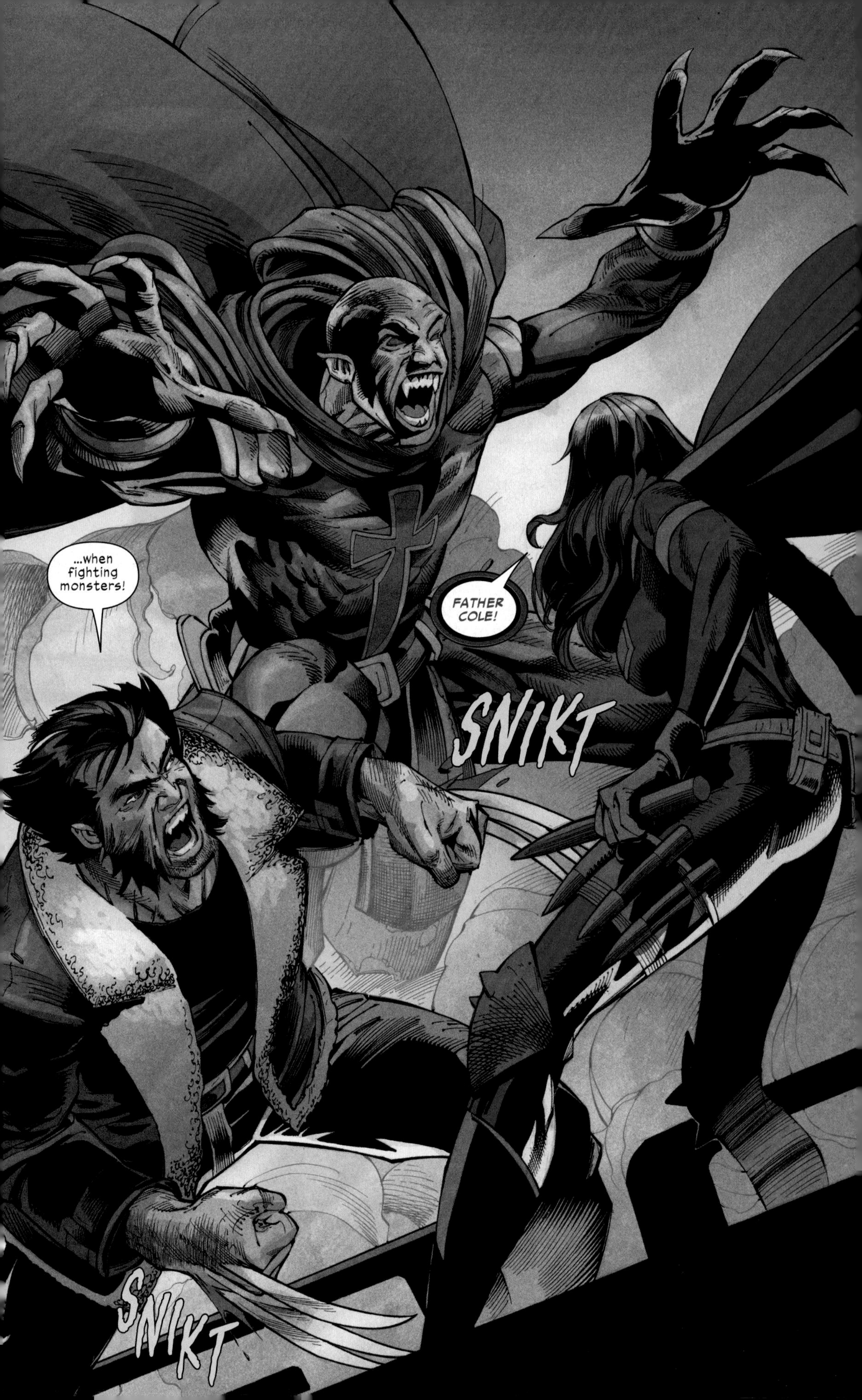

...when fighting monsters!
FATHER COLE!
SNIKT
SNIKT

BLOOD IN THE BANK

The Vampire Nation has been amassing power and resources under the leadership of Dracula. Among these resources: samples of Wolverine's blood, use of which allows the vamps to daywalk. Now Wolverine is out for blood. To take the fight directly to Drac, Wolverine sought out Louise, his friend in the vampire-hunting Nightguard -- but was stunned to find she seems to be becoming a vampire herself!

Meanwhile, Beast and X-Force have been tracking the mutant traitor Omega Red, who has been aiding Dracula in his plot...

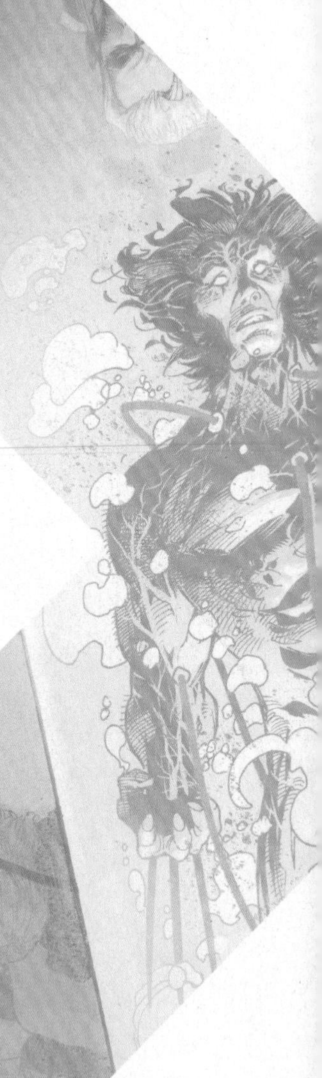

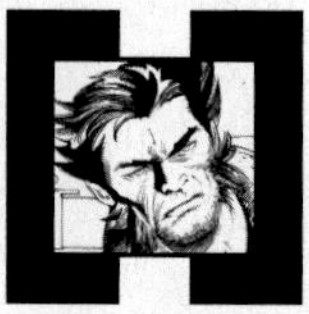
Wolverine

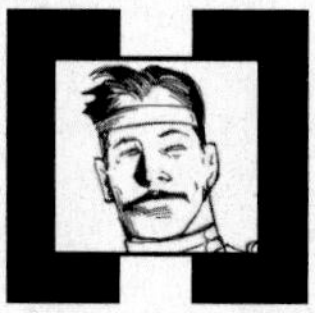
Forge

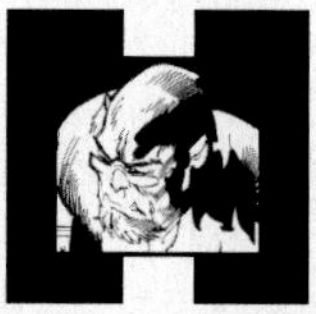
Beast

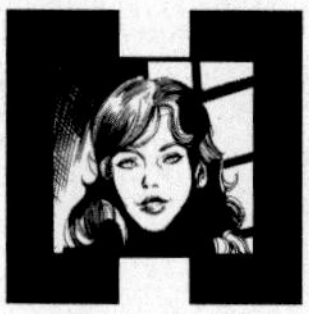
Louise

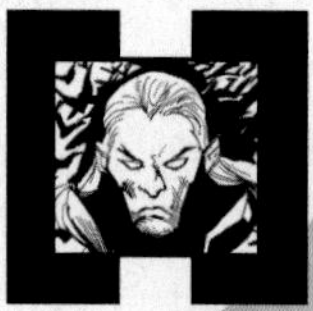
Dracula

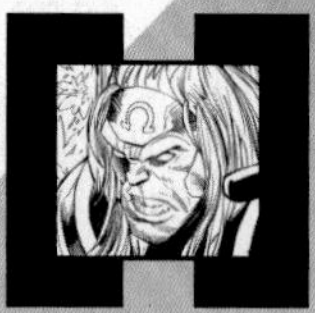
Omega Red

WOLVERINE

[X_12]

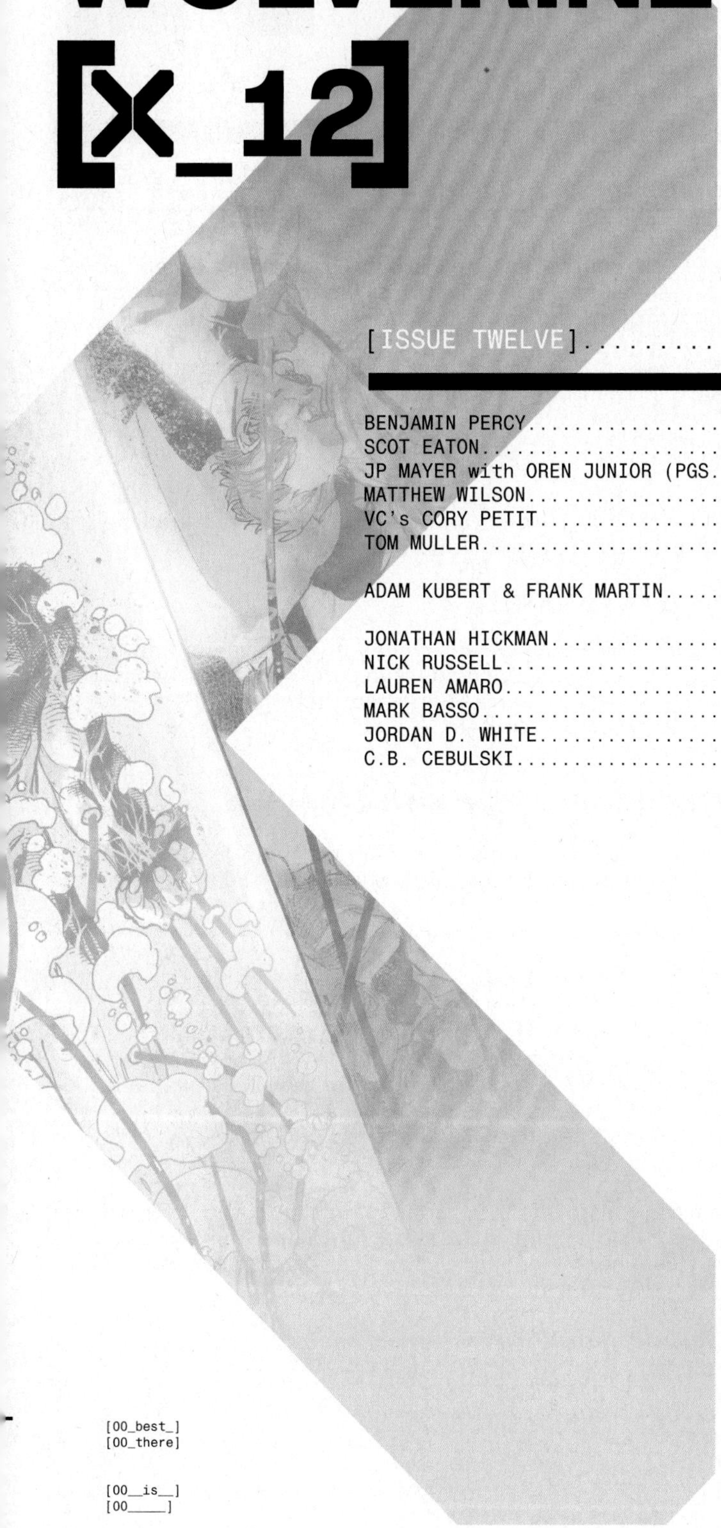

[ISSUE TWELVE]........................ PENUMBRA

BENJAMIN PERCY....................................[WRITER]
SCOT EATON..[PENCILER]
JP MAYER with OREN JUNIOR (PGS. 15-20).............[INKERS]
MATTHEW WILSON.............................[COLOR ARTIST]
VC's CORY PETIT...................................[LETTERER]
TOM MULLER..[DESIGN]

ADAM KUBERT & FRANK MARTIN.................[COVER ARTISTS]

JONATHAN HICKMAN..............................[HEAD OF X]
NICK RUSSELL...............................[PRODUCTION]
LAUREN AMARO.........................[ASSISTANT EDITOR]
MARK BASSO...[EDITOR]
JORDAN D. WHITE.........................[SENIOR EDITOR]
C.B. CEBULSKI...........................[EDITOR IN CHIEF]

[00_best_]
[00_there]

[00__is__]
[00_____]

[00_bub_]

[00____X]

X-FORCE: EVIDENCE LOG

Notebook: Dr. James Boggs, Don of Microbiology, Oxford University

To say that the blood sample -- culled from the mutant known as Wolverine -- is abnormal would be an understatement. Its complexity is unguessable on a number of levels, and if I spent the next ten years studying it, I don't know that I would --

But what am I even saying? I don't have ten years. I don't know that I have ten days. And Timothy...poor Timothy... I daresay he might not last another ten hours.

Help me.

The antigen structure is unlike any other I've encountered. If a normal blood cell is a cardboard box -- simple, flexible, but sturdy in its structure -- Wolverine's is a brick house of many rooms and hallways with a fireplace roaring at its center.

I can hear him. Always. Whispering in my ear. Dracul.

Disease- and temperature-resistant, the muscular antibodies aggressively stand up to and wipe out any foreign intrusion. The exogenous polypeptides defy categorization. The hemoglobin count is an astonishing 30 grams per deciliter, so that one could say he is carrying around in his veins a nuclear arsenal of protein.

I see him in the mist oozing across the campus green, in the rat scurrying through the alley, in the bat clinging to an attic rafter. Dracul. His name is my command.

If only I could study the source himself, if only I could sample his bone marrow, things might be different. The answer -- to what some might call a veritable fountain of youth -- is in his stem cells.

Help me.

The lifespan of a standard red blood cell is 120 days. The lifespan of a vampire's is roughly one day. Whatever power comes with their virulence weakens the RBC membrane. The swift degradation of hemoglobin requires constant transfusion. A kind of daily dialysis. Thus their permanent thirst. They have to refresh their systems or they will collapse.

I saw a fly on a windowsill earlier today. I snatched it and shoved it in my mouth before I knew what I was doing.

An infusion of Wolverine's blood controls the standard antagonistic effects of phosphatidylserine, CD47, infrared, visible, and ultraviolet light. And the bloodclocks manage to replicate -- poorly but serviceably enough -- the liver and spleen, creating a sustainable environment, prolonging the healing factor's potential.

He's going to kill me soon. Please, God, forgive me for helping him.

—

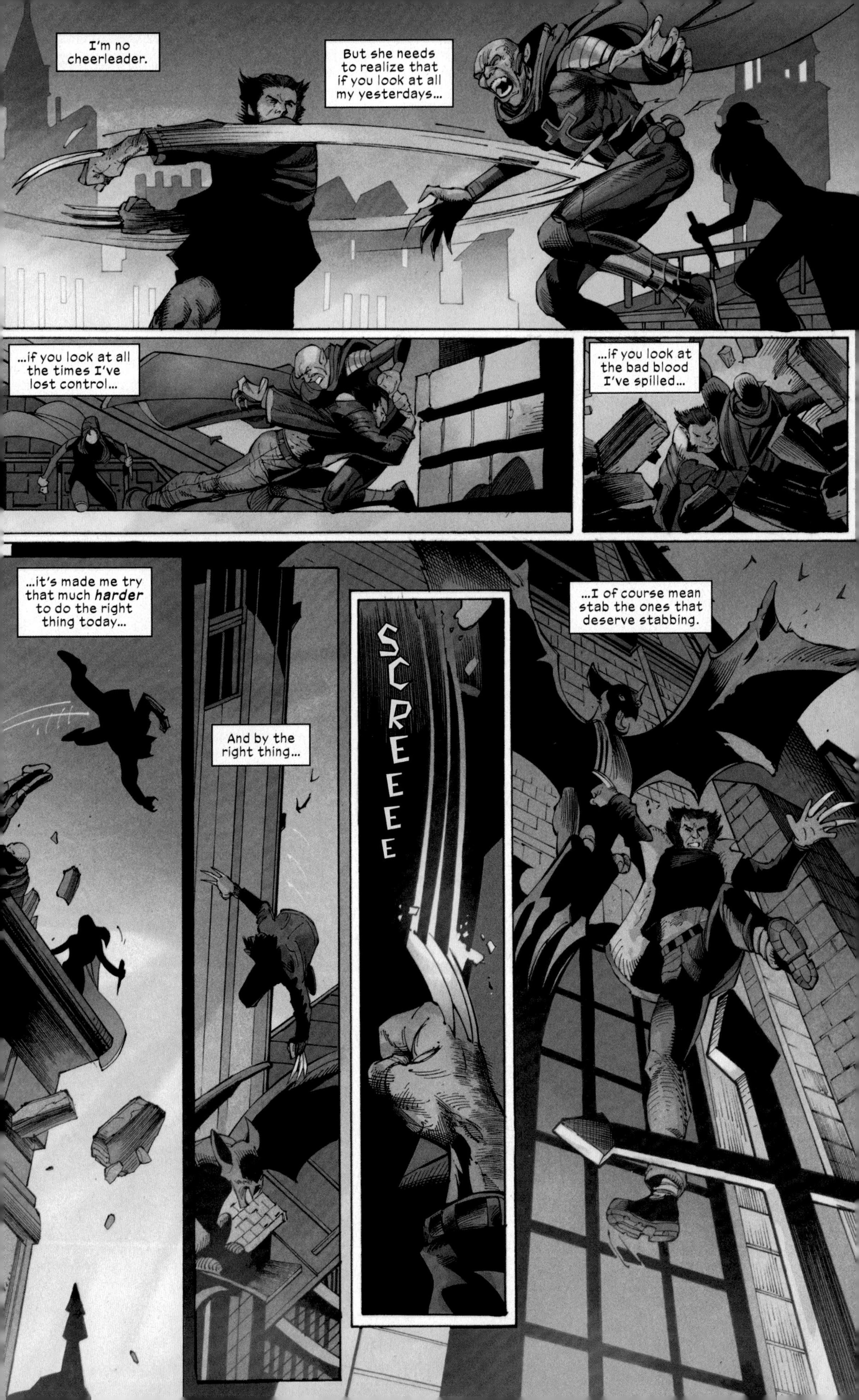
I'm no cheerleader.
But she needs to realize that if you look at all my yesterdays...
...if you look at all the times I've lost control...
...if you look at the bad blood I've spilled...
...it's made me try that much *harder* to do the right thing today...
And by the right thing...
SCREEEE
...I of course mean stab the ones that deserve stabbing.

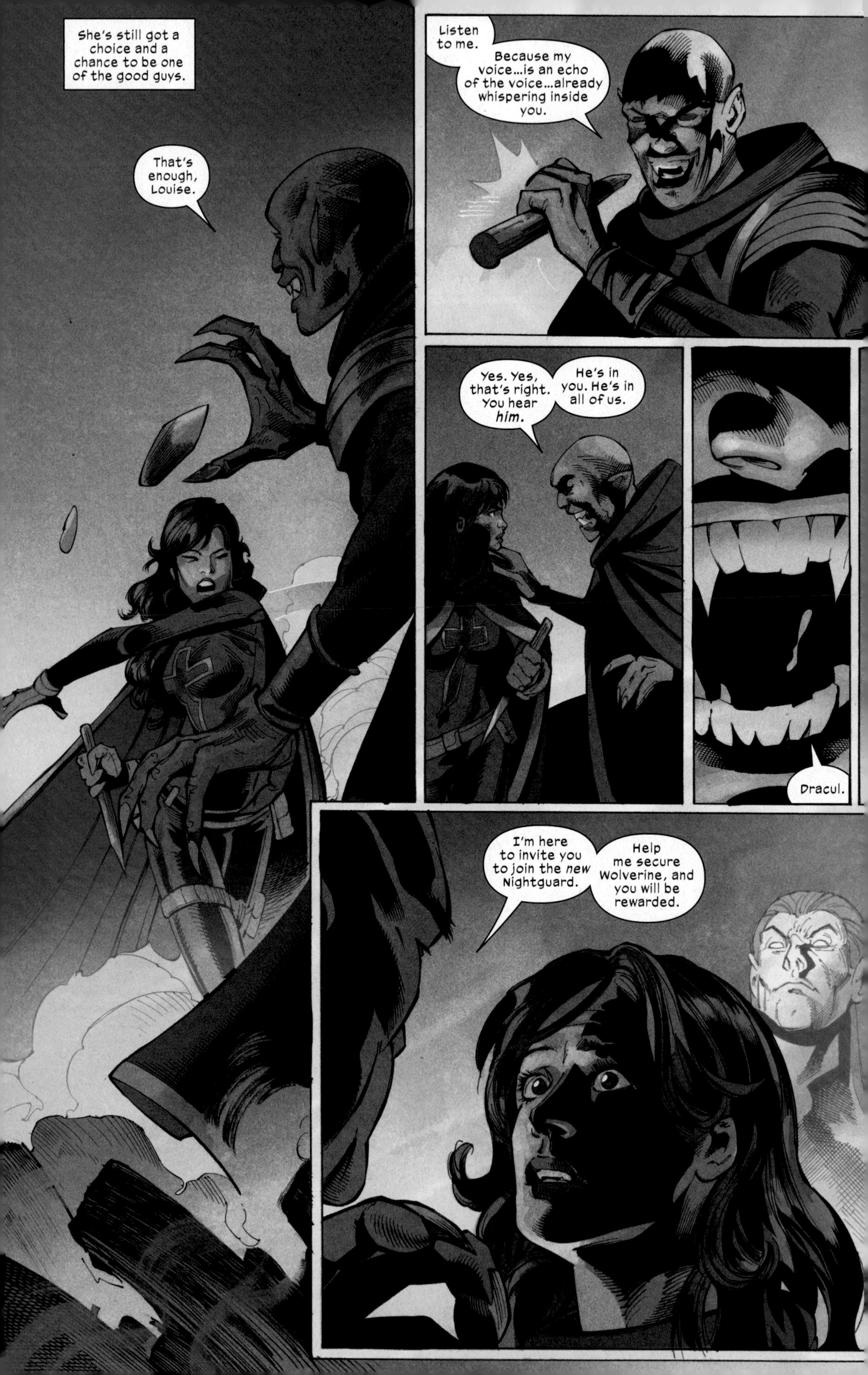
She's still got a choice and a chance to be one of the good guys.
That's enough, Louise.
Listen to me.
Because my voice...is an echo of the voice...already whispering inside you.
Yes. Yes, that's right. You hear *him*.
He's in you. He's in all of us.
Dracul.
I'm here to invite you to join the *new* Nightguard.
Help me secure Wolverine, and you will be rewarded.

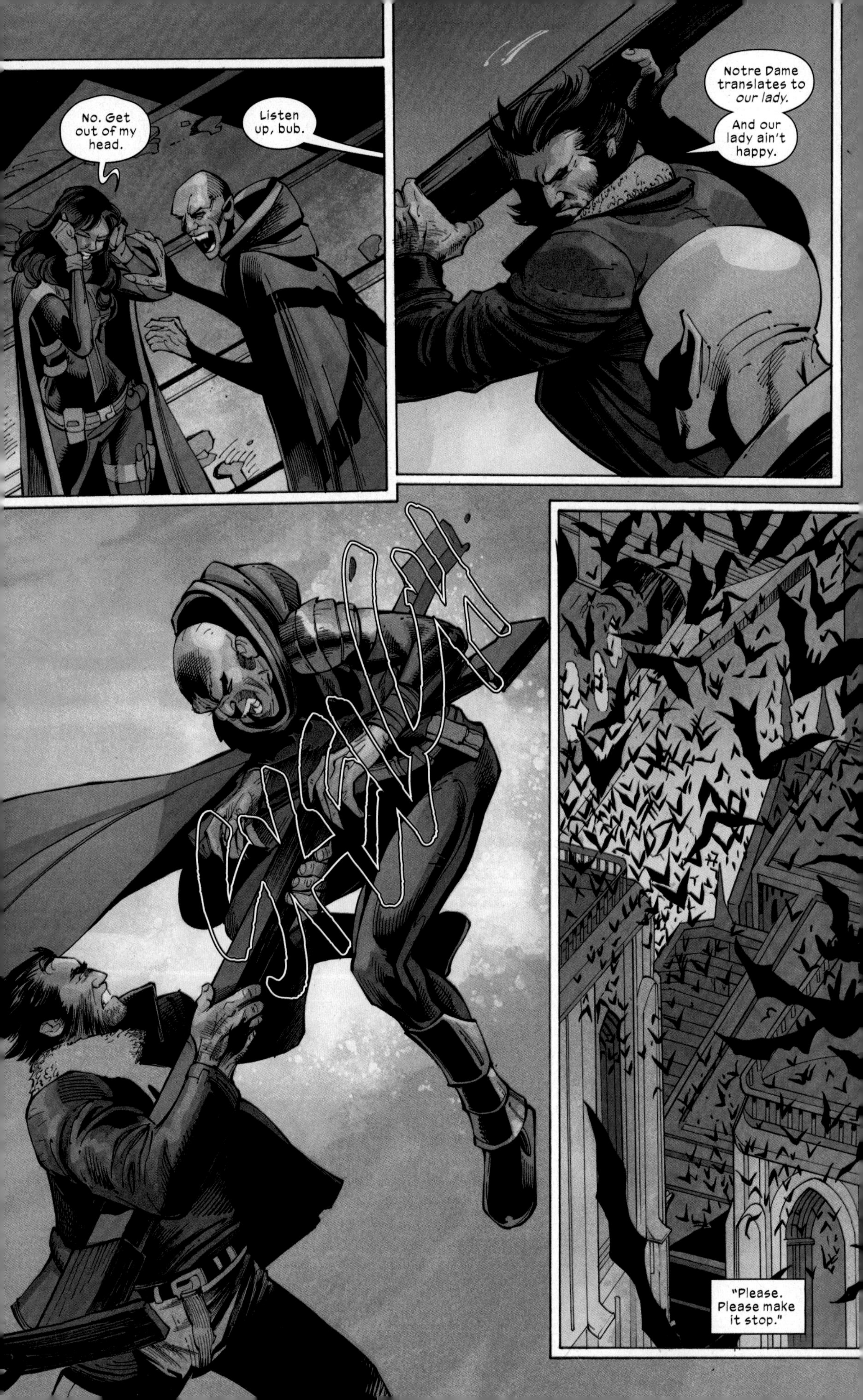
No. Get out of my head.
Listen up, bub.
Notre Dame translates to *our lady.*
And our lady ain't happy.
"Please. Please make it stop."

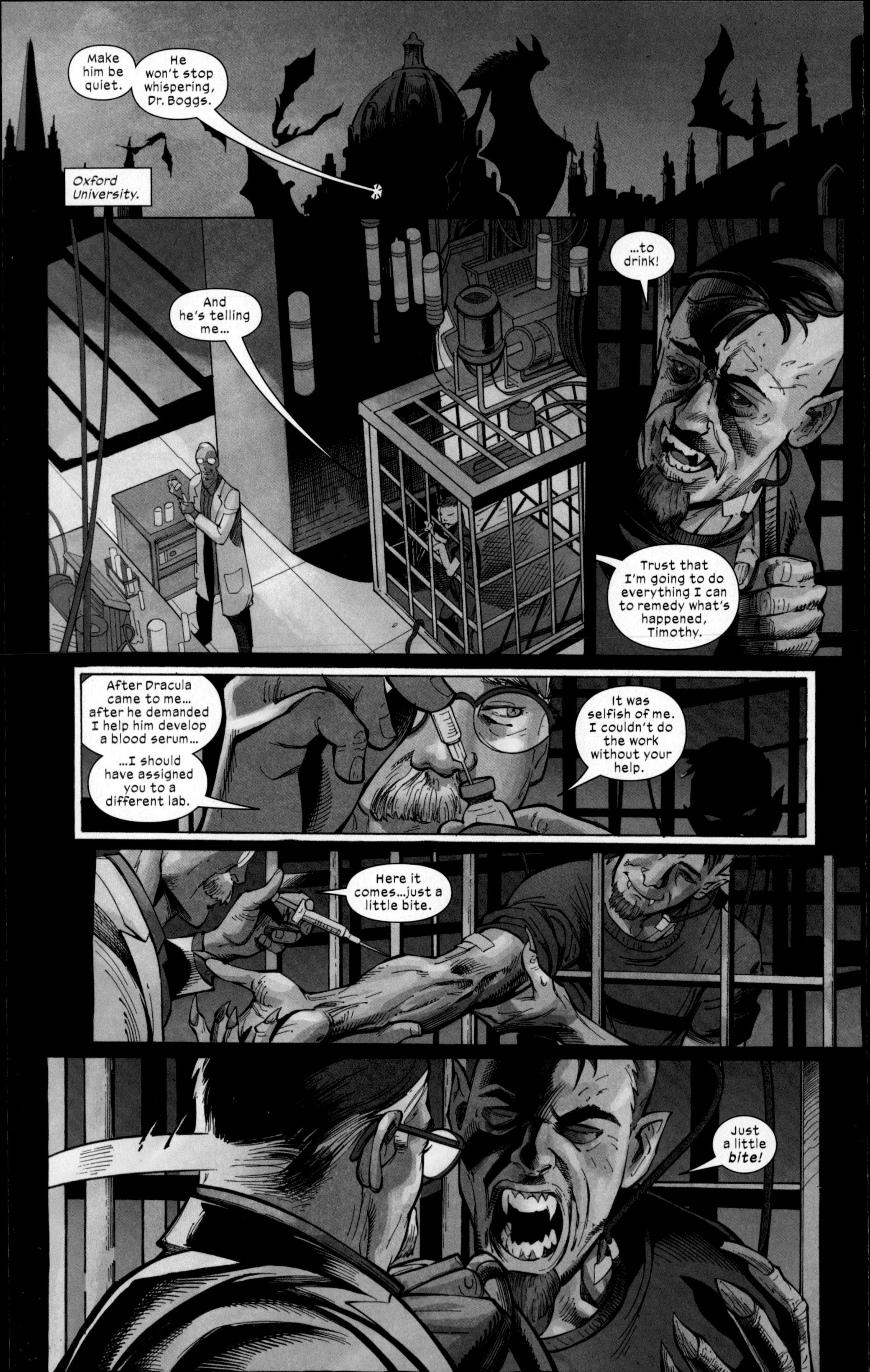
Make him be quiet.
He won't stop whispering, Dr. Boggs.
Oxford University.
And he's telling me...
...to drink!
Trust that I'm going to do everything I can to remedy what's happened, Timothy.
After Dracula came to me... after he demanded I help him develop a blood serum...
...I should have assigned you to a different lab.
It was selfish of me. I couldn't do the work without your help.
Here it comes...just a little bite.
Just a little *bite!*

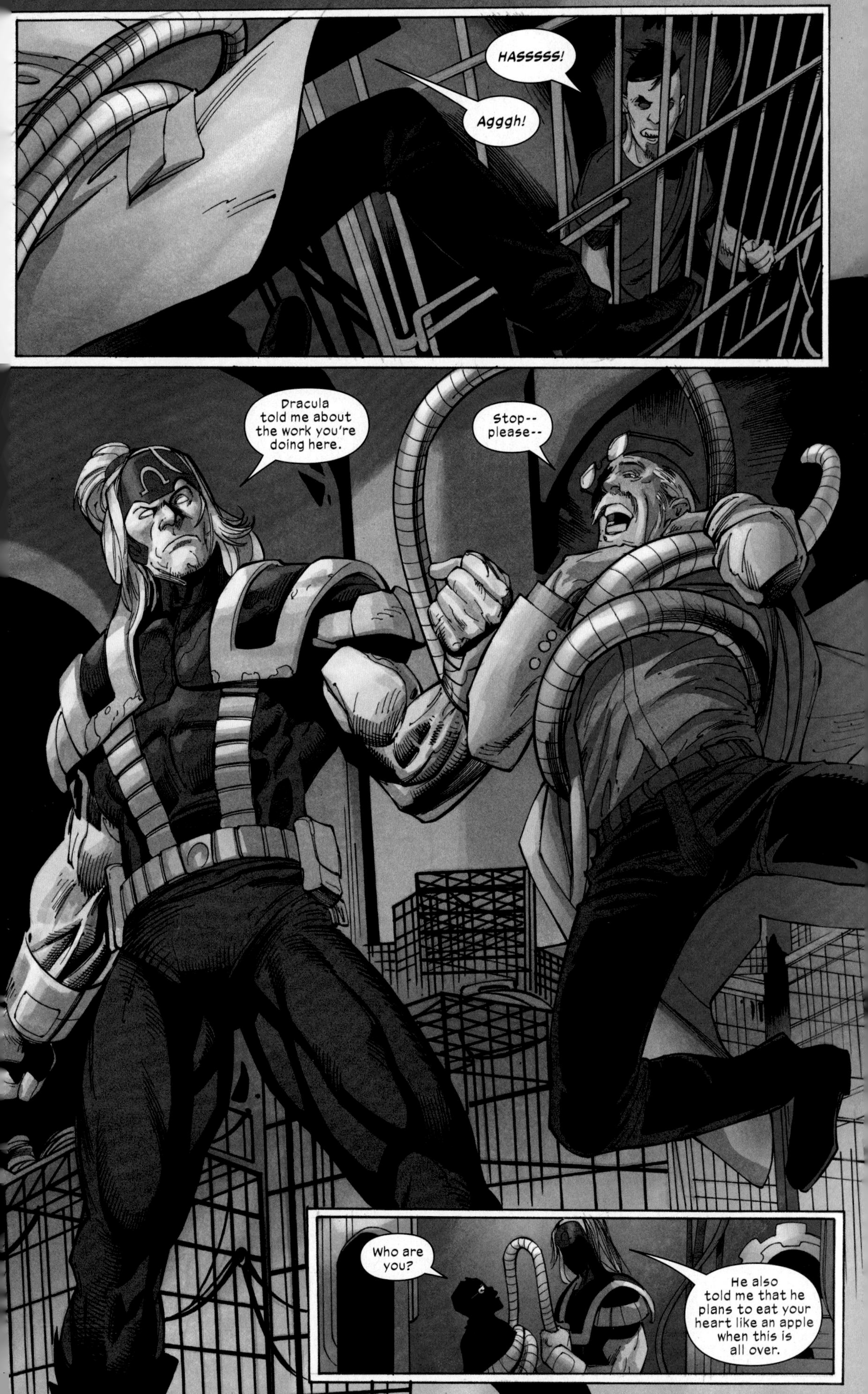
HASSSSS!
Agggh!
Dracula told me about the work you're doing here.
Stop-- please--
Who are you?
He also told me that he plans to eat your heart like an apple when this is all over.

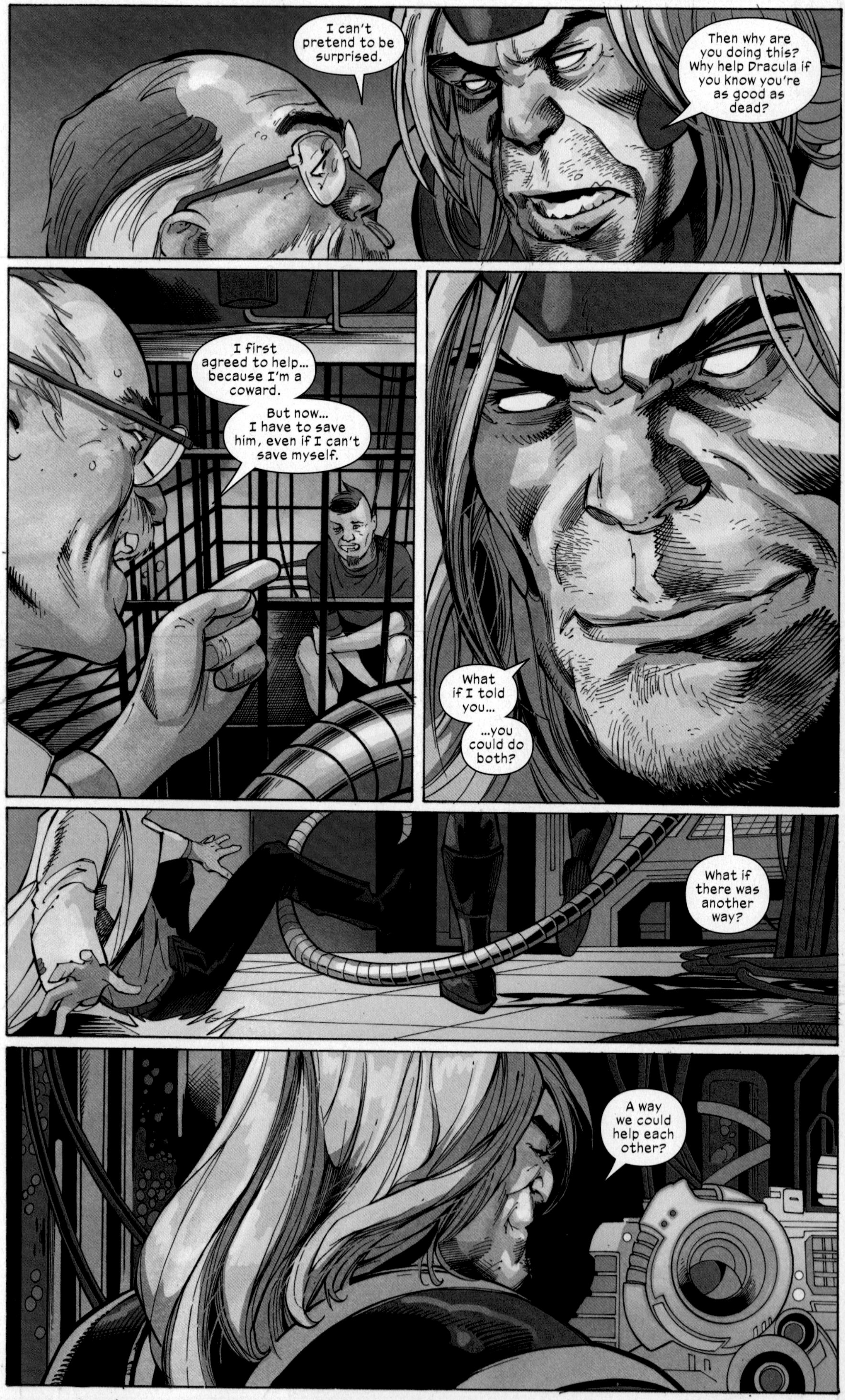

I can't pretend to be surprised.
Then why are you doing this? Why help Dracula if you know you're as good as dead?
I first agreed to help... because I'm a coward.
But now... I have to save him, even if I can't save myself.
What if I told you...
...you could do both?
What if there was another way?
A way we could help each other?

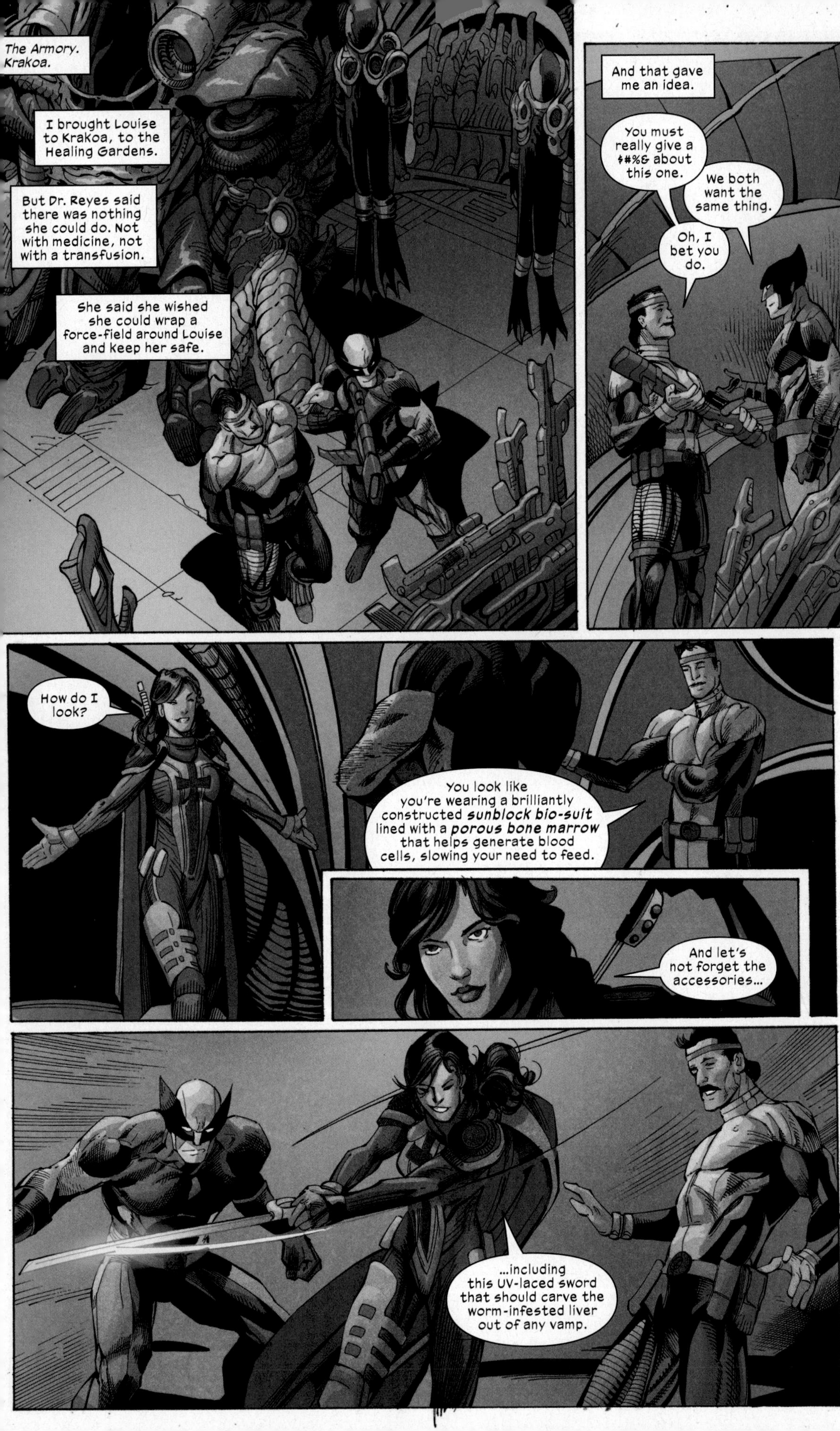

The Armory.
Krakoa.
I brought Louise to Krakoa, to the Healing Gardens.
But Dr. Reyes said there was nothing she could do. Not with medicine, not with a transfusion.
She said she wished she could wrap a force-field around Louise and keep her safe.
And that gave me an idea.
You must really give a $#%& about this one.
We both want the same thing.
Oh, I bet you do.
How do I look?
You look like you're wearing a brilliantly constructed *sunblock bio-suit* lined with a *porous bone marrow* that helps generate blood cells, slowing your need to feed.
And let's not forget the accessories...
...including this UV-laced sword that should carve the worm-infested liver out of any vamp.

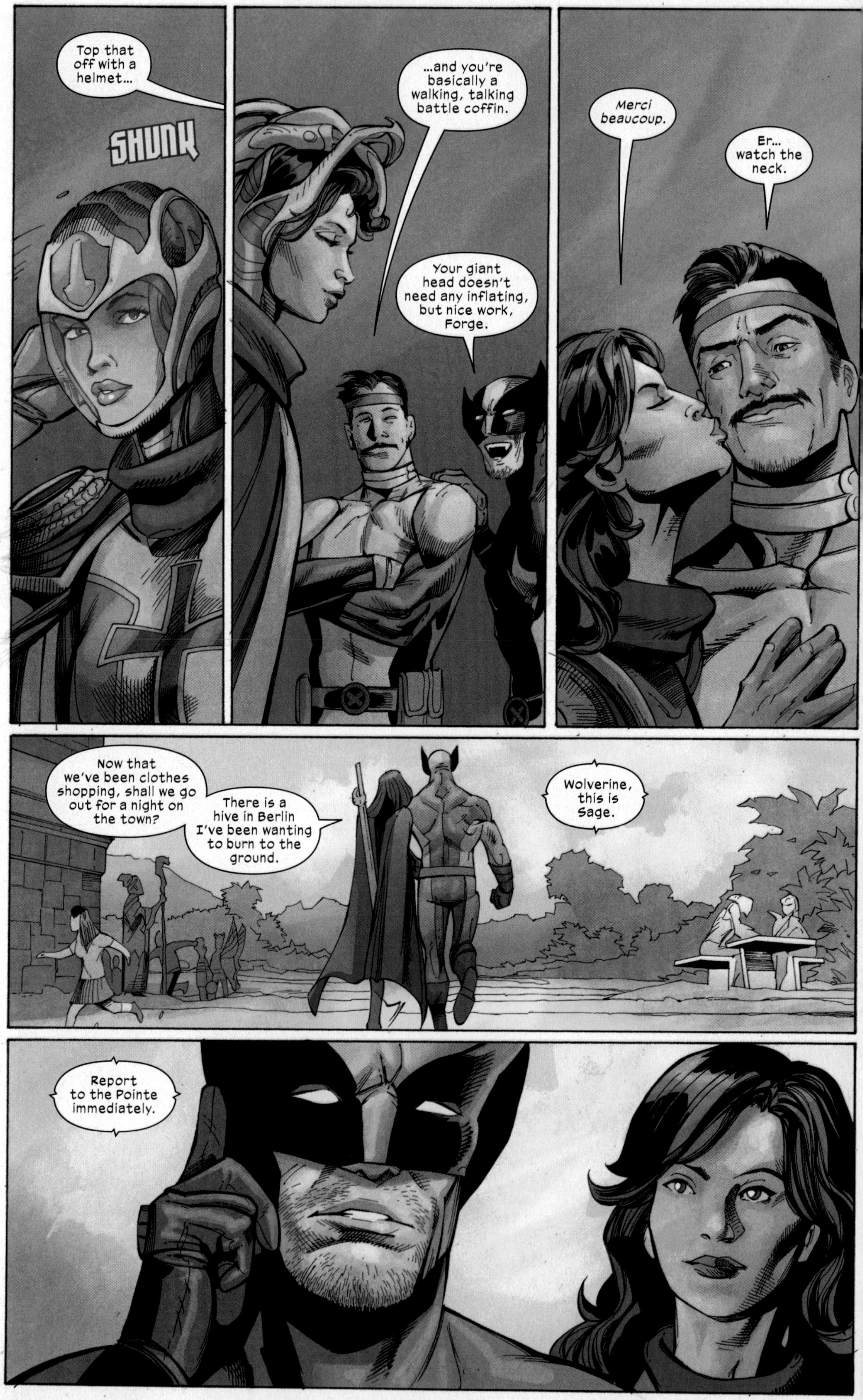
Top that off with a helmet...
SHUNK
...and you're basically a walking, talking battle coffin.
Your giant head doesn't need any inflating, but nice work, Forge.
Merci beaucoup.
Er... watch the neck.
Now that we've been clothes shopping, shall we go out for a night on the town?
There is a hive in Berlin I've been wanting to burn to the ground.
Wolverine, this is Sage.
Report to the Pointe immediately.

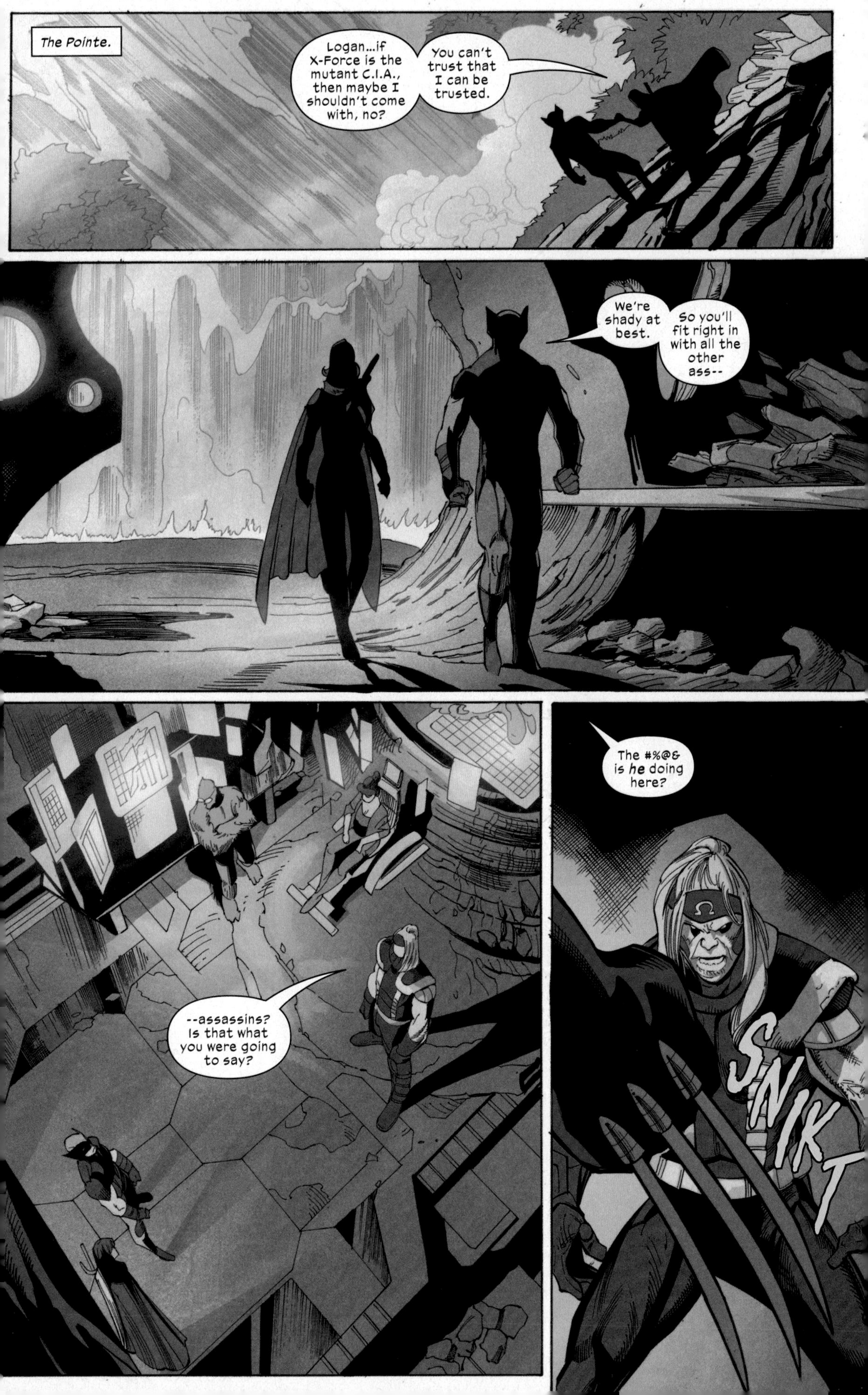
The Pointe.
Logan...if X-Force is the mutant C.I.A., then maybe I shouldn't come with, no?
You can't trust that I can be trusted.
We're shady at best.
So you'll fit right in with all the other ass--
--assassins? Is that what you were going to say?
The #%@& is he doing here?
SNIKT

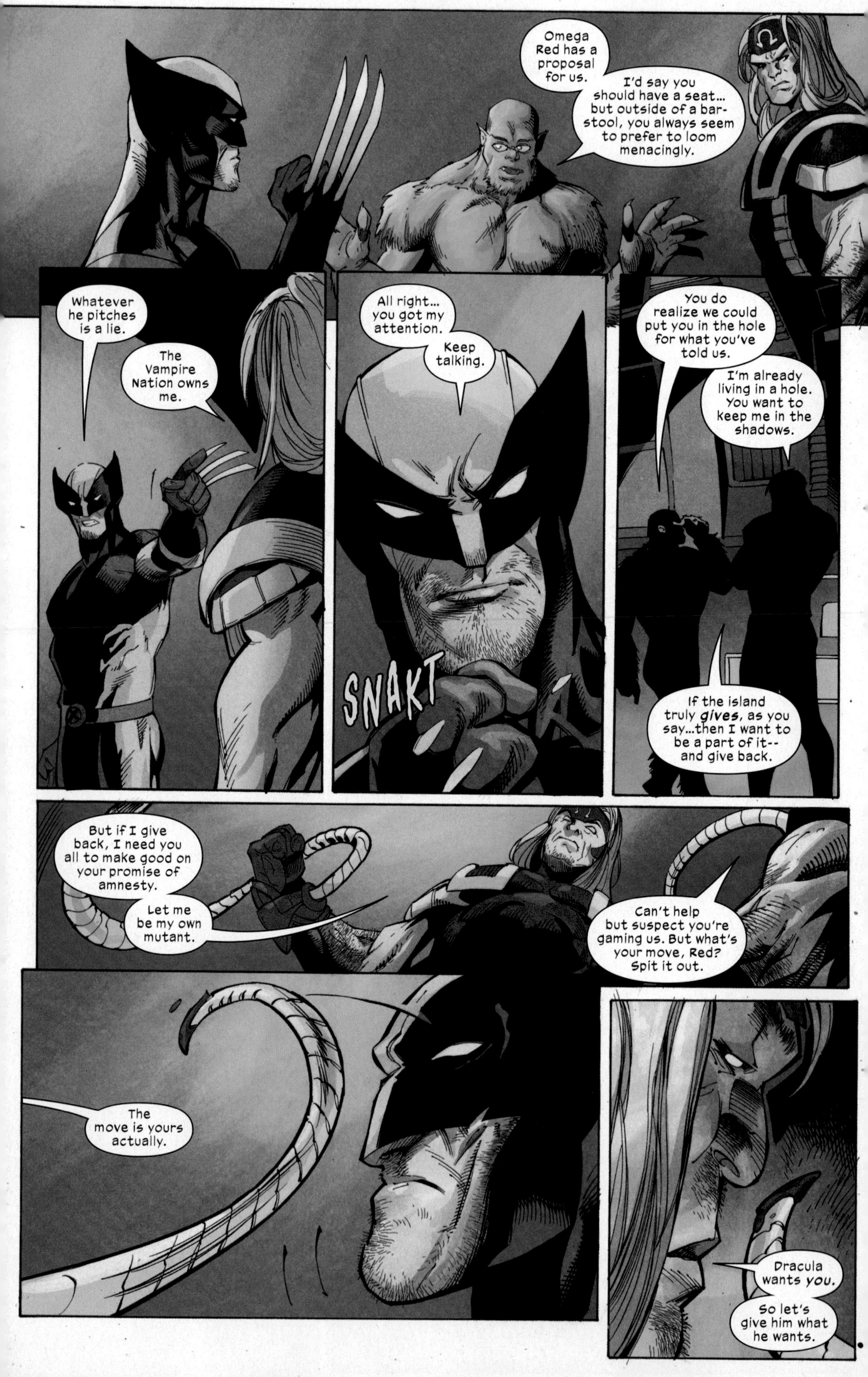
Omega Red has a proposal for us.
I'd say you should have a seat... but outside of a bar-stool, you always seem to prefer to loom menacingly.
Whatever he pitches is a lie.
The Vampire Nation owns me.
All right... you got my attention.
Keep talking.
SNAKT
You do realize we could put you in the hole for what you've told us.
I'm already living in a hole. You want to keep me in the shadows.
If the island truly *gives*, as you say...then I want to be a part of it--and give back.
But if I give back, I need you all to make good on your promise of amnesty.
Let me be my own mutant.
Can't help but suspect you're gaming us. But what's your move, Red? Spit it out.
The move is yours actually.
Dracula wants *you*.
So let's give him what he wants.

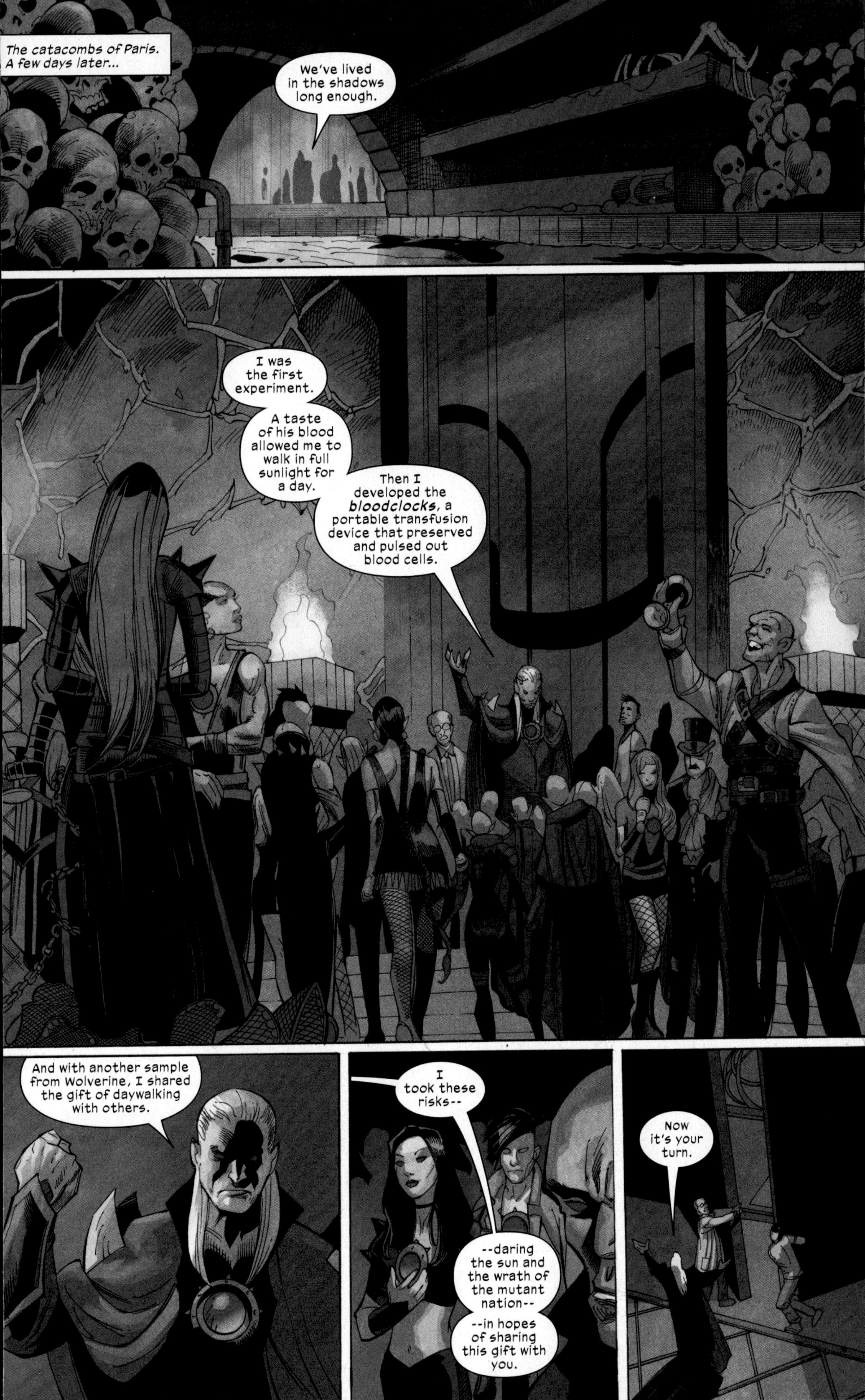
The catacombs of Paris. A few days later...
We've lived in the shadows long enough.
I was the first experiment.
A taste of his blood allowed me to walk in full sunlight for a day.
Then I developed the *bloodclocks*, a portable transfusion device that preserved and pulsed out blood cells.
And with another sample from Wolverine, I shared the gift of daywalking with others.
I took these risks--
--daring the sun and the wrath of the mutant nation--
--in hopes of sharing this gift with you.
Now it's your turn.

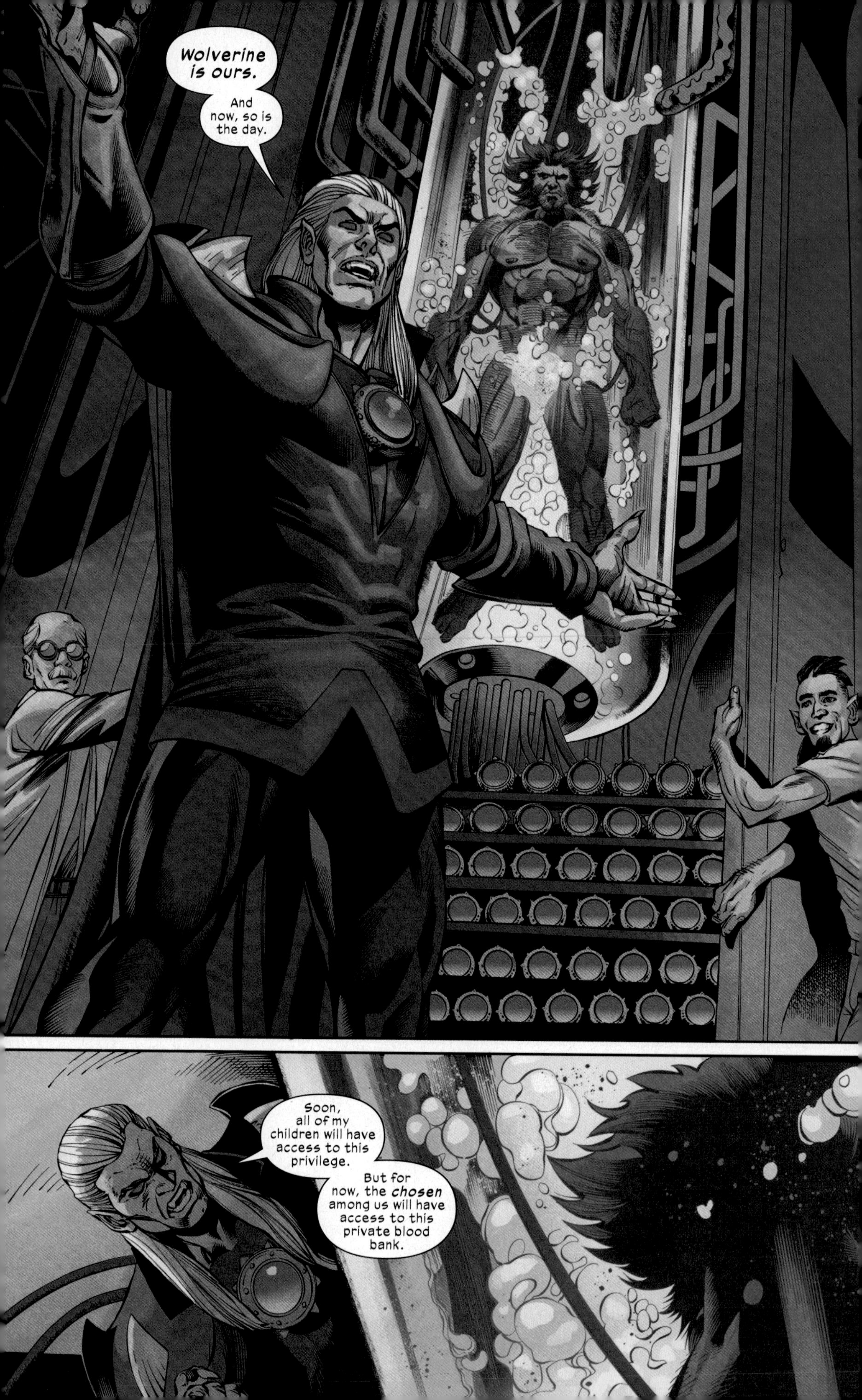
Wolverine is ours.
And now, so is the day.
Soon, all of my children will have access to this privilege.
But for now, the *chosen* among us will have access to this private blood bank.

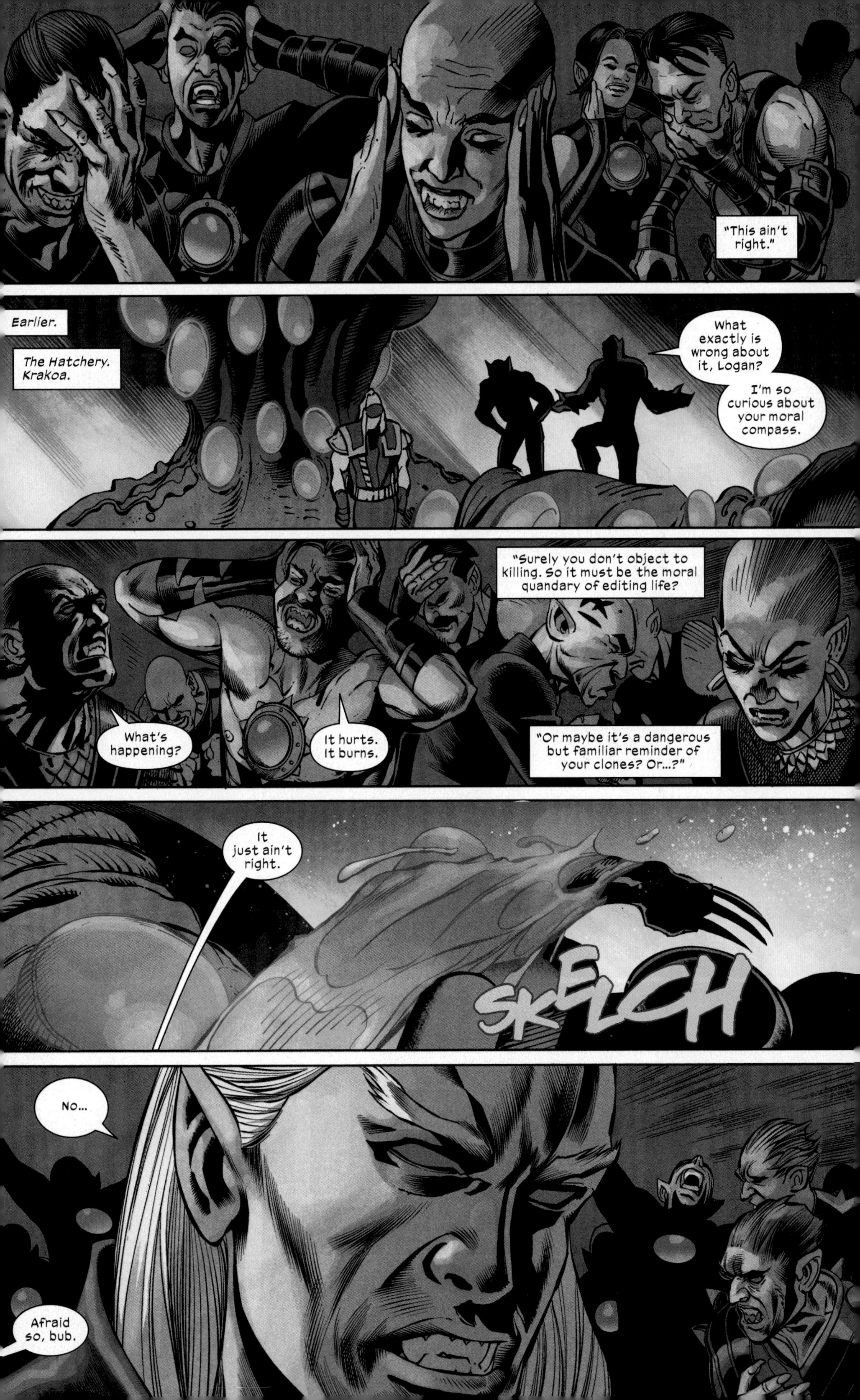
"This ain't right."
Earlier.
The Hatchery. Krakoa.
What exactly is wrong about it, Logan?
I'm so curious about your moral compass.
"Surely you don't object to killing. So it must be the moral quandary of editing life?
What's happening?
It hurts. It burns.
"Or maybe it's a dangerous but familiar reminder of your clones? Or...?"
It just ain't right.
SKELCH
No...
Afraid so, bub.

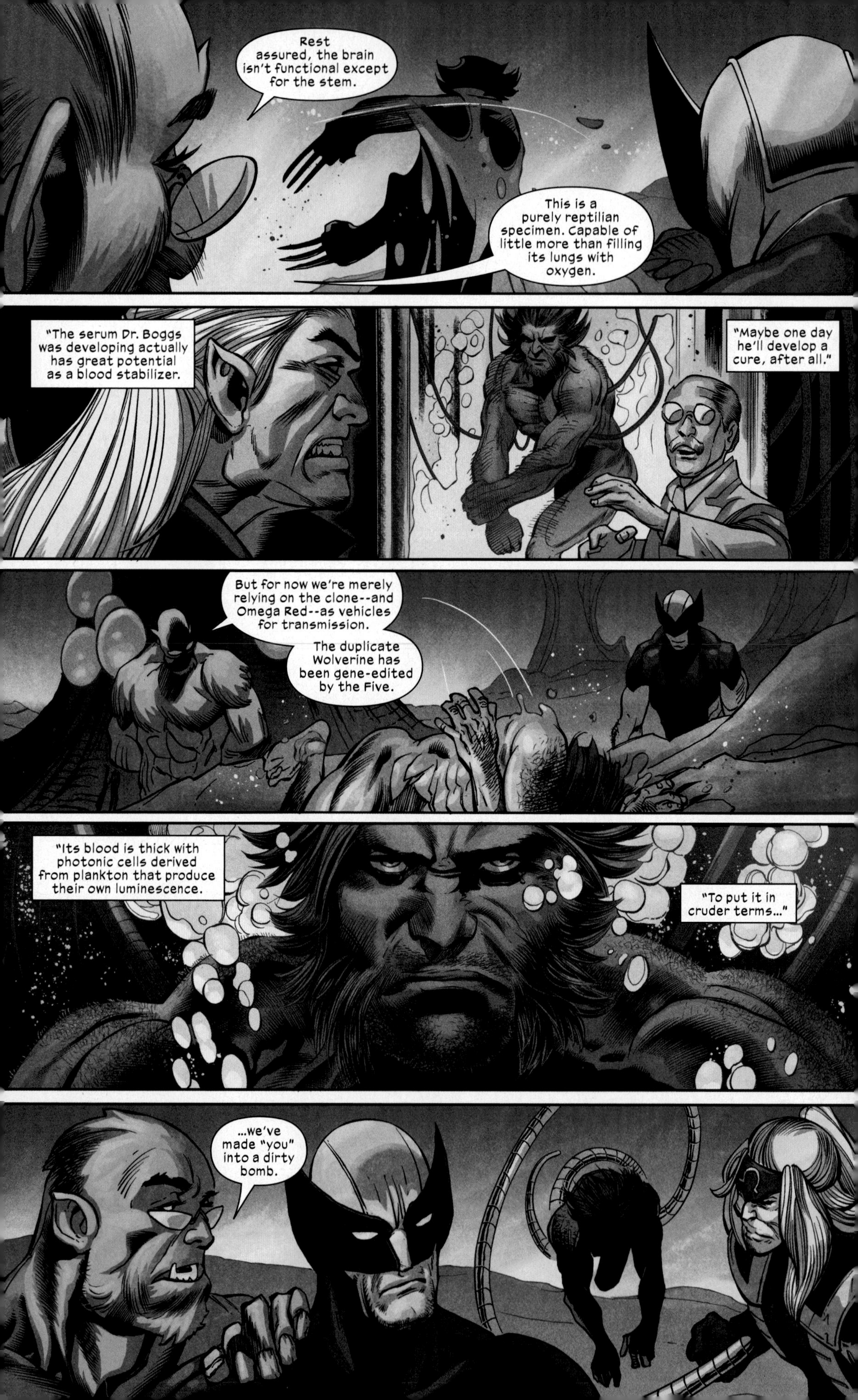
Rest assured, the brain isn't functional except for the stem.
This is a purely reptilian specimen. Capable of little more than filling its lungs with oxygen.
"The serum Dr. Boggs was developing actually has great potential as a blood stabilizer.
"Maybe one day he'll develop a cure, after all."
But for now we're merely relying on the clone--and Omega Red--as vehicles for transmission.
The duplicate Wolverine has been gene-edited by the Five.
"Its blood is thick with photonic cells derived from plankton that produce their own luminescence.
"To put it in cruder terms..."
...we've made "you" into a dirty bomb.

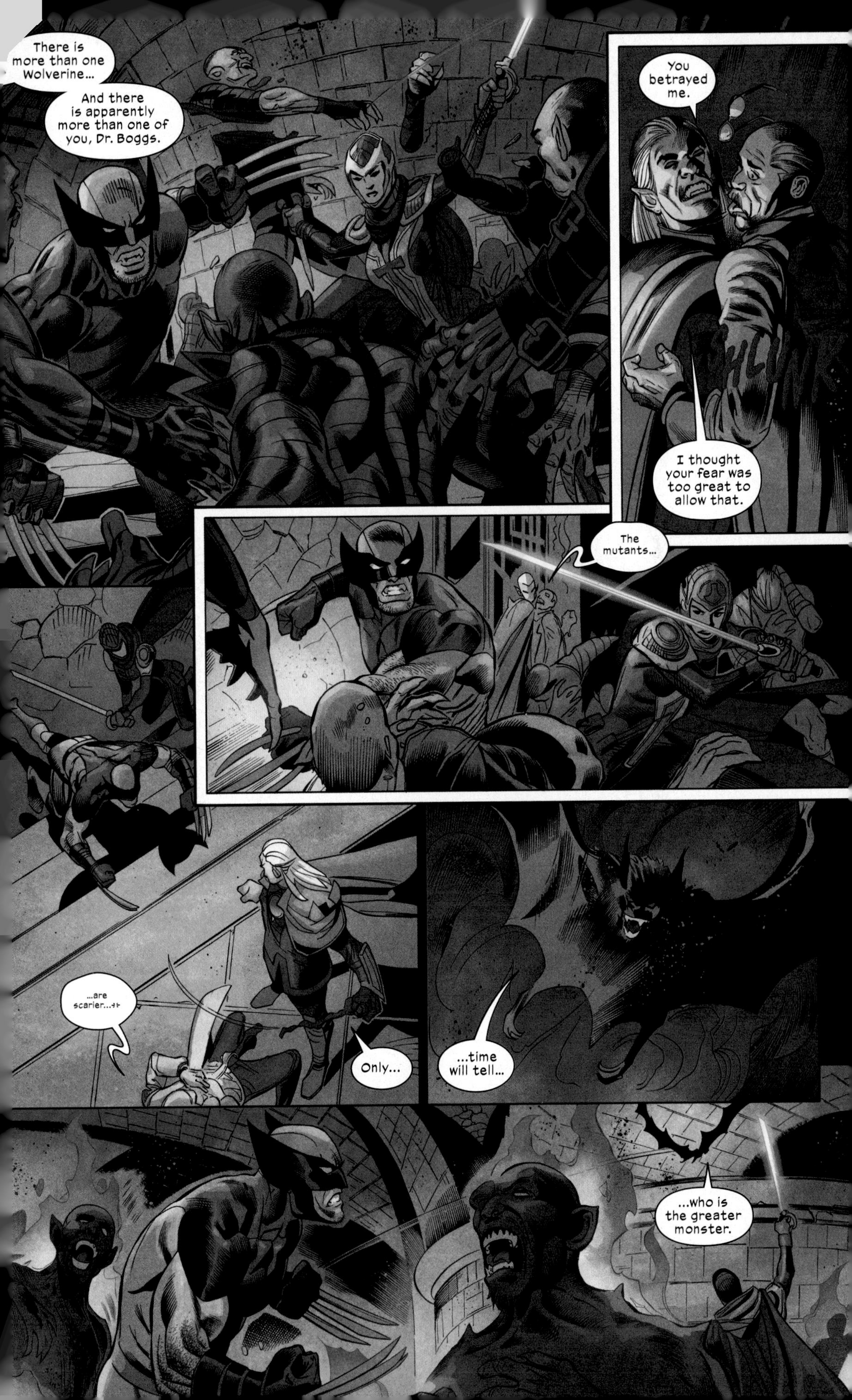
There is more than one Wolverine...
And there is apparently more than one of you, Dr. Boggs.
You betrayed me.
I thought your fear was too great to allow that.
The mutants...
...are scarier...
Only...
...time will tell...
...who is the greater monster.

[wolv__[0.12]
[erine_[0.12]

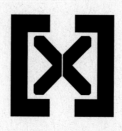

Not sure what I hate more:
vegetables, whiners, or
#@$% vampires.

-- WOLVERINE

[wolv__[0.XX]
[erine_[0.XX]

[wolv__[0.12].....]
[erine_[0.12].....]

[Wolverine_alpha.]

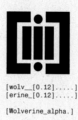

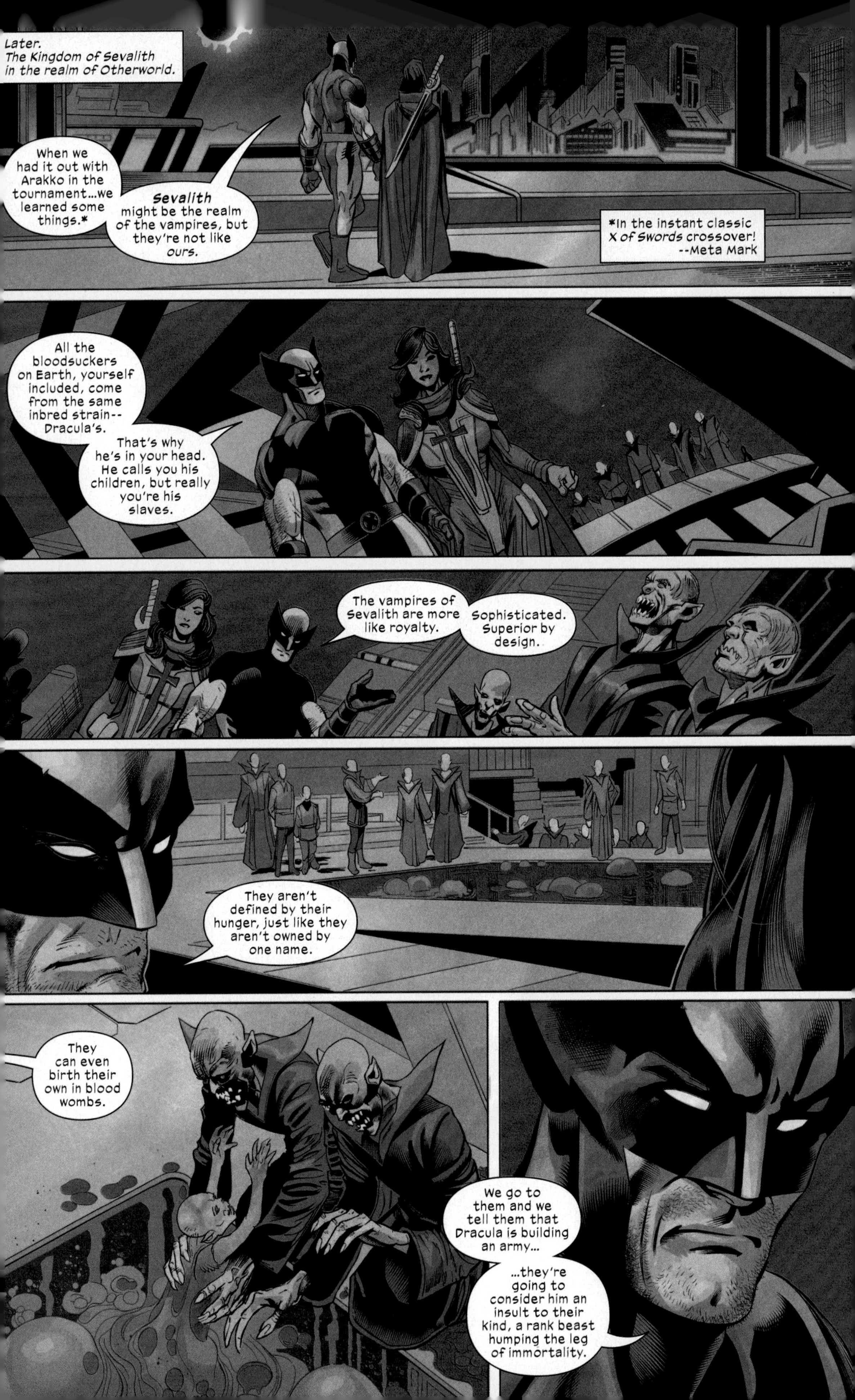
Later.
The Kingdom of Sevalith in the realm of Otherworld.
When we had it out with Arakko in the tournament...we learned some things.*
Sevalith might be the realm of the vampires, but they're not like ours.
*In the instant classic X of Swords crossover! --Meta Mark
All the bloodsuckers on Earth, yourself included, come from the same inbred strain--Dracula's.
That's why he's in your head. He calls you his children, but really you're his slaves.
The vampires of Sevalith are more like royalty.
Sophisticated. Superior by design.
They aren't defined by their hunger, just like they aren't owned by one name.
They can even birth their own in blood wombs.
We go to them and we tell them that Dracula is building an army...
...they're going to consider him an insult to their kind, a rank beast humping the leg of immortality.

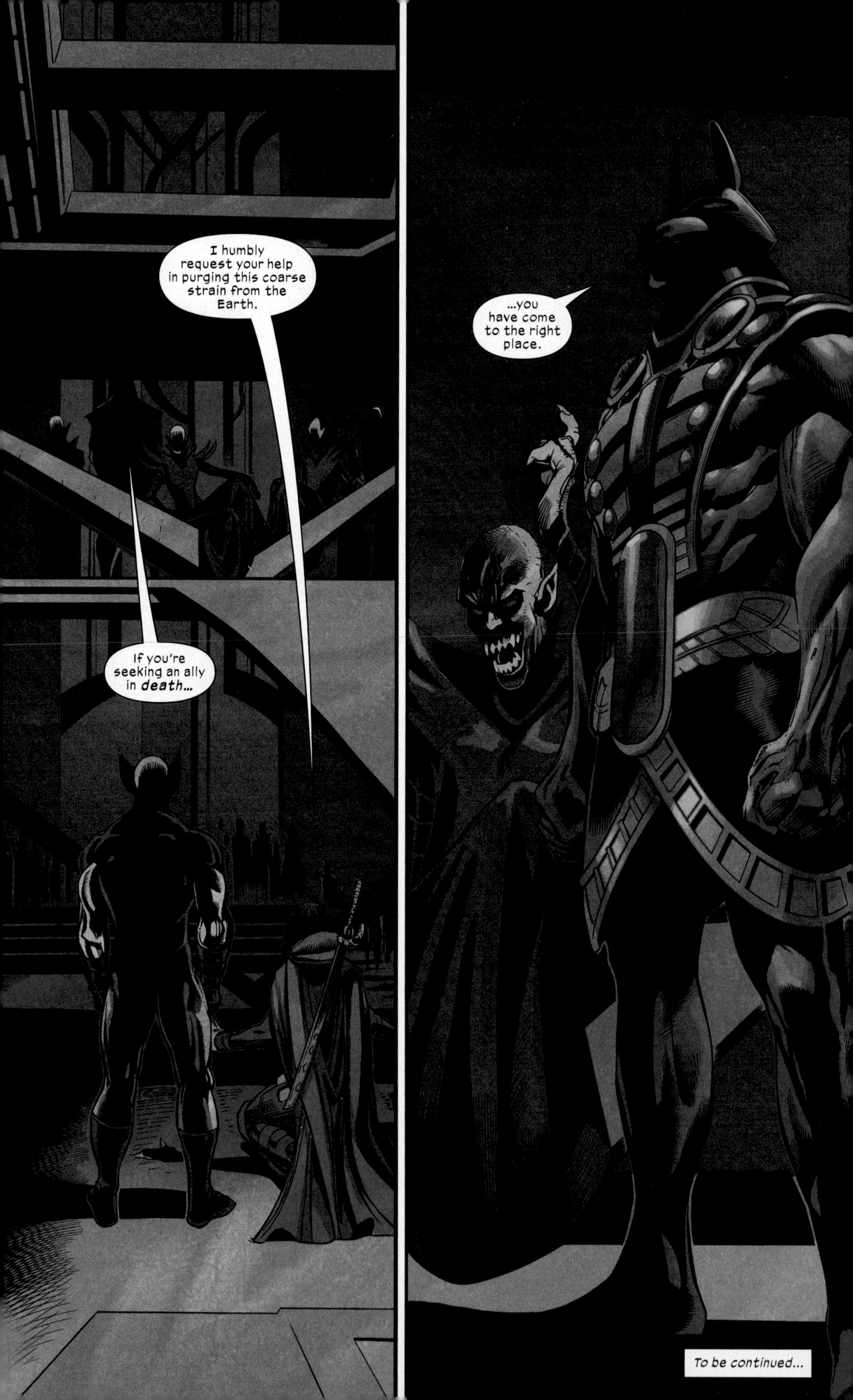
I humbly request your help in purging this coarse strain from the Earth.
If you're seeking an ally in *death*...
...you have come to the right place.
To be continued...

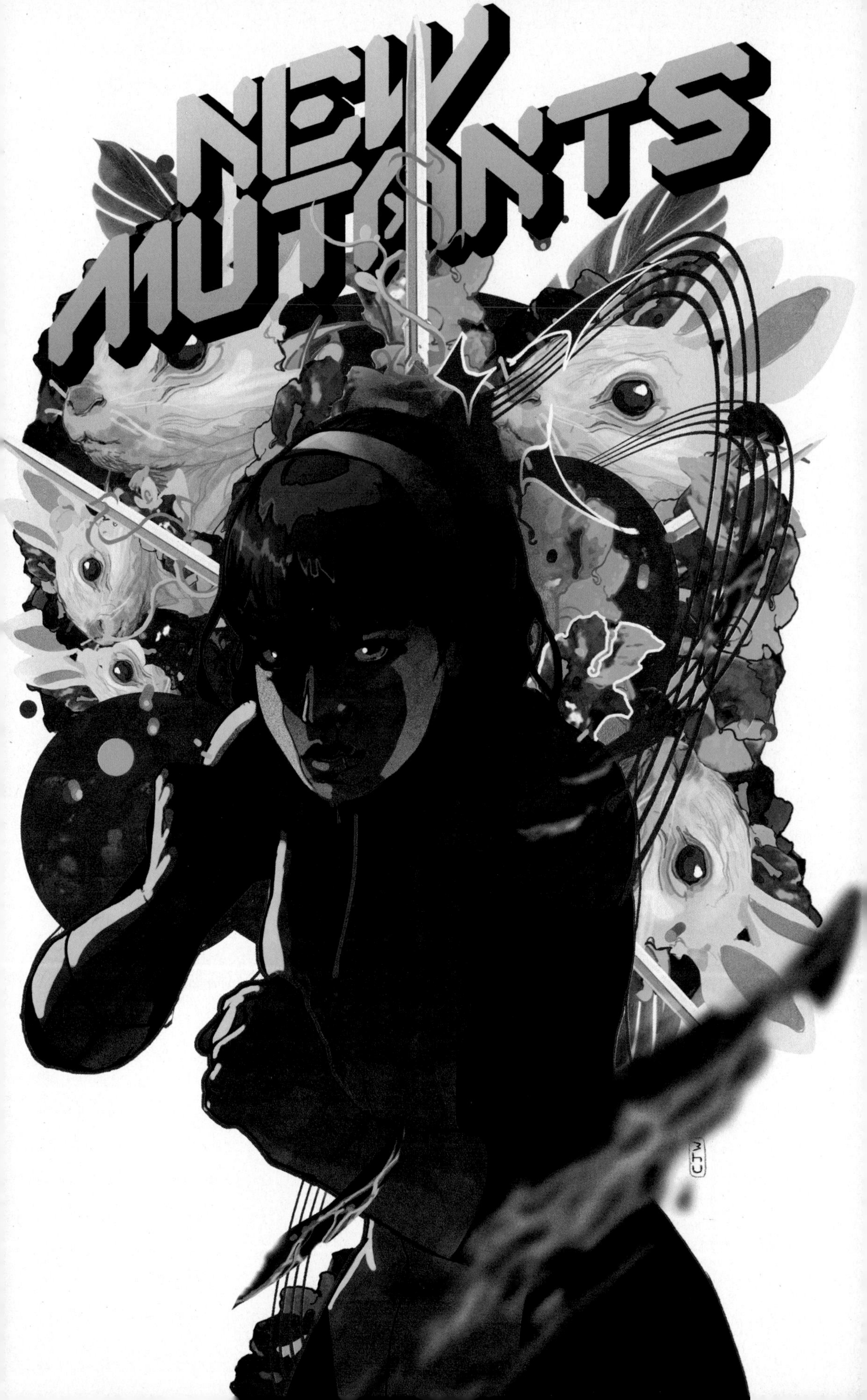
NEW
MUTANTS
CJW

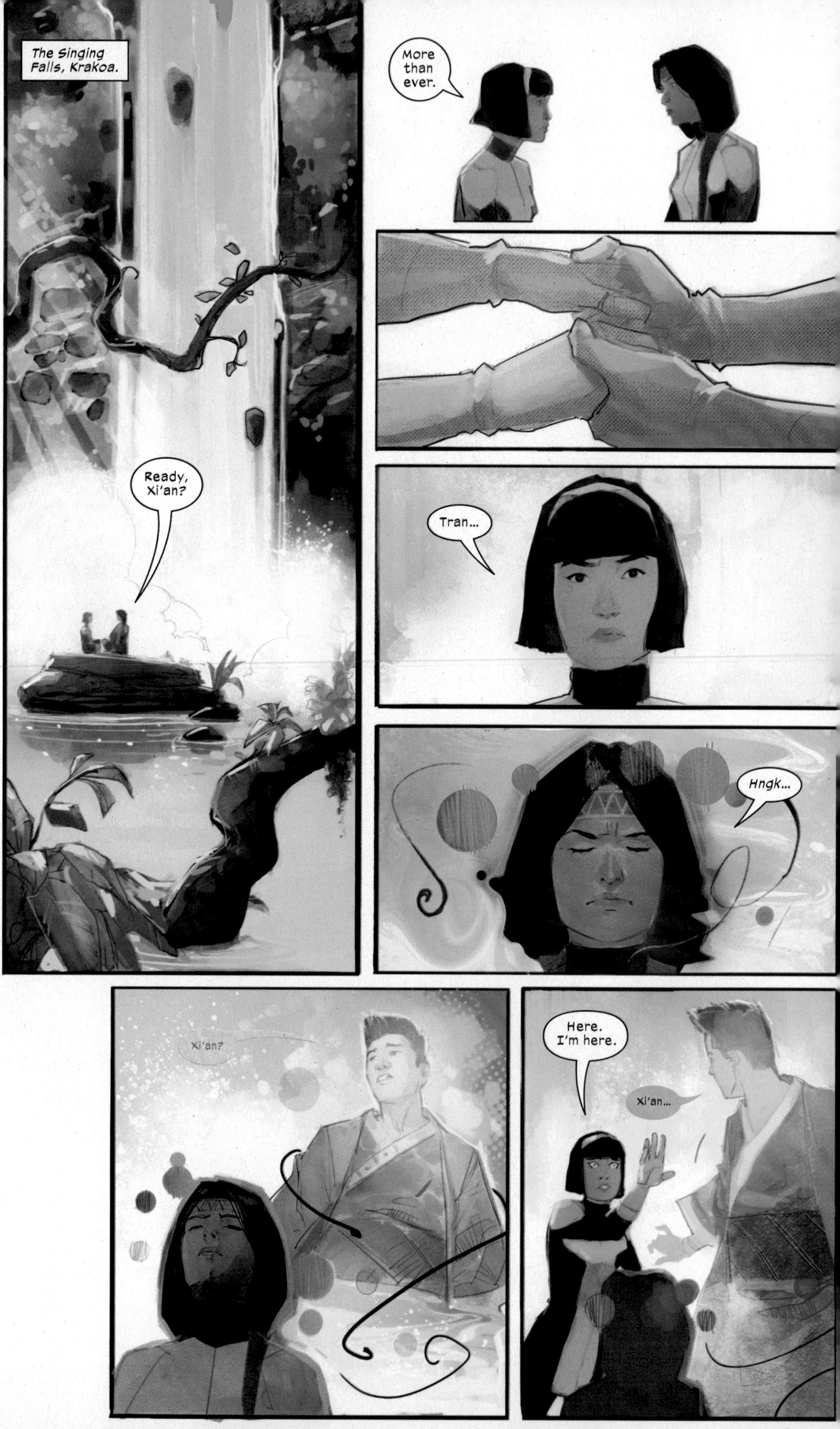

The Singing Falls, Krakoa.
Ready, Xi'an?
More than ever.
Tran...
Hngk...
Xi'an?
Here. I'm here.
Xi'an...

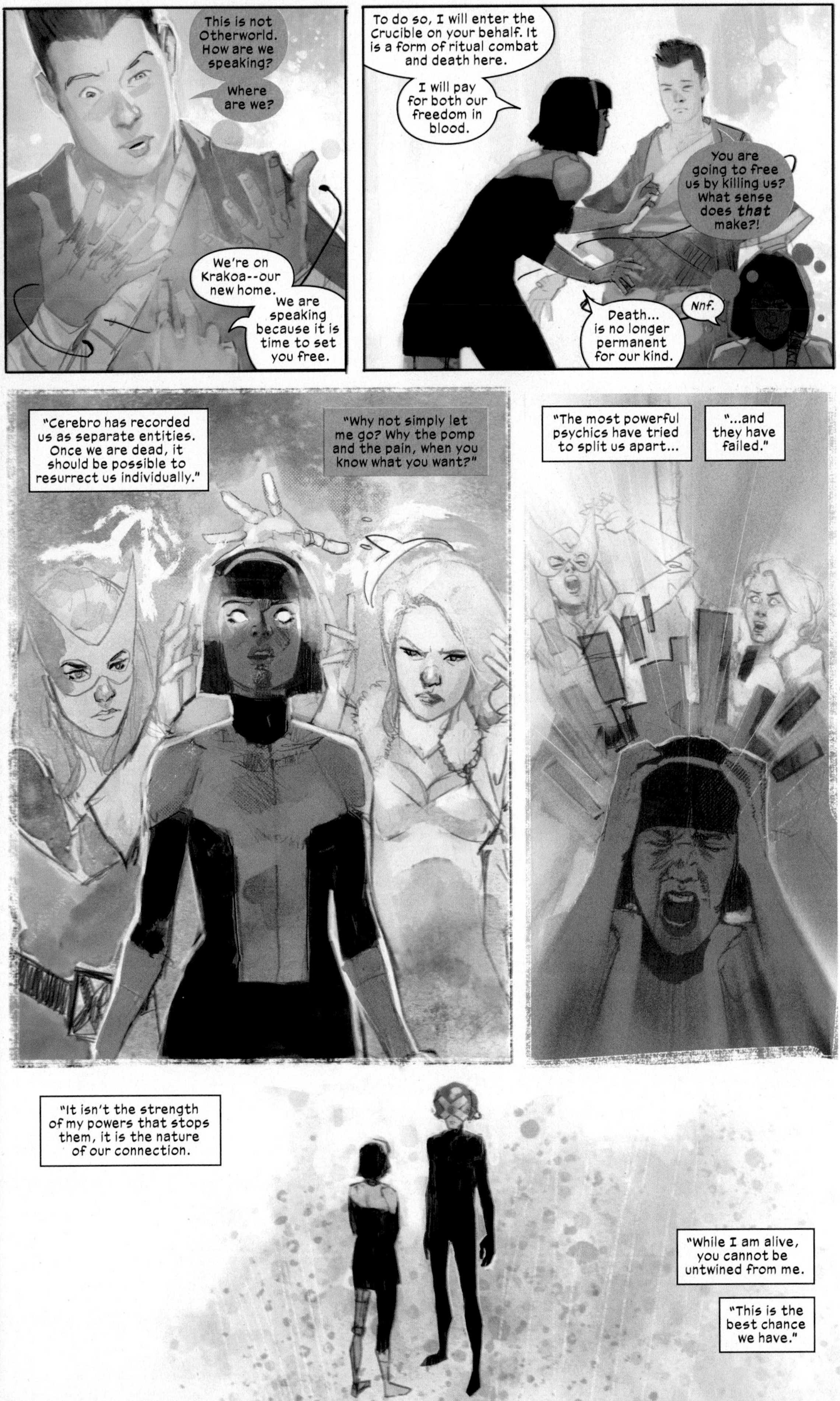
This is not Otherworld. How are we speaking?
Where are we?
We're on Krakoa--our new home.
We are speaking because it is time to set you free.
To do so, I will enter the Crucible on your behalf. It is a form of ritual combat and death here.
I will pay for both our freedom in blood.
You are going to free us by killing us? What sense does *that* make?!
Death... is no longer permanent for our kind.
Nnf.
"Cerebro has recorded us as separate entities. Once we are dead, it should be possible to resurrect us individually."
"Why not simply let me go? Why the pomp and the pain, when you know what you want?"
"The most powerful psychics have tried to split us apart...
"...and they have failed."
"It isn't the strength of my powers that stops them, it is the nature of our connection.
"While I am alive, you cannot be untwined from me.
"This is the best chance we have."

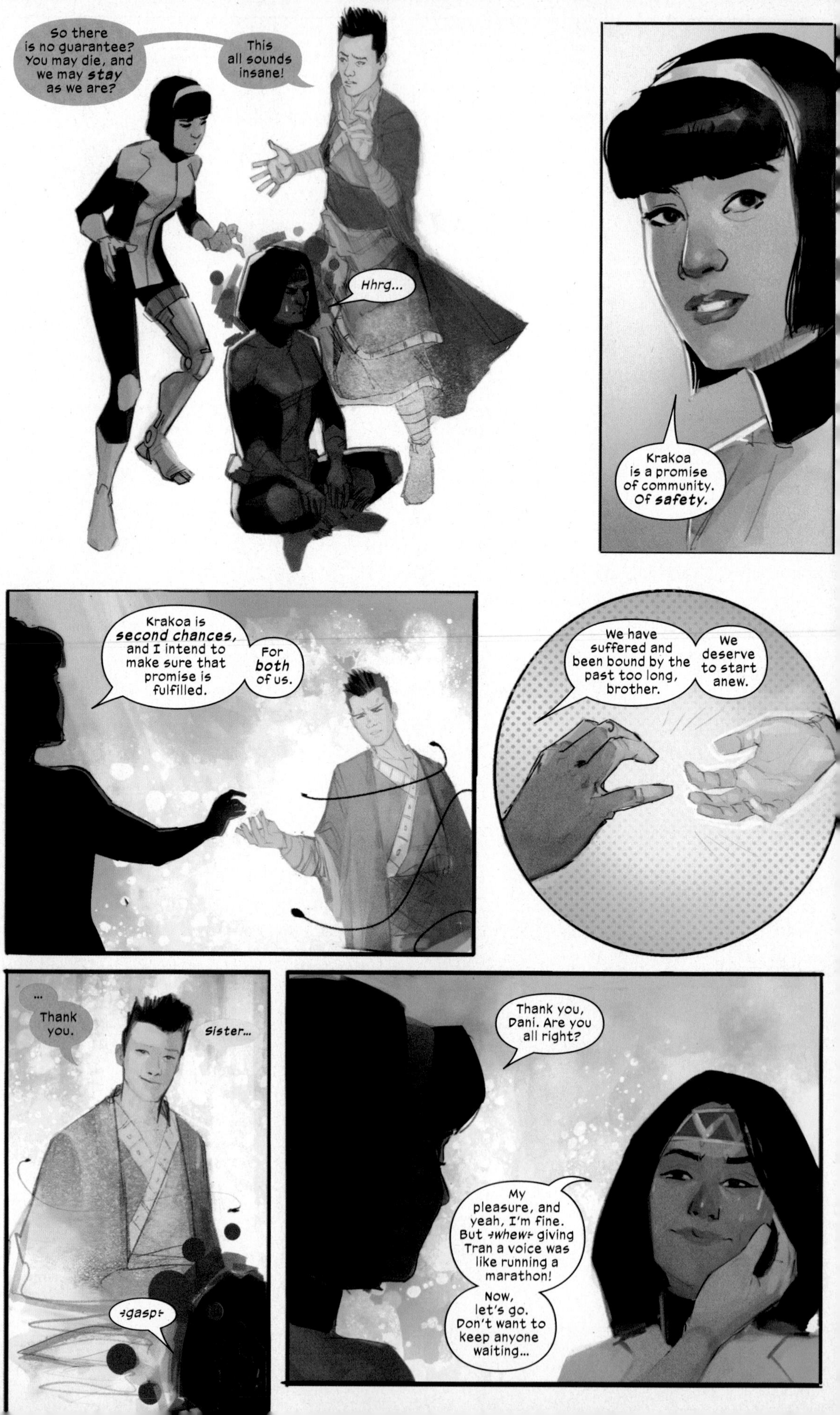
So there is no guarantee? You may die, and we may stay as we are?
This all sounds insane!
Hhrg...
Krakoa is a promise of community. Of safety.
Krakoa is second chances, and I intend to make sure that promise is fulfilled.
For both of us.
We have suffered and been bound by the past too long, brother.
We deserve to start anew.
... Thank you.
Sister...
‡gasp‡
Thank you, Dani. Are you all right?
My pleasure, and yeah, I'm fine. But ‡whew‡ giving Tran a voice was like running a marathon!
Now, let's go. Don't want to keep anyone waiting...

PSYCHIC RESCUE REPORT (FAILURE)

SUBJECTS: Karma (Xi'an Coy Manh), Tran Coy Manh

RELEVANT CONTEXT:

- Subjects are twin siblings who share a similar power set.

- Initial psychic bonding occurred during a conflict, in which Karma absorbed Tran's "life essence" in total.

- Tran gained influence over Karma for a time and succeeded in releasing his "soul" from her through magical interference.

- A secondary bonding incident occurred, through magical intervention involving Magik's soulsword.

- This bonding suppressed Tran's ability to influence Karma.

PROCEDURE(S): Psychic extraction

PARTICIPANTS: Karma [& Tran], Psylocke (Kwannon), Prestige (Rachel Summers), Marvel Girl (Jean Grey) & White Queen (Emma Frost) [in tandem], Professor X

ATTEMPTS: 4

PROCEDURE(S): Magical/soulsword extraction

PARTICIPANTS: Karma [& Tran], Magik (Illyana Rasputina)

ATTEMPTS: 1

NOTES: The connection forged through the power of the soulsword seems to have activated a reciprocal consciousness latch between the subjects, which cannot be undone while they are both alive. All attempts have resulted in failure. Pushing beyond would likely result in permanent psychic damage to all involved (and possibly anyone within a "blast" radius of a few miles).

Further, it appears that even though Magik's sword was involved in re-binding Tran to Karma, it cannot undo it.

That Cerebro reads the twins as separate entities is hopeful, however. Theoretically, with the proper attention and intention during the Resurrection process, separation **should** be possible, though there is a real possibility that the two will be changed permanently even if they are. Karma has been informed of this risk and has chosen to move forward with her plans for the Crucible.

May her faith in us be rewarded.

-- Professor X

[00_synergy_X]
[X__power__00]

LET THE LIVING GO ON

The NEW MUTANTS have been tasked with training the youth of Krakoa -- teaching them to use and combine their mutant abilities! But basic training isn't working for everyone -- a group of young mutants have fallen in with the Shadow King, who's been using his psychic powers to experiment with body-swapping, though Scout became suspicious of his motives. Meanwhile, a mysterious psychic presence has been haunting Karma -- her brother Tran, whose soul is bound to her own. And she will go to any lengths to free him...and to become free herself.

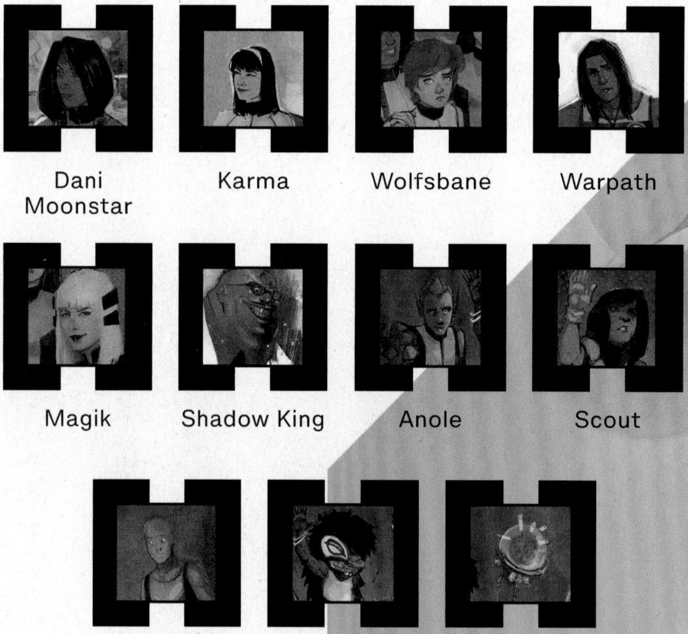

Dani Moonstar, Karma, Wolfsbane, Warpath
Magik, Shadow King, Anole, Scout
Rain Boy, Cosmar, No-Girl

NEW MUTANTS

[X_18]

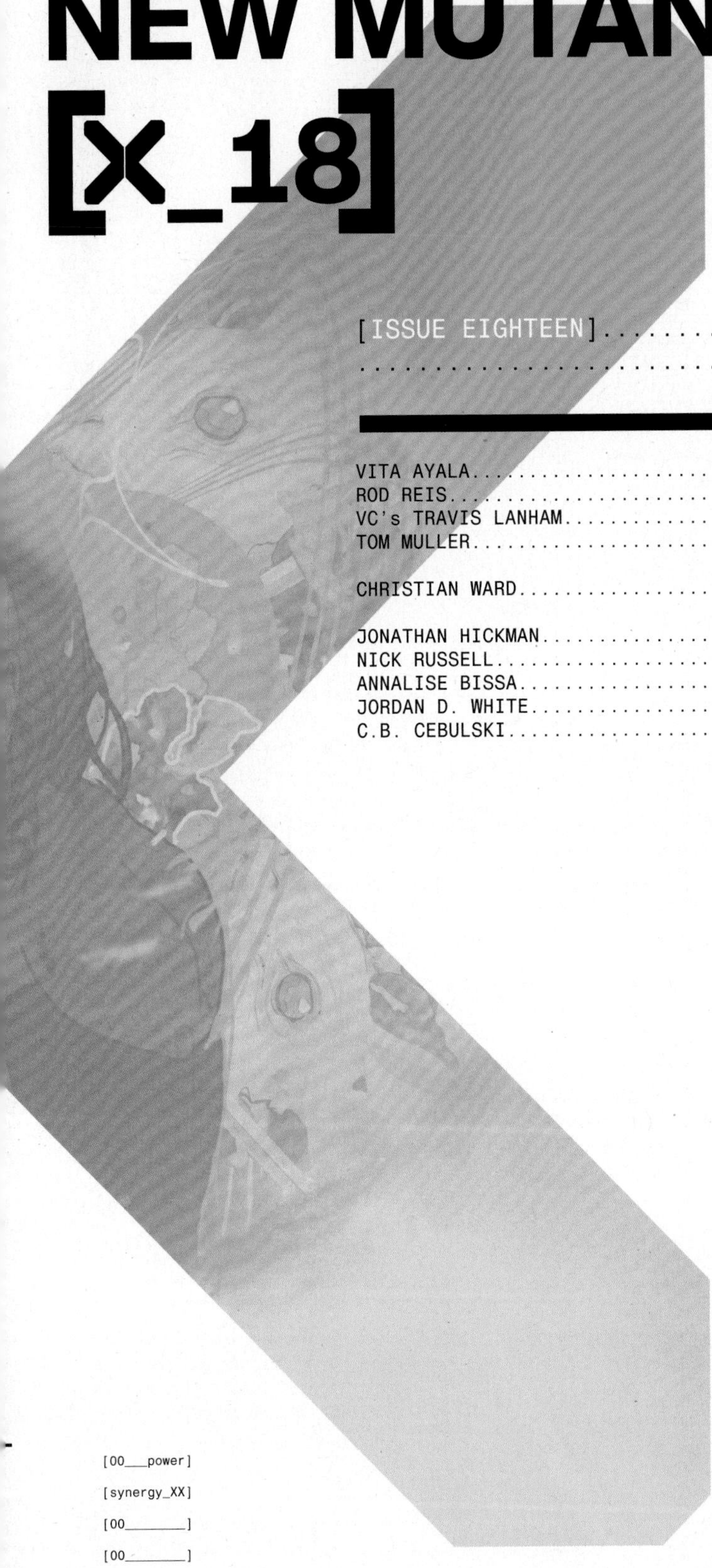

[ISSUE EIGHTEEN]....................................
....................................HOMECOMING

VITA AYALA....................................[WRITER]
ROD REIS....................................[ARTIST]
VC's TRAVIS LANHAM....................................[LETTERER]
TOM MULLER....................................[DESIGN]

CHRISTIAN WARD....................................[COVER ARTIST]

JONATHAN HICKMAN....................................[HEAD OF X]
NICK RUSSELL....................................[PRODUCTION]
ANNALISE BISSA....................................[EDITOR]
JORDAN D. WHITE....................................[SENIOR EDITOR]
C.B. CEBULSKI....................................[EDITOR IN CHIEF]

[00___power]
[synergy_XX]
[00________]
[00________]
[00______in]
[00_____the]
[00____wild]
[00____hunt]

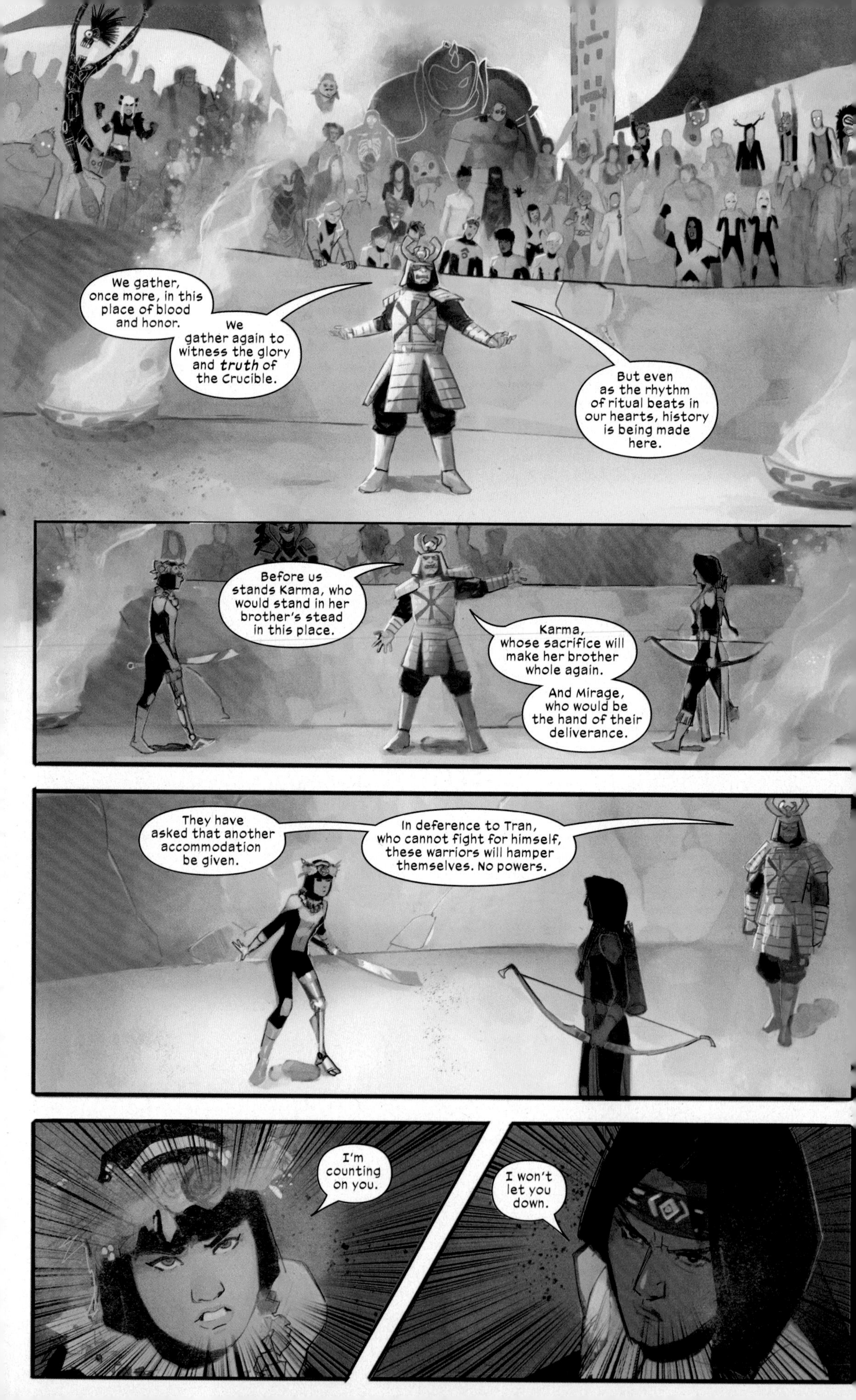
We gather, once more, in this place of blood and honor.
We gather again to witness the glory and *truth* of the Crucible.
But even as the rhythm of ritual beats in our hearts, history is being made here.
Before us stands Karma, who would stand in her brother's stead in this place.
Karma, whose sacrifice will make her brother whole again.
And Mirage, who would be the hand of their deliverance.
They have asked that another accommodation be given.
In deference to Tran, who cannot fight for himself, these warriors will hamper themselves. No powers.
I'm counting on you.
I won't let you down.

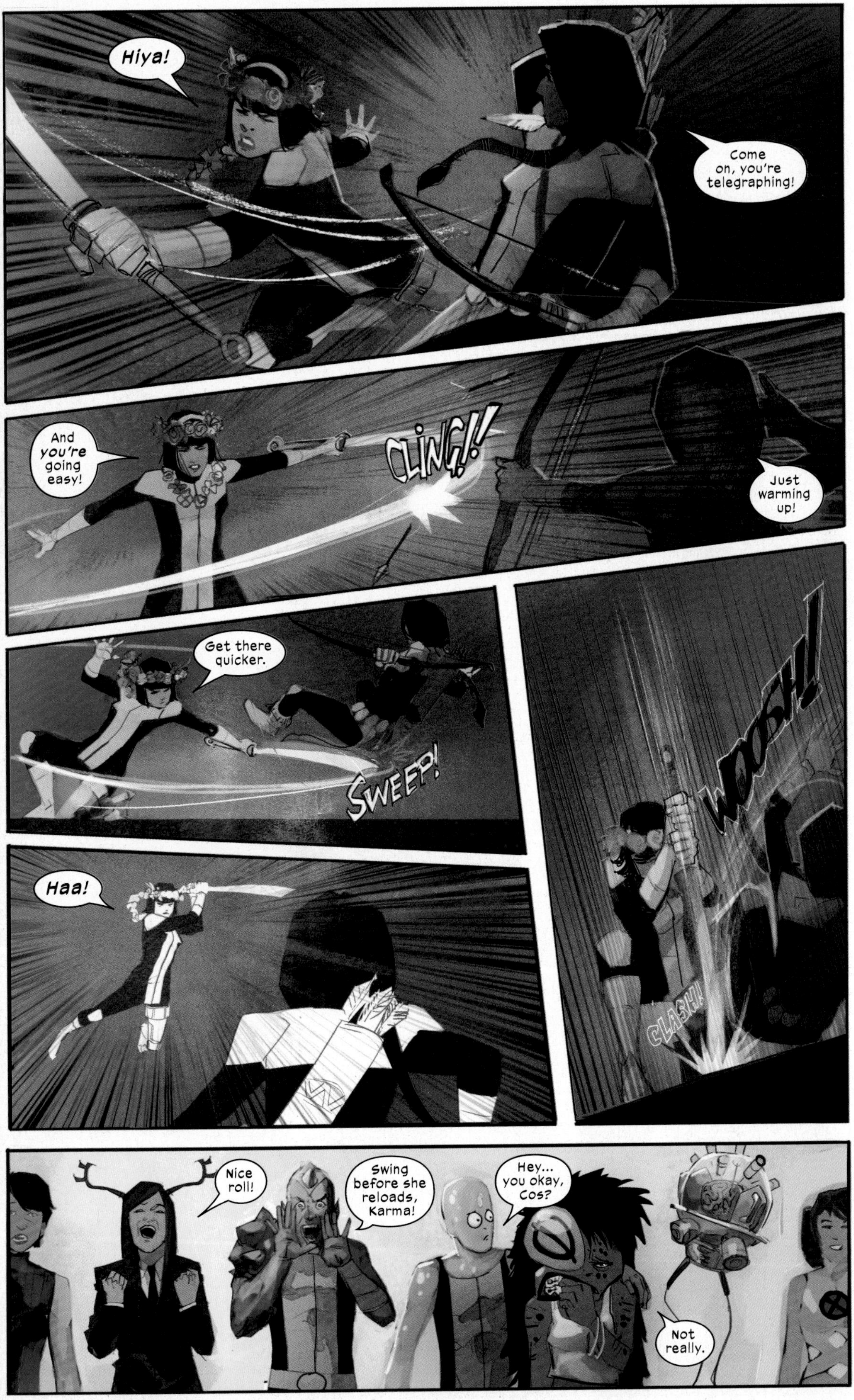
Hiya!
Come on, you're telegraphing!
And you're going easy!
CLING!!
Just warming up!
Get there quicker.
SWEEP!
Haa!
WOOSH!
CLASH!
Nice roll!
Swing before she reloads, Karma!
Hey... you okay, Cos?
Not really.

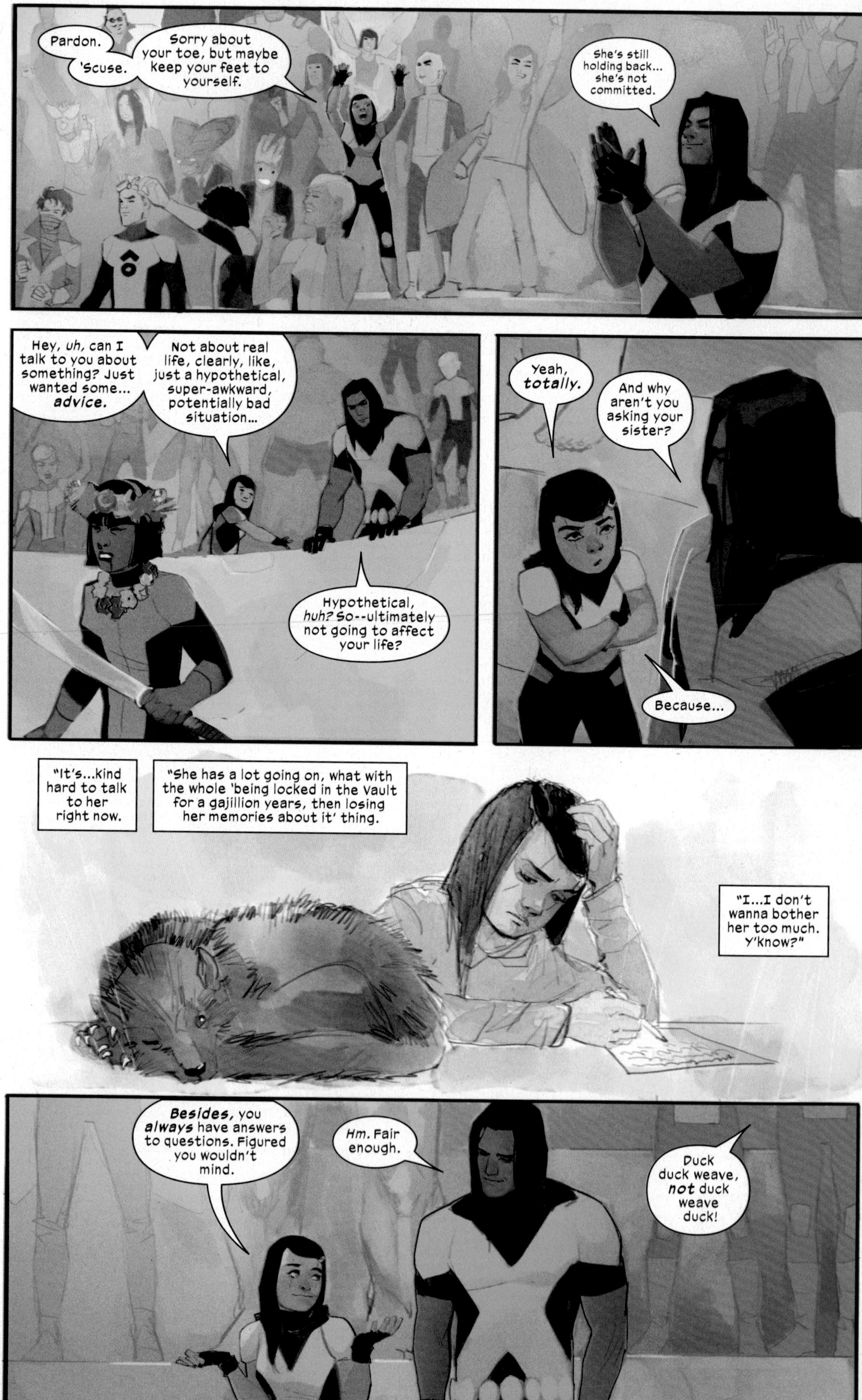
Pardon.
'Scuse.
Sorry about your toe, but maybe keep your feet to yourself.
She's still holding back... she's not committed.
Hey, uh, can I talk to you about something? Just wanted some... advice.
Not about real life, clearly, like, just a hypothetical, super-awkward, potentially bad situation...
Hypothetical, huh? So--ultimately not going to affect your life?
Yeah, totally.
And why aren't you asking your sister?
Because...
"It's...kind hard to talk to her right now.
"She has a lot going on, what with the whole 'being locked in the Vault for a gajillion years, then losing her memories about it' thing.
"I...I don't wanna bother her too much. Y'know?"
Besides, you always have answers to questions. Figured you wouldn't mind.
Hm. Fair enough.
Duck duck weave, not duck weave duck!

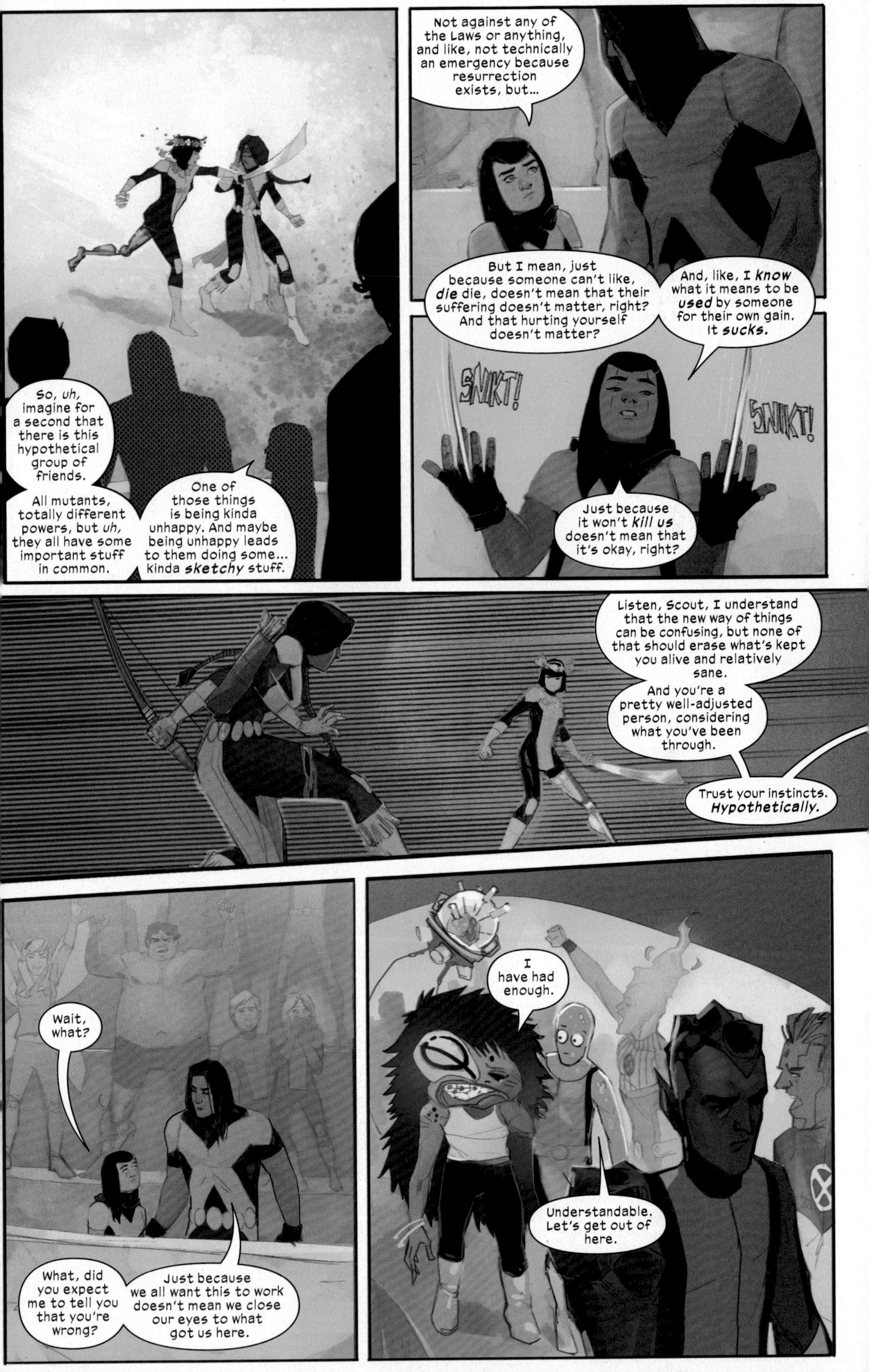
So, uh, imagine for a second that there is this hypothetical group of friends.
All mutants, totally different powers, but uh, they all have some important stuff in common.
One of those things is being kinda unhappy. And maybe being unhappy leads to them doing some... kinda sketchy stuff.
Not against any of the Laws or anything, and like, not technically an emergency because resurrection exists, but...
But I mean, just because someone can't like, die die, doesn't mean that their suffering doesn't matter, right? And that hurting yourself doesn't matter?
And, like, I know what it means to be used by someone for their own gain. It sucks.
SNIKT!
SNIKT!
Just because it won't kill us doesn't mean that it's okay, right?
Listen, Scout, I understand that the new way of things can be confusing, but none of that should erase what's kept you alive and relatively sane.
And you're a pretty well-adjusted person, considering what you've been through.
Trust your instincts. Hypothetically.
Wait, what?
What, did you expect me to tell you that you're wrong?
Just because we all want this to work doesn't mean we close our eyes to what got us here.
I have had enough.
Understandable. Let's get out of here.

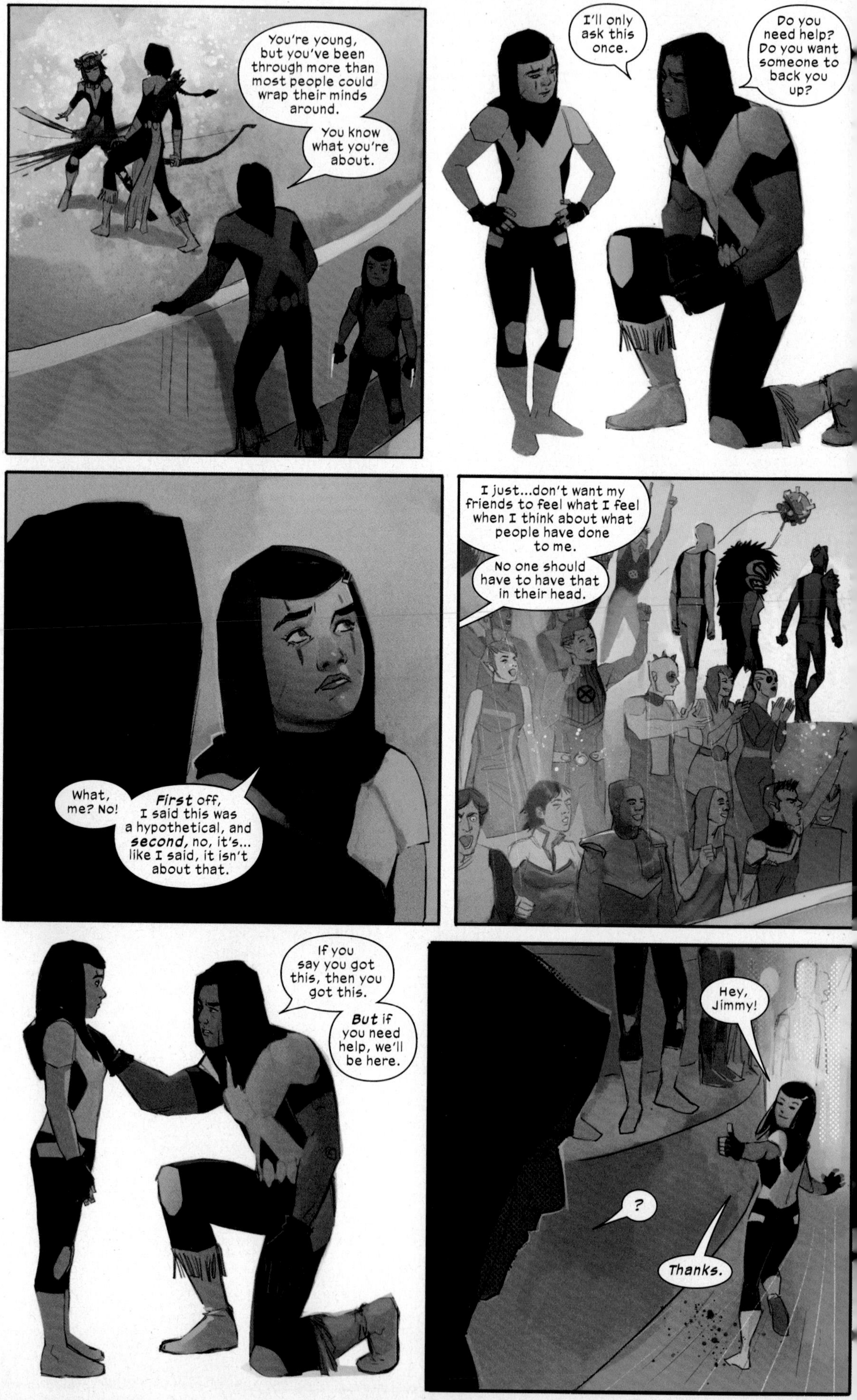

You're young, but you've been through more than most people could wrap their minds around.
You know what you're about.
I'll only ask this once.
Do you need help? Do you want someone to back you up?
What, me? No!
First off, I said this was a hypothetical, and *second,* no, it's... like I said, it isn't about that.
I just...don't want my friends to feel what I feel when I think about what people have done to me.
No one should have to have that in their head.
If you say you got this, then you got this.
But if you need help, we'll be here.
Hey, Jimmy!
?
Thanks.

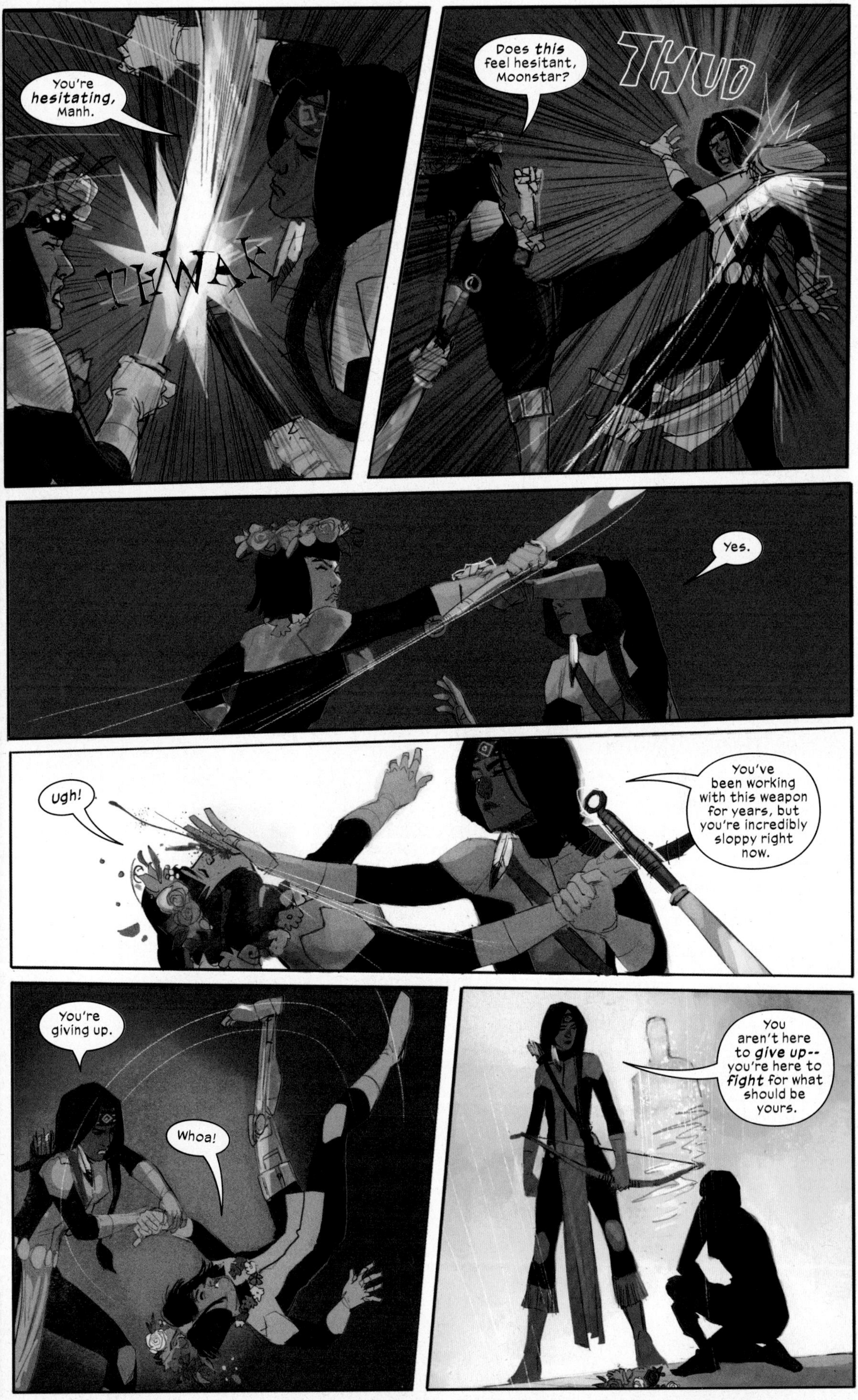
You're *hesitating,* Manh.
THWAK
Does *this* feel hesitant, Moonstar?
THUD
Yes.
Ugh!
You've been working with this weapon for years, but you're incredibly sloppy right now.
You're giving up.
Whoa!
You aren't here to *give up--* you're here to *fight* for what should be yours.

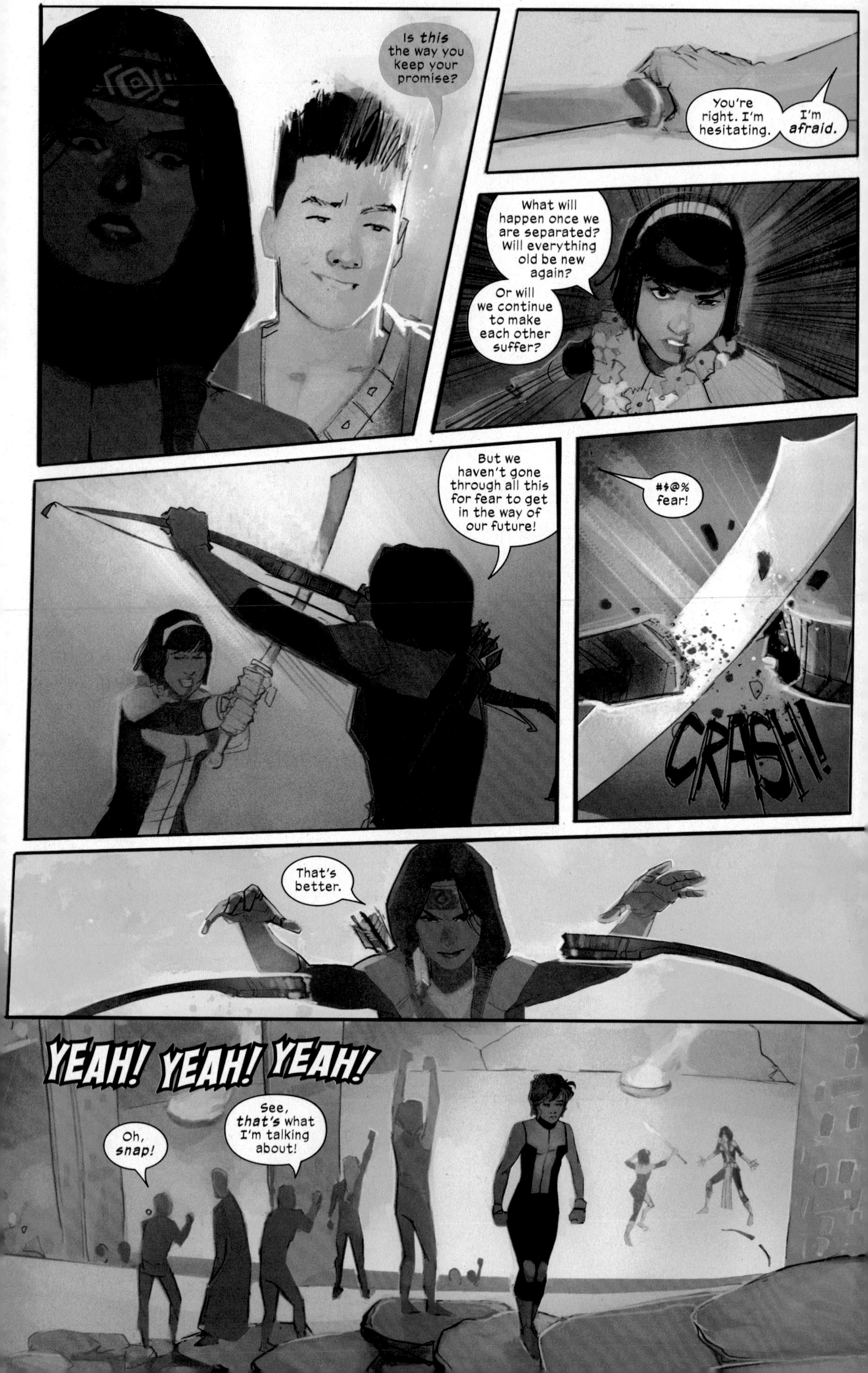
Is this the way you keep your promise?
You're right. I'm hesitating.
I'm afraid.
What will happen once we are separated? Will everything old be new again?
Or will we continue to make each other suffer?
But we haven't gone through all this for fear to get in the way of our future!
#$@% fear!
CRASH!
That's better.
YEAH! YEAH! YEAH!
Oh, snap!
See, that's what I'm talking about!

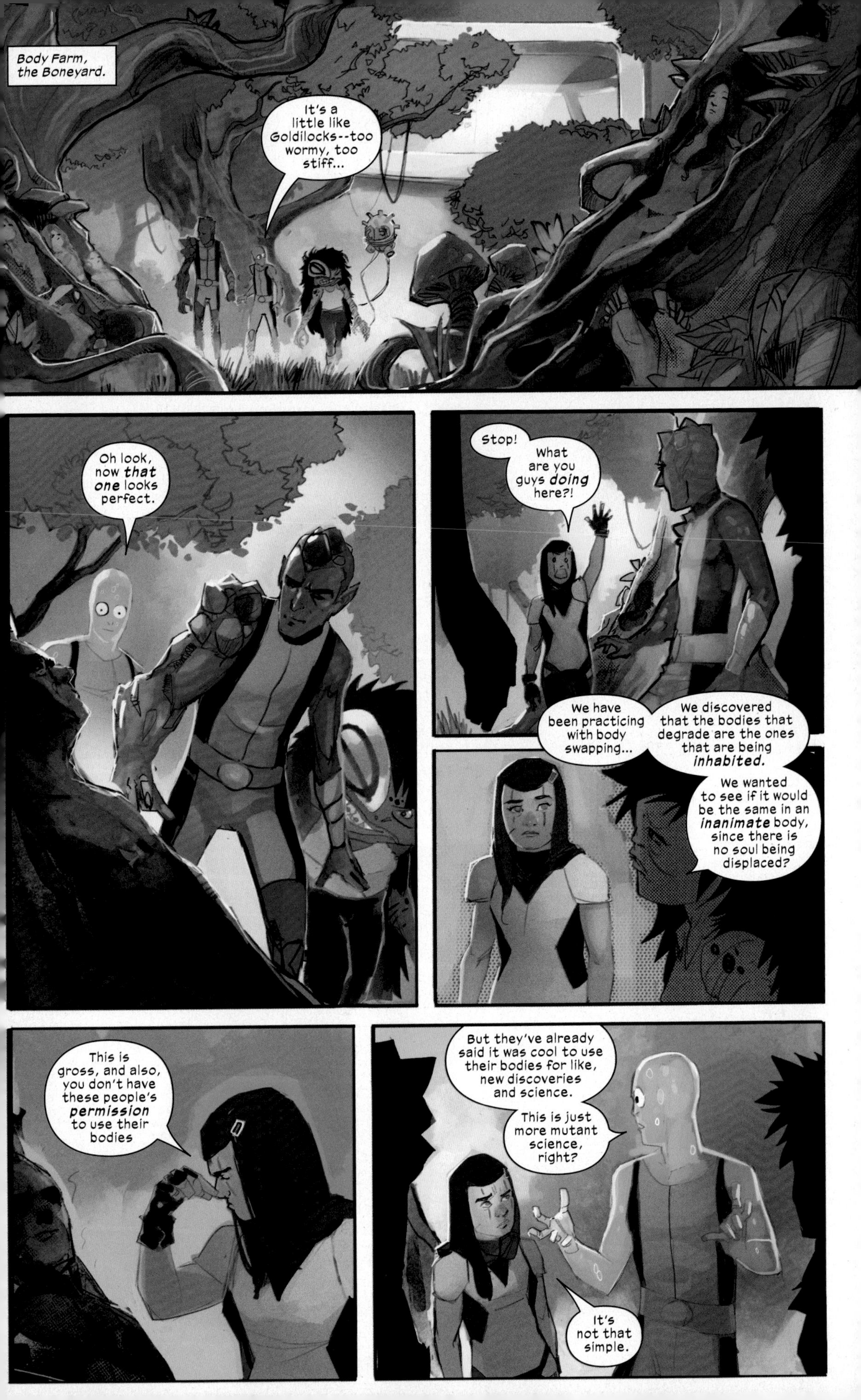
Body Farm, the Boneyard.
It's a little like Goldilocks--too wormy, too stiff...
Oh look, now that one looks perfect.
Stop! What are you guys doing here?!
We have been practicing with body swapping...
We discovered that the bodies that degrade are the ones that are being inhabited.
We wanted to see if it would be the same in an inanimate body, since there is no soul being displaced?
This is gross, and also, you don't have these people's permission to use their bodies
But they've already said it was cool to use their bodies for like, new discoveries and science.
This is just more mutant science, right?
It's not that simple.

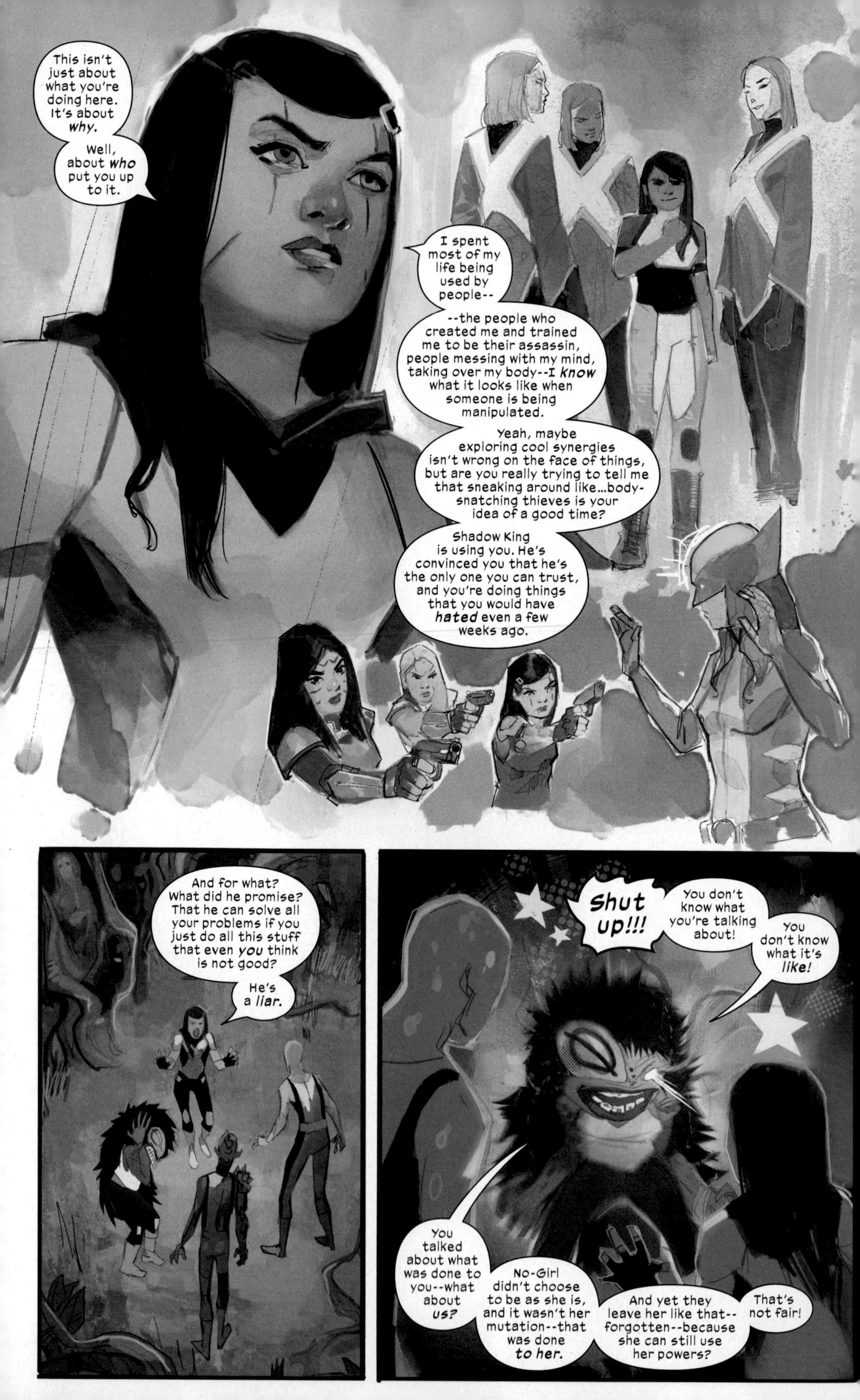

This isn't just about what you're doing here. It's about *why.*
Well, about *who* put you up to it.
I spent most of my life being used by people--
--the people who created me and trained me to be their assassin, people messing with my mind, taking over my body--I *know* what it looks like when someone is being manipulated.
Yeah, maybe exploring cool synergies isn't wrong on the face of things, but are you really trying to tell me that sneaking around like...body-snatching thieves is your idea of a good time?
Shadow King is using you. He's convinced you that he's the only one you can trust, and you're doing things that you would have *hated* even a few weeks ago.
And for what? What did he promise? That he can solve all your problems if you just do all this stuff that even *you* think is not good?
He's a *liar.*
Shut up!!!
You don't know what you're talking about!
You don't know what it's *like!*
You talked about what was done to you--what about *us?*
No-Girl didn't choose to be as she is, and it wasn't her mutation--that was done *to her.*
And yet they leave her like that--forgotten--because she can still use her powers?
That's not fair!

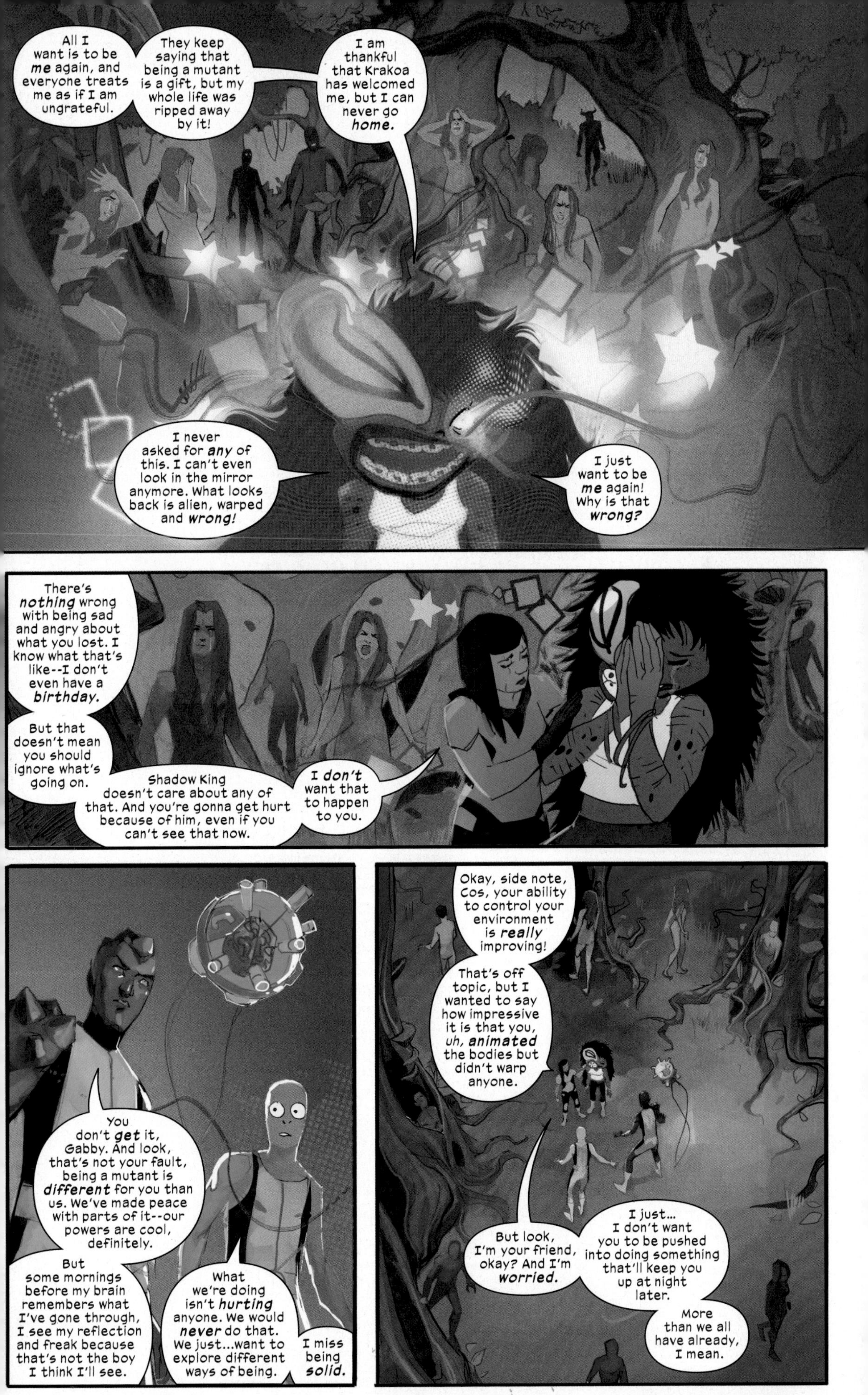

All I want is to be *me* again, and everyone treats me as if I am ungrateful.
They keep saying that being a mutant is a gift, but my whole life was ripped away by it!
I am thankful that Krakoa has welcomed me, but I can never go *home.*
I never asked for *any* of this. I can't even look in the mirror anymore. What looks back is alien, warped and *wrong!*
I just want to be *me* again! Why is that *wrong?*
There's *nothing* wrong with being sad and angry about what you lost. I know what that's like--I don't even have a *birthday.*
But that doesn't mean you should ignore what's going on.
Shadow King doesn't care about any of that. And you're gonna get hurt because of him, even if you can't see that now.
I *don't* want that to happen to you.
You don't *get* it, Gabby. And look, that's not your fault, being a mutant is *different* for you than us. We've made peace with parts of it--our powers are cool, definitely.
But some mornings before my brain remembers what I've gone through, I see my reflection and freak because that's not the boy I think I'll see.
What we're doing isn't *hurting* anyone. We would *never* do that. We just...want to explore different ways of being.
I miss being *solid.*
Okay, side note, Cos, your ability to control your environment is *really* improving!
That's off topic, but I wanted to say how impressive it is that you, *uh, animated* the bodies but didn't warp anyone.
But look, I'm your friend, okay? And I'm *worried.*
I just... I don't want you to be pushed into doing something that'll keep you up at night later.
More than we all have already, I mean.

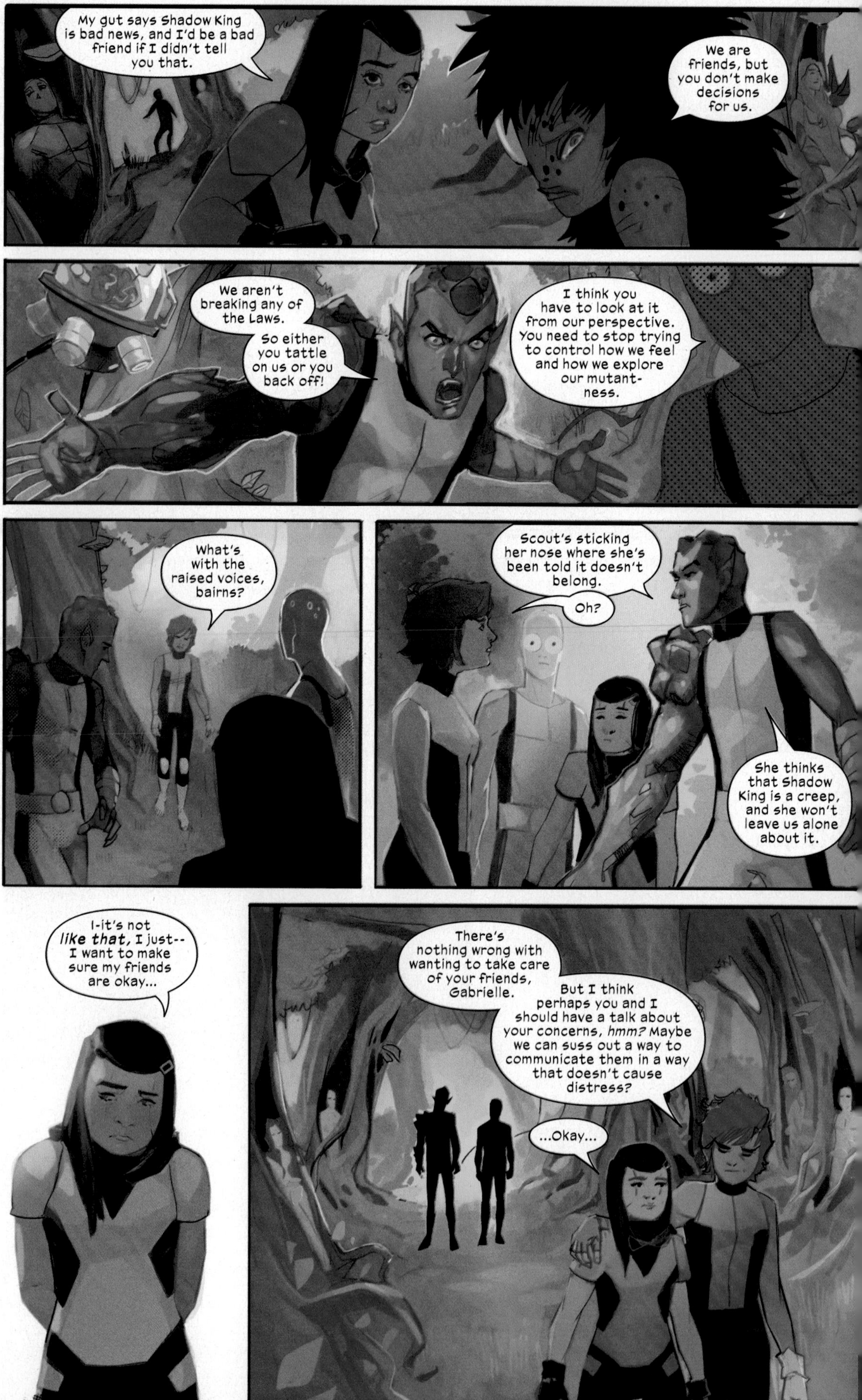

My gut says Shadow King is bad news, and I'd be a bad friend if I didn't tell you that.
We are friends, but you don't make decisions for us.
We aren't breaking any of the Laws.
So either you tattle on us or you back off!
I think you have to look at it from our perspective. You need to stop trying to control how we feel and how we explore our mutant-ness.
What's with the raised voices, bairns?
Scout's sticking her nose where she's been told it doesn't belong.
Oh?
She thinks that Shadow King is a creep, and she won't leave us alone about it.
I-it's not *like that,* I just-- I want to make sure my friends are okay...
There's nothing wrong with wanting to take care of your friends, Gabrielle.
But I think perhaps you and I should have a talk about your concerns, *hmm?* Maybe we can suss out a way to communicate them in a way that doesn't cause distress?
...Okay...

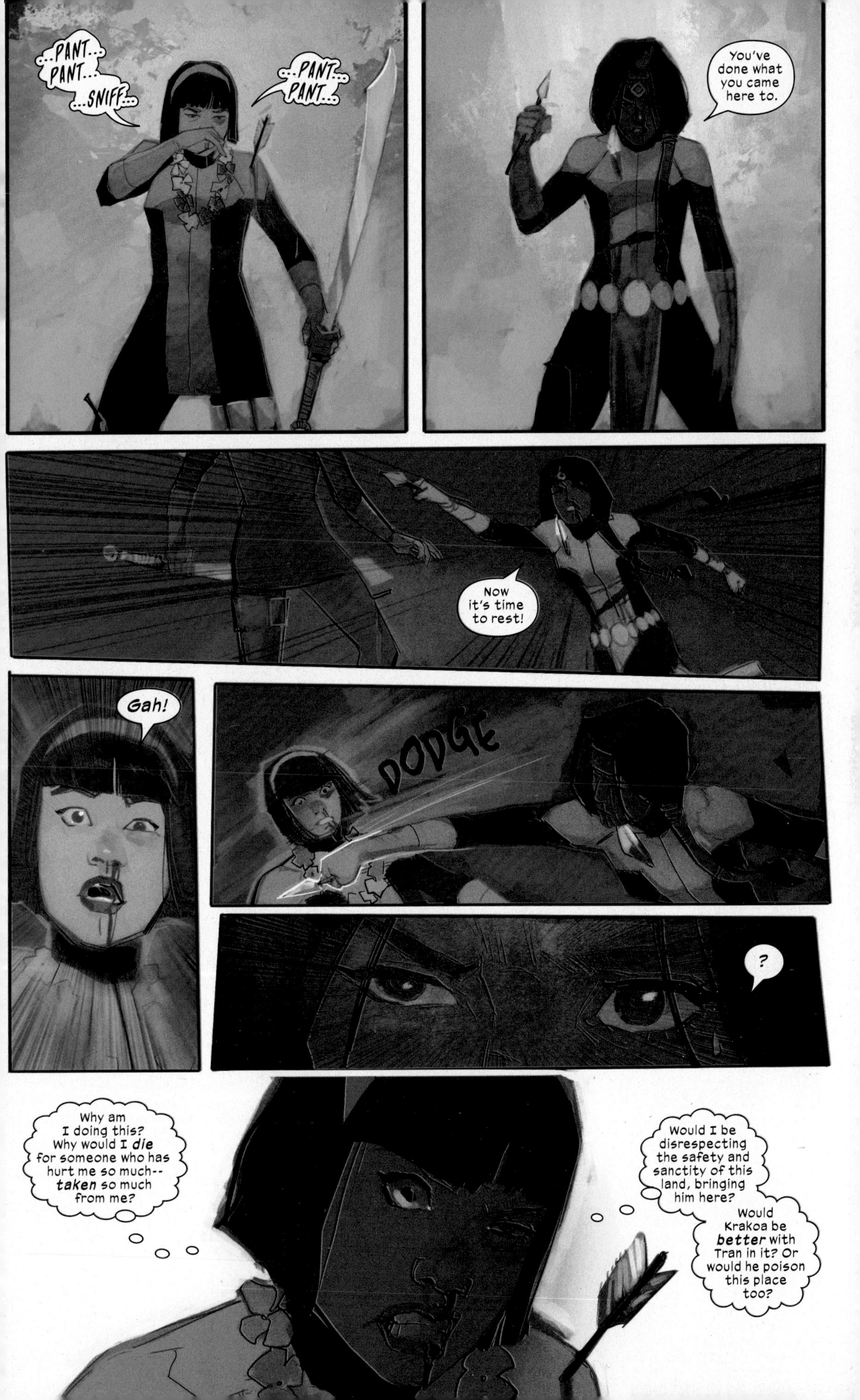
...PANT... PANT... ...SNIFF...
...PANT... PANT...
You've done what you came here to.
Now it's time to rest!
Gah!
DODGE
?
Why am I doing this? Why would I *die* for someone who has hurt me so much-- *taken* so much from me?
Would I be disrespecting the safety and sanctity of this land, bringing him here?
Would Krakoa be *better* with Tran in it? Or would he poison this place too?

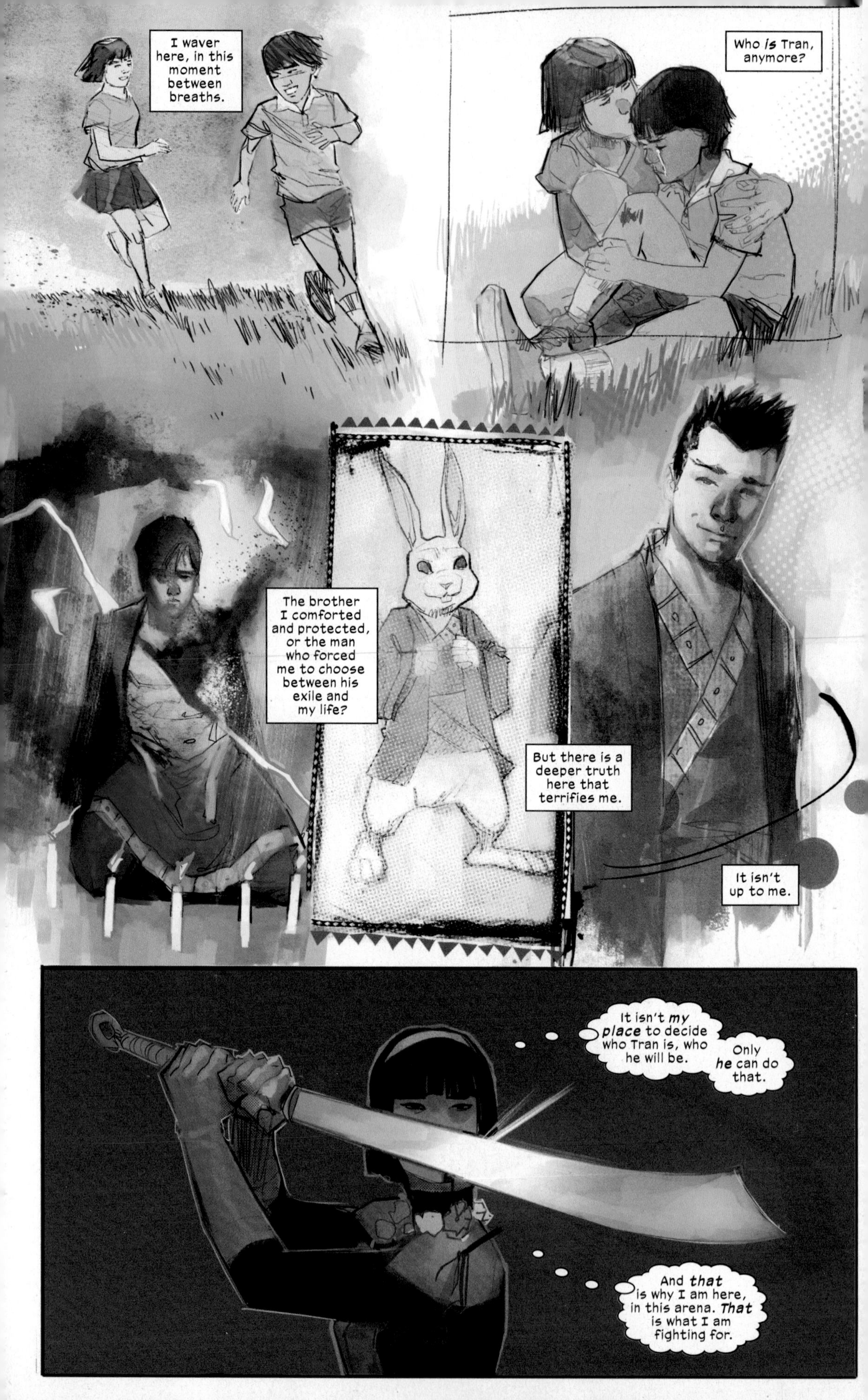
I waver here, in this moment between breaths.
Who *is* Tran, anymore?
The brother I comforted and protected, or the man who forced me to choose between his exile and my life?
But there is a deeper truth here that terrifies me.
It isn't up to me.
It isn't *my* *place* to decide who Tran is, who he will be.
Only *he* can do that.
And *that* is why I am here, in this arena. *That* is what I am fighting for.

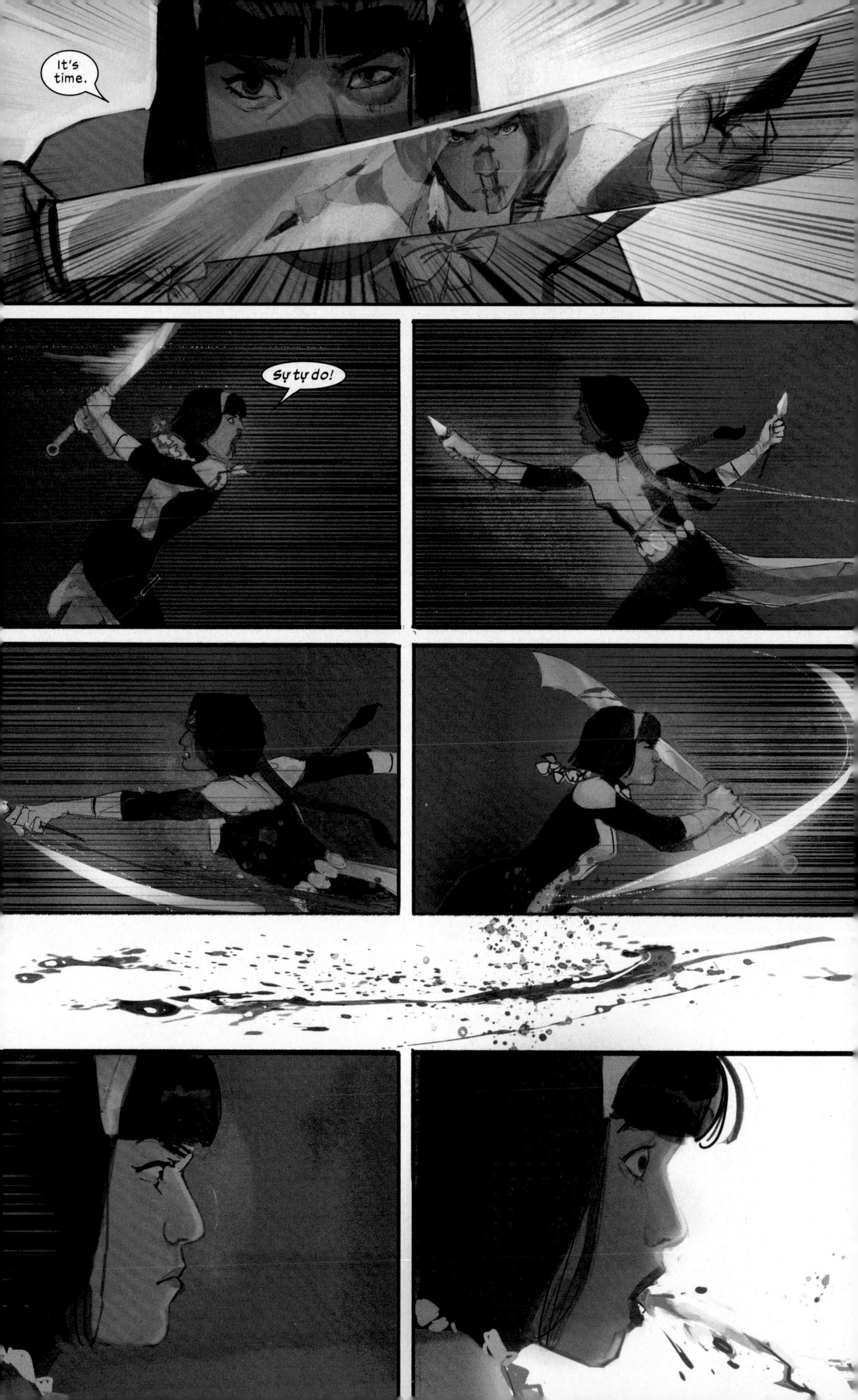
It's time.
Sự tự do!

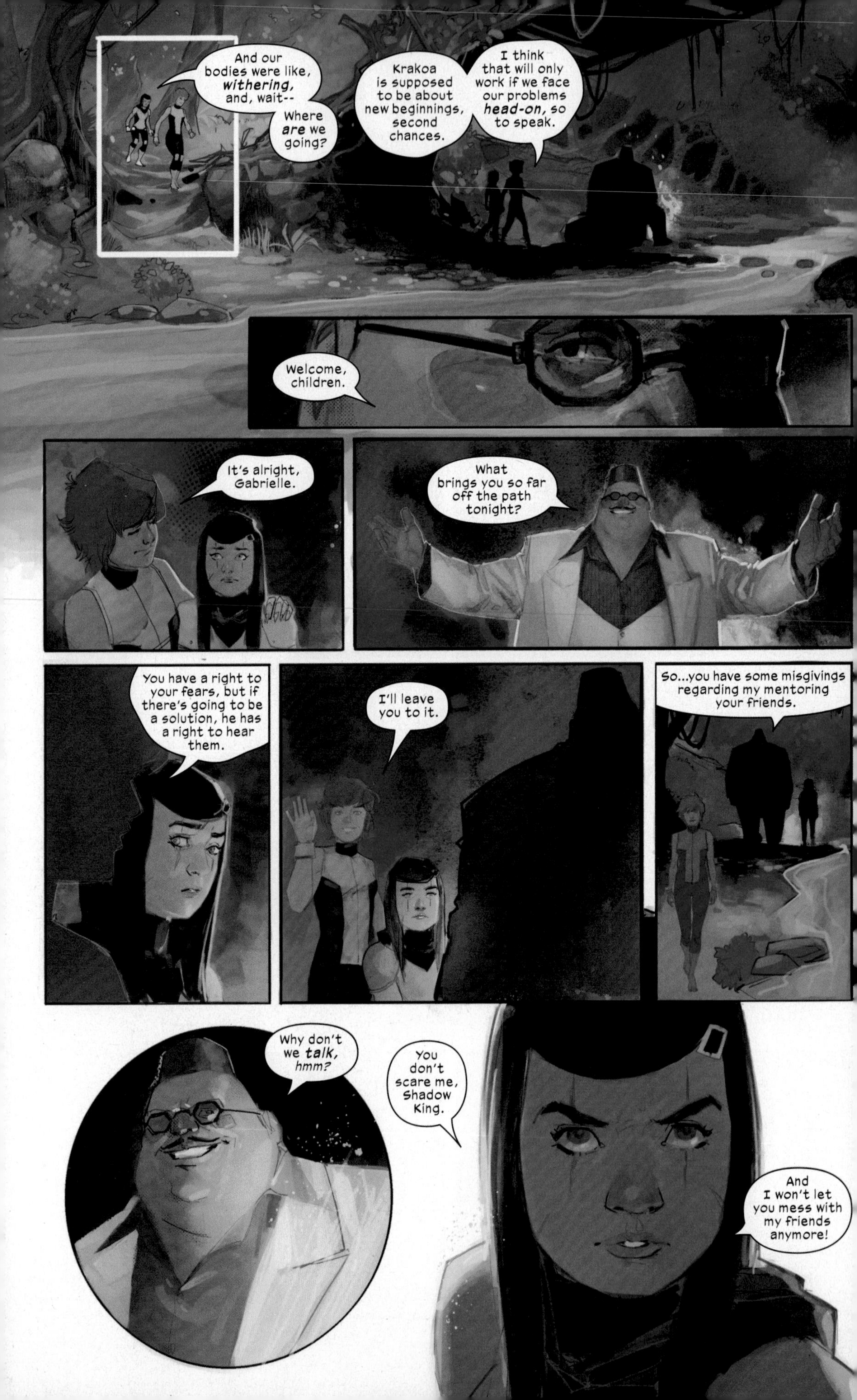
And our bodies were like, *withering,* and, wait--
Where *are* we going?
Krakoa is supposed to be about new beginnings, second chances.
I think that will only work if we face our problems *head-on,* so to speak.
Welcome, children.
It's alright, Gabrielle.
What brings you so far off the path tonight?
You have a right to your fears, but if there's going to be a solution, he has a right to hear them.
I'll leave you to it.
So...you have some misgivings regarding my mentoring your friends.
Why don't we *talk,* *hmm?*
You don't scare me, Shadow King.
And I won't let you mess with my friends anymore!

[ACTION....[quietc]_00]
[REPORT....[ouncil]_18]

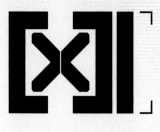

(NON) ACTION REPORT TO THE QUIET COUNCIL

I'll make this quick.

When we came to you with concern about how dangerous the bored mutants running around the island were, you turned it around pretty masterfully and made it our problem to handle. I was ~~butter~~bitter at first, but I'll admit, it turned out to be a smart move--the people on the ground seeing the issue will have a better idea of how to fix it.

But the thing is, <u>we</u> were raised by <u>you</u>. We got our understanding of what it means to be mutants -- of how to deal with the world and each other -- from <u>you</u>. So we ~~appraoched~~ approached the problem like you would.

And we were wrong.

It's not enough to train mutants to "use their powers ~~efficiantyly~~ ~~efficiantly~~ efficiently" and how to fight. These people aren't soldiers or an army, they are supposed to be citizens in a new nation (that already has a pretty well-developed defensive force).

These people (half of them <u>kids</u>) don't need to learn how to kill, they need purpose. They need to feel like they are contributing <u>meaningfully</u> to their new society. They need to feel like a community.

So you're going to start getting requests for more resources, equipment, etc. Jimmy and I are developing a new program, not centered around making child soldiers. Expect some "field trip" requests too.

You ~~gavae~~ gave us this job so that we could do better than you would. So we will.

-- Magik

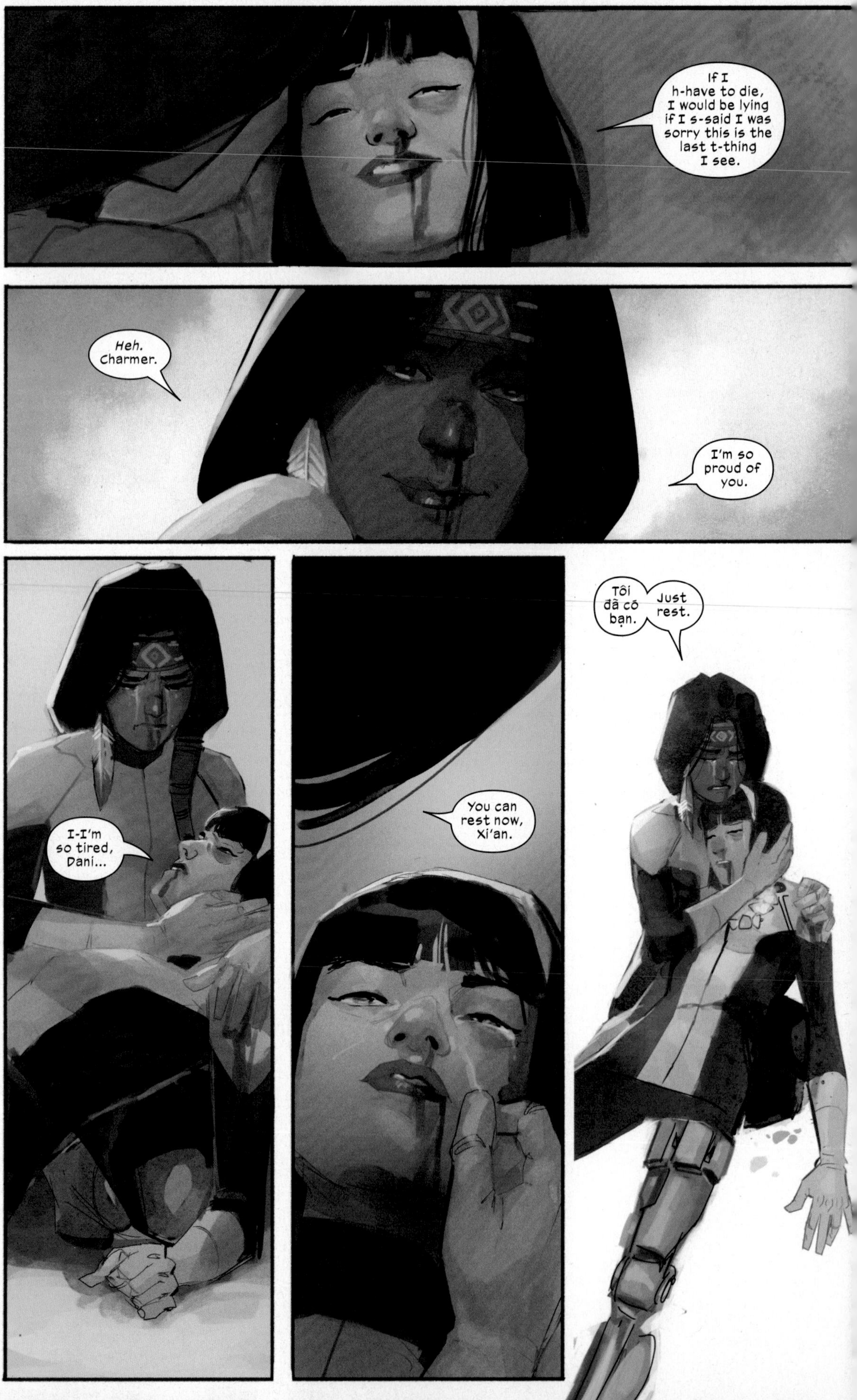
If I h-have to die, I would be lying if I s-said I was sorry this is the last t-thing I see.
Heh. Charmer.
I'm so proud of you.
I-I'm so tired, Dani...
You can rest now, Xi'an.
Tôi đã có bạn.
Just rest.

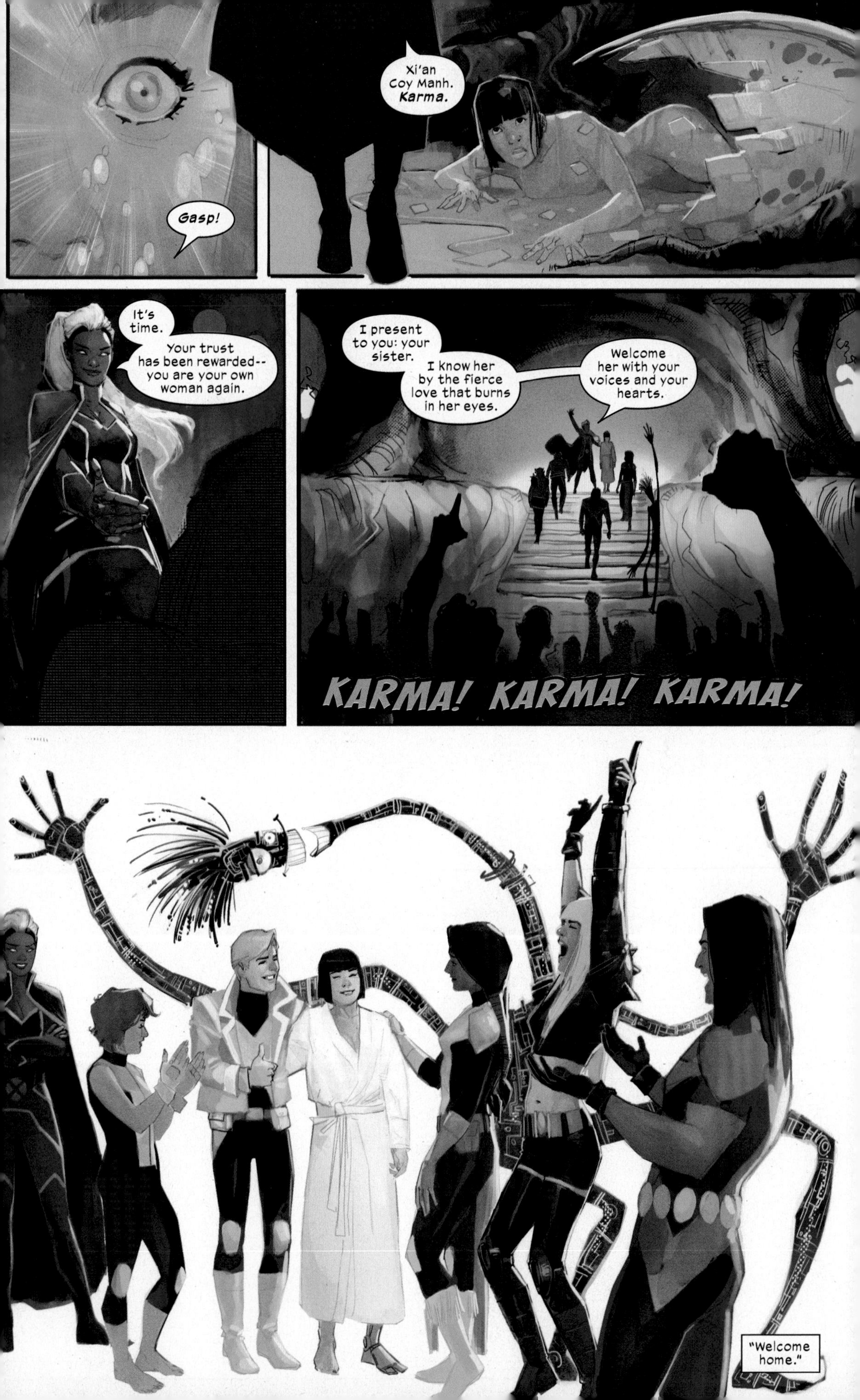
Gasp!
Xi'an Coy Manh. Karma.
It's time.
Your trust has been rewarded-- you are your own woman again.
I present to you: your sister.
I know her by the fierce love that burns in her eyes.
Welcome her with your voices and your hearts.
KARMA! KARMA! KARMA!
"Welcome home."

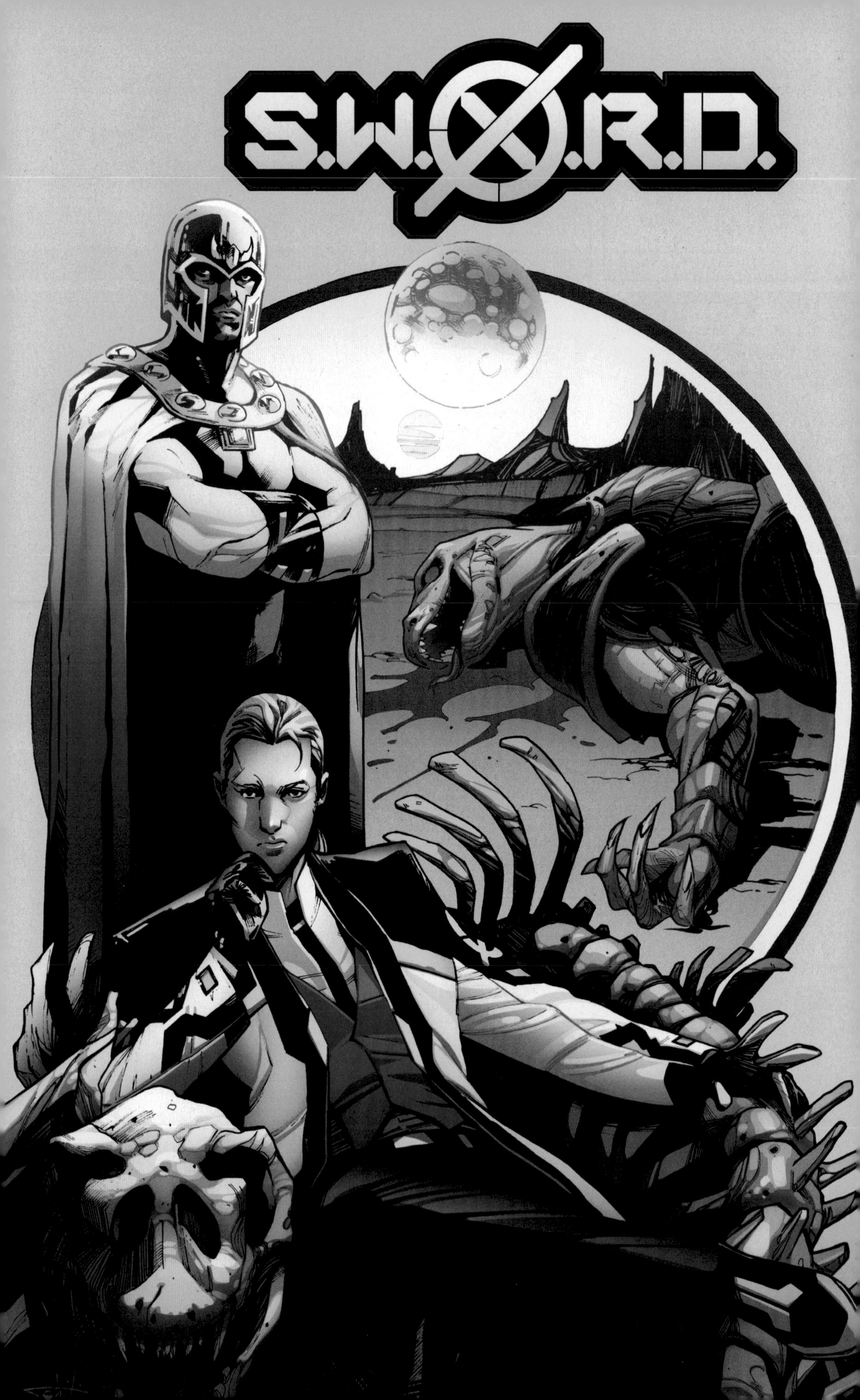
S.W.O.R.D.

///////////WE-PLEX SUPREME INTELLIGENCE SYSTEM ACTIVE

h Kree Diplomatic Gestalt // Reality 616 // Utopia Protocols Engage

Self-Identification Loop // SYSTEM IS

/////delusions inexhaustible ////////////////// *end them all*

sentient beings numberless //// ///////////////////// *// save them all*

gates of creation manifold /////////// /////////////////////// */// open them all*

utopian kree way supreme ////////// /////////////////////// *////// complete it*

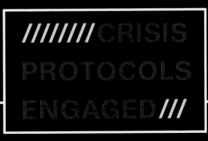

////////CRISIS PROTOCOLS ENGAGED///

KNULL////////////////////////// ///////////NEUTRALIZED

OLYMPIAN GODS/////// ///////////NEUTRALIZED

KREE IMPERIUM//////// ///////CRISIS INACTIVE

KORVAC APOTHEOSIS /////////AWAITING DATA

SNARKWAR/////////////// ///////////CRISIS ACTIVE

////////U-KREE COLONY J-453 OVERTAKEN BY ZN'RX FORCES////////// ///////////CALCULATING RESPONSE/////////////// ////////REQUEST DATA?

COLONIST EVACUATION DATA///// ////////// 593 sentients evacuated // *save them all* 98.83% success in current instance ///////////////////// // OPPOSING FORCE DATA////////////// ///////////////commanded by WEZEL of CHITA CLAN ///////////////////////////// ///////////combat strength 64.22% of U-Kree max combat strength/// /// //////////ODDS OF SUCCESSFULLY RETAKING COLONY//////////////////// ////79.1% with 38% casualty rate ////////*casualty rate unacceptable* /// ODDS OF FURTHER SUCCESSFUL INCURSION BY ZN'RX FORCES//// /////2.22% with current defenses /// ///////////STRATEGY CALCULATED ENGAGE SIEGE PROTOCOL

UPDATE ////////// NEW DATA

SIEGE PROTOCOL RESULT //////////////incursion attempts 8 //////////successful incursions 0 /////////RECENT INCURSIONS 0 ////*end them all* 100% success in current instance///////////////

UPDATE /// NEW DATA ///Wezel is requesting safe passage through U-Kree space/////////// ALLOW ///// Y/N?

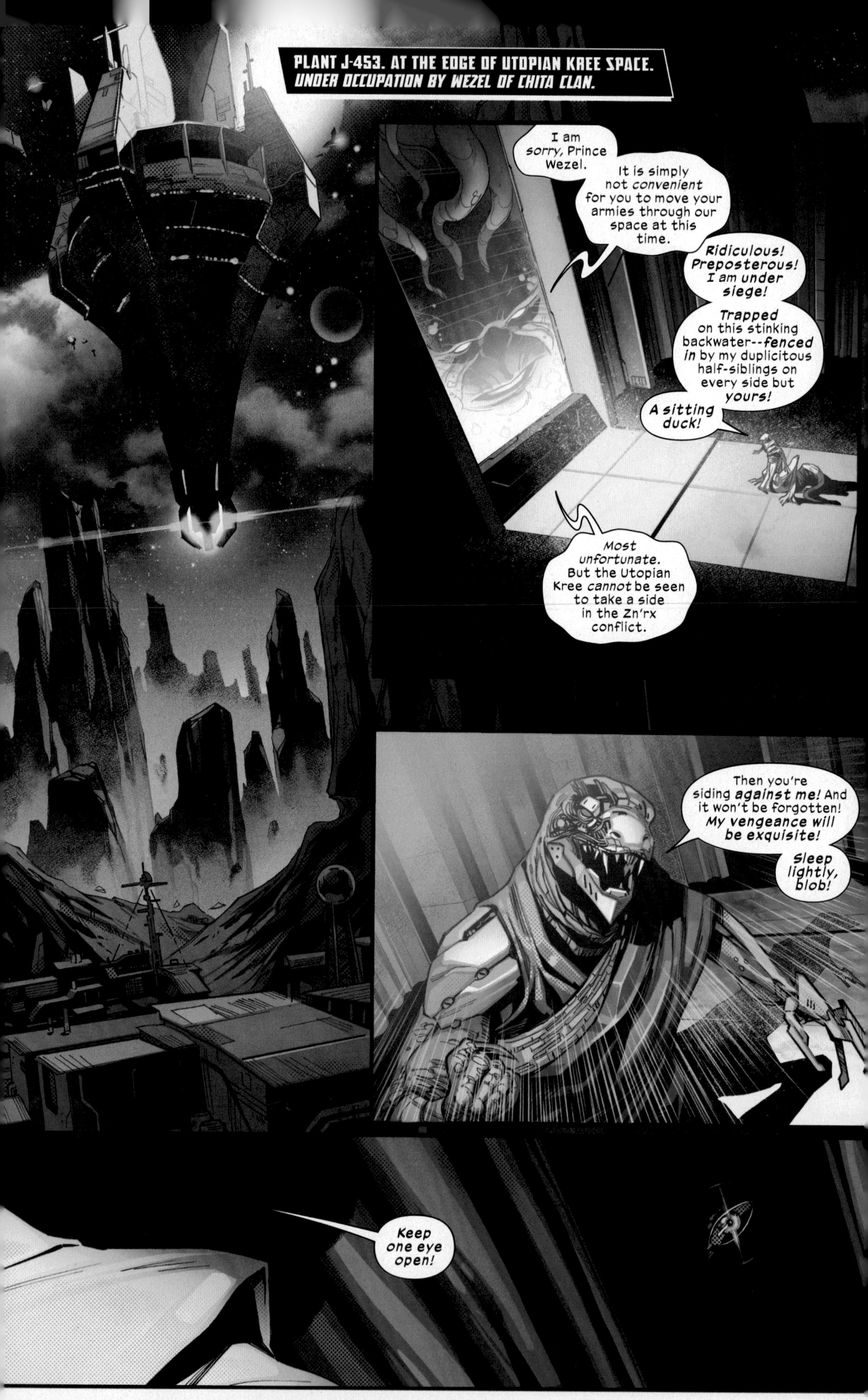
PLANT J-453. AT THE EDGE OF UTOPIAN KREE SPACE.
UNDER OCCUPATION BY WEZEL OF CHITA CLAN.
I am sorry, Prince Wezel.
It is simply not convenient for you to move your armies through our space at this time.
Ridiculous! Preposterous! I am under siege!
Trapped on this stinking backwater--fenced in by my duplicitous half-siblings on every side but yours!
A sitting duck!
Most unfortunate. But the Utopian Kree cannot be seen to take a side in the Zn'rx conflict.
Then you're siding against me! And it won't be forgotten! My vengeance will be exquisite!
Sleep lightly, blob!
Keep one eye open!

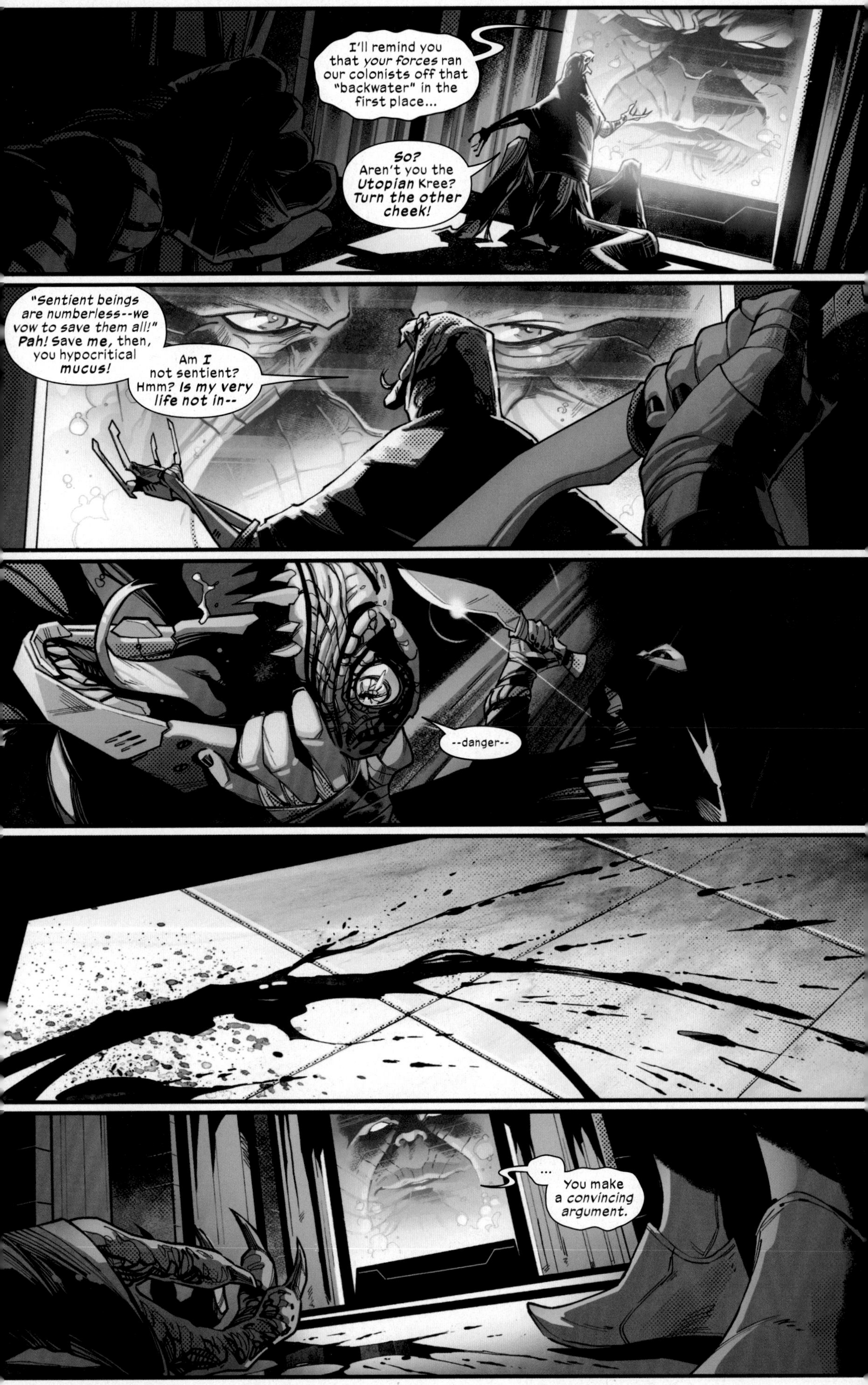

I'll remind you that *your forces* ran our colonists off that "backwater" in the first place...
So? Aren't you the *Utopian* Kree? *Turn the other cheek!*
"Sentient beings are numberless--we vow to save them all!" Pah! Save *me,* then, you hypocritical *mucus!*
Am *I* not sentient? Hmm? *Is my very life not in--*
--danger--
... You make a *convincing* argument.

MURDER DRESSES IN GOLD

Fabian Cortez distinguished himself during Knull's assault on Krakoa, giving his life in service of mutantkind. In recognition, Magneto has allowed him to address the Quiet Council following his resurrection -- on the matter of Krakoa's second law: **Murder no man.**

Meanwhile, the Snarkwar -- the war of succession for the throne of the Zn'rx Empire -- is expanding across the galaxy. More and more innocent worlds are being sucked into the conflict as the heirs to the throne spread death in their wake... And in turn, death stalks them.

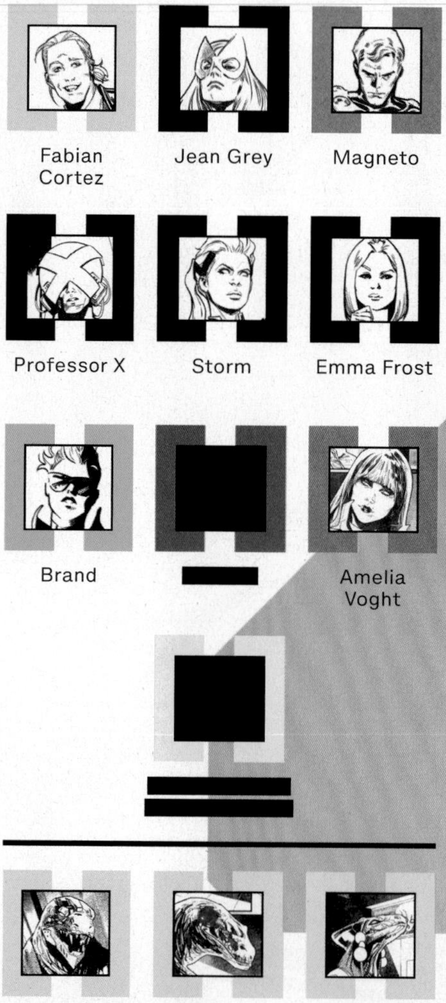

Fabian
Cortez

Jean Grey

Magneto

Professor X

Storm

Emma Frost

Brand

Amelia
Voght

Wezel

Khondor

Lyga

[00__snar]
[00__kwar]

S.W.O.R.D.

[X_05]

[ISSUE FIVE]........................... GIALLO

AL EWING.......................................[WRITER]
VALERIO SCHITI.................................[ARTIST]
MARTE GRACIA..........................[COLOR ARTIST]
VC's ARIANA MAHER........................[LETTERER]
TOM MULLER.....................................[DESIGN]

VALERIO SCHITI & MARTE GRACIA..............[COVER ARTISTS]

STEFANO CASELLI & FEDERICO BLEE.....[VARIANT COVER ARTISTS]

JONATHAN HICKMAN..............................[HEAD OF X]
NICK RUSSELL...............................[PRODUCTION]
ANNALISE BISSA.........................[ASSOCIATE EDITOR]
JORDAN D. WHITE................................[EDITOR]
C.B. CEBULSKI...........................[EDITOR IN CHIEF]

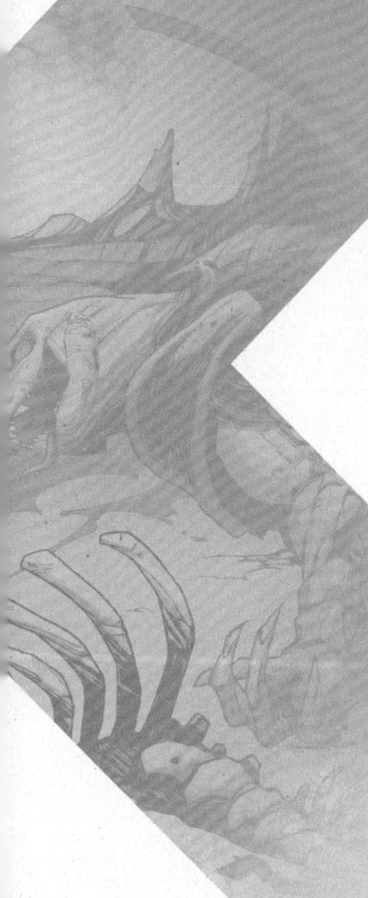

[00__snar]
[00__kwar]

[00_00....0]
[00_00...05]

[00_death_]
[00__is___]

[00__near_]

[00______X]

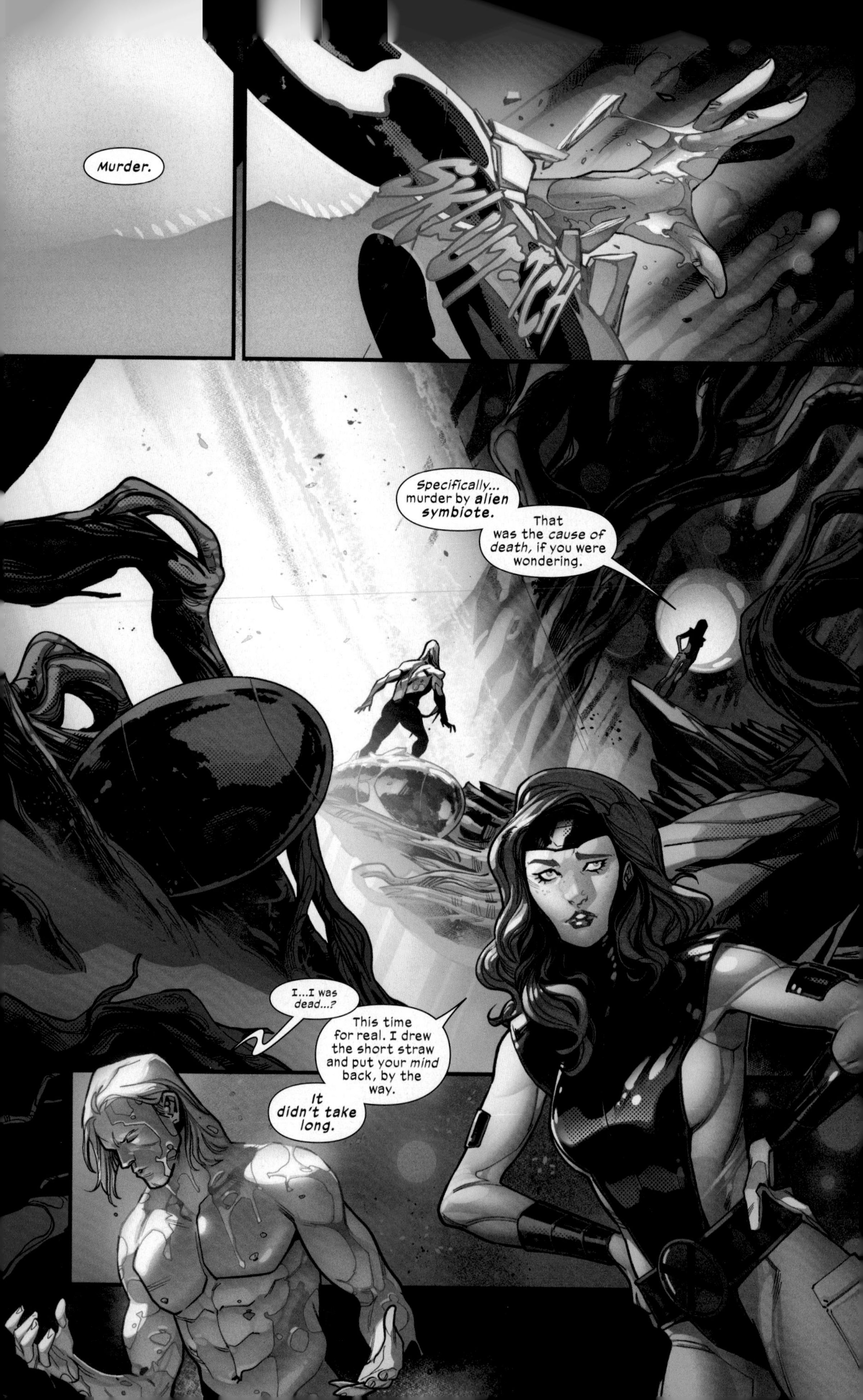

Murder.
SKLUTCH
Specifically... murder by alien symbiote.
That was the cause of death, if you were wondering.
I...I was dead...?
This time for real. I drew the short straw and put your mind back, by the way.
It didn't take long.

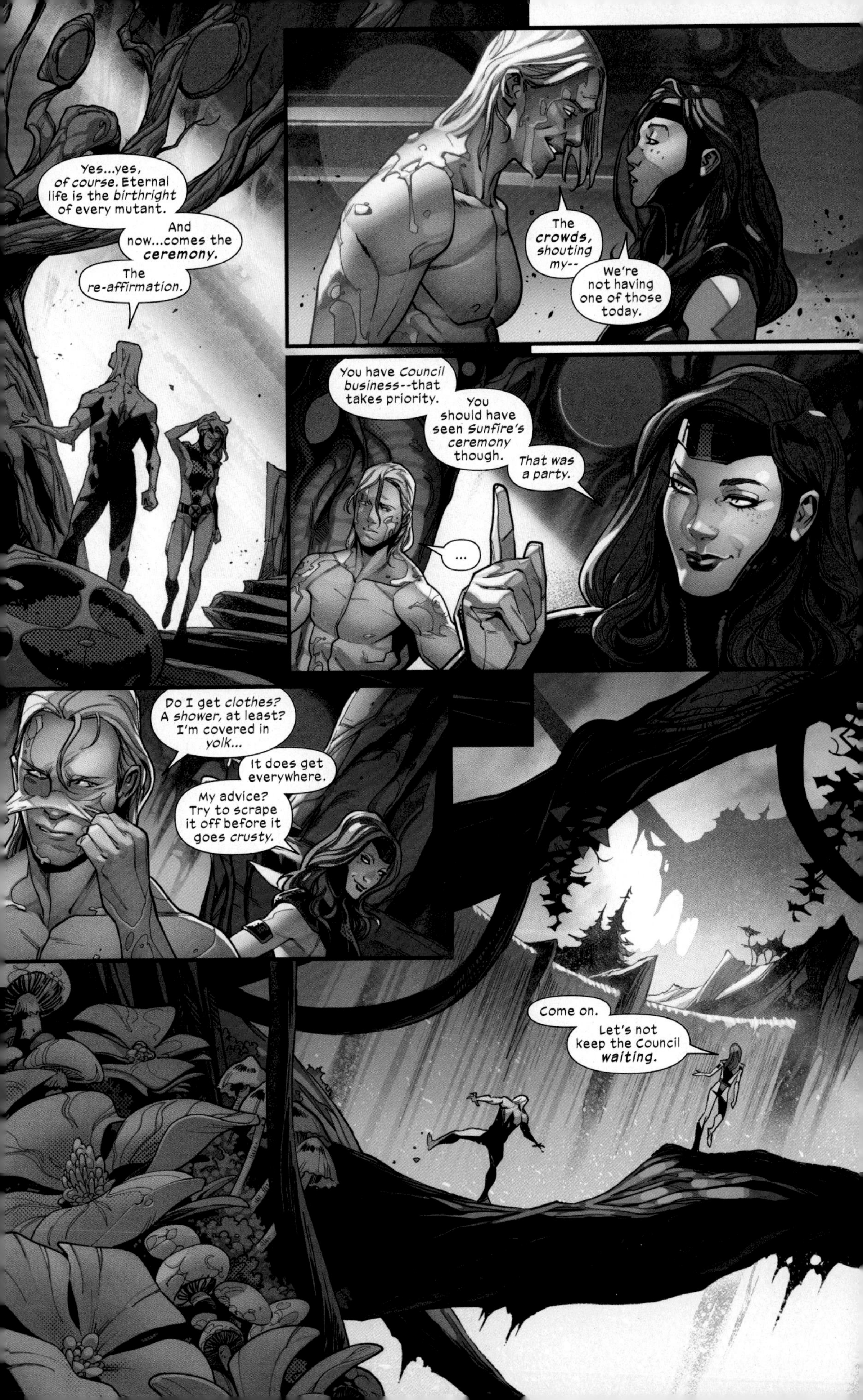
Yes...yes, of course. Eternal life is the birthright of every mutant.
And now...comes the ceremony.
The re-affirmation.
The crowds, shouting my--
We're not having one of those today.
You have Council business--that takes priority.
You should have seen Sunfire's ceremony though.
That was a party.
...
Do I get clothes? A shower, at least? I'm covered in yolk...
It does get everywhere.
My advice? Try to scrape it off before it goes crusty.
Come on.
Let's not keep the Council waiting.

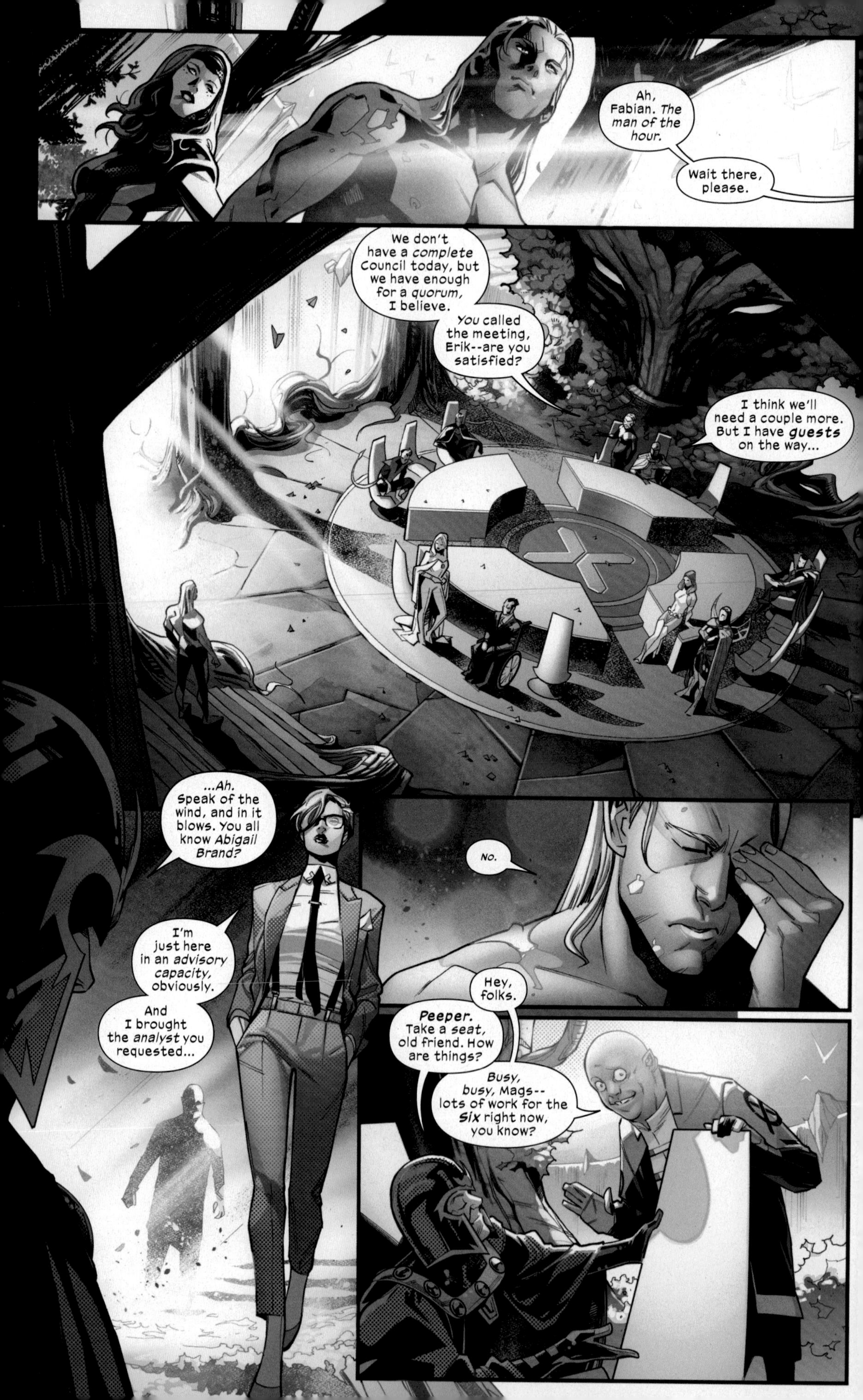

Ah, Fabian. *The man of the hour.*
Wait there, please.
We don't have a *complete* Council today, but we have enough for a *quorum,* I believe.
You called the meeting, Erik--are you satisfied?
I think we'll need a couple more. But I have ***guests*** on the way...
...Ah. Speak of the wind, and in it blows. You all know *Abigail Brand?*
NO.
I'm just here in an *advisory capacity,* obviously.
And I brought the *analyst* you requested...
Hey, folks.
Peeper. Take a *seat,* old friend. How are things?
Busy, busy, Mags--lots of work for the ***Six*** right now, you know?

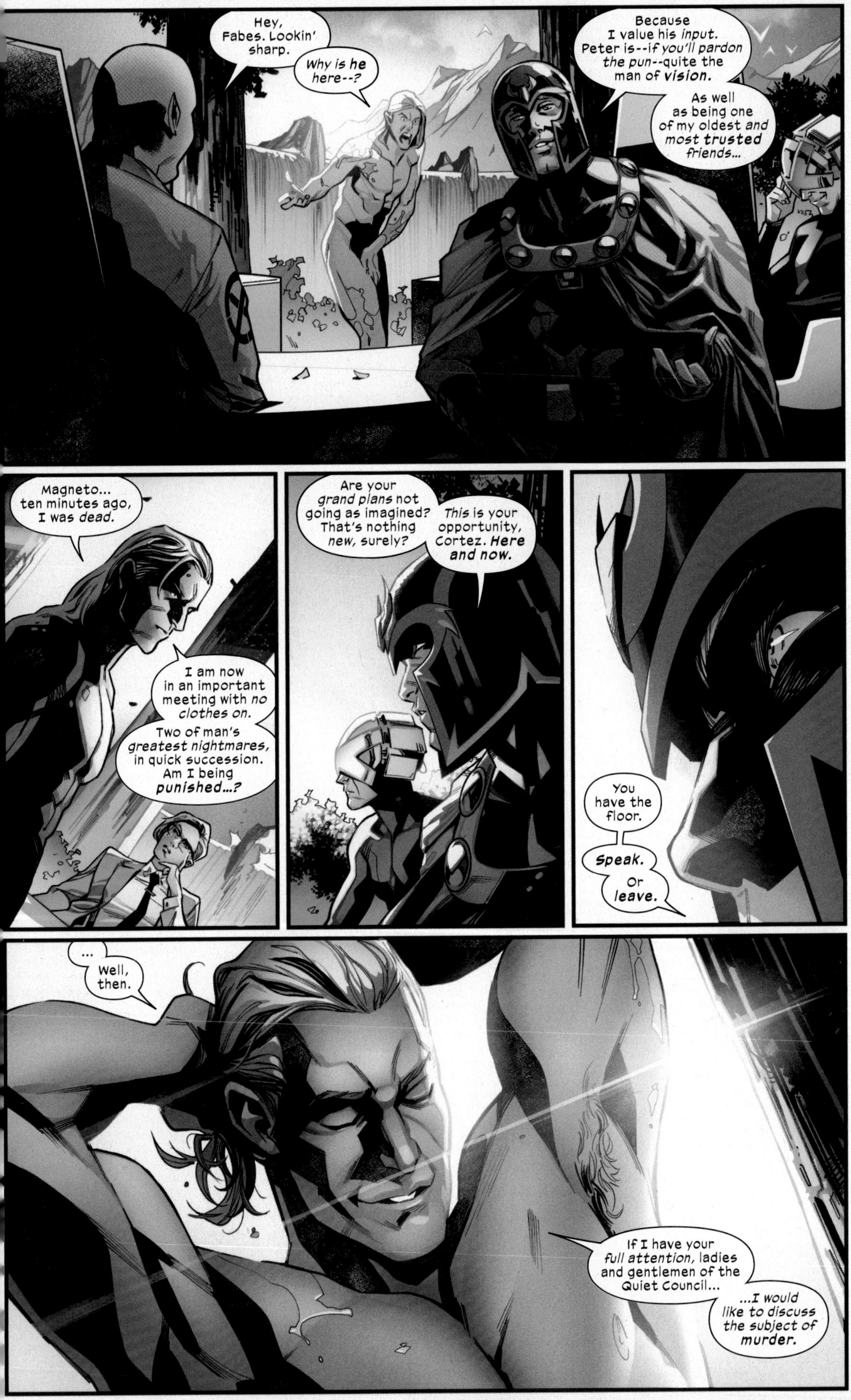
Hey, Fabes. Lookin' sharp.
Why is he here--?
Because I value his input. Peter is--if you'll pardon the pun--quite the man of vision.
As well as being one of my oldest and most trusted friends...
Magneto... ten minutes ago, I was dead.
I am now in an important meeting with no clothes on.
Two of man's greatest nightmares, in quick succession. Am I being punished...?
Are your grand plans not going as imagined? That's nothing new, surely?
This is your opportunity, Cortez. Here and now.
You have the floor.
Speak.
Or leave.
...
Well, then.
If I have your full attention, ladies and gentlemen of the Quiet Council...
...I would like to discuss the subject of murder.

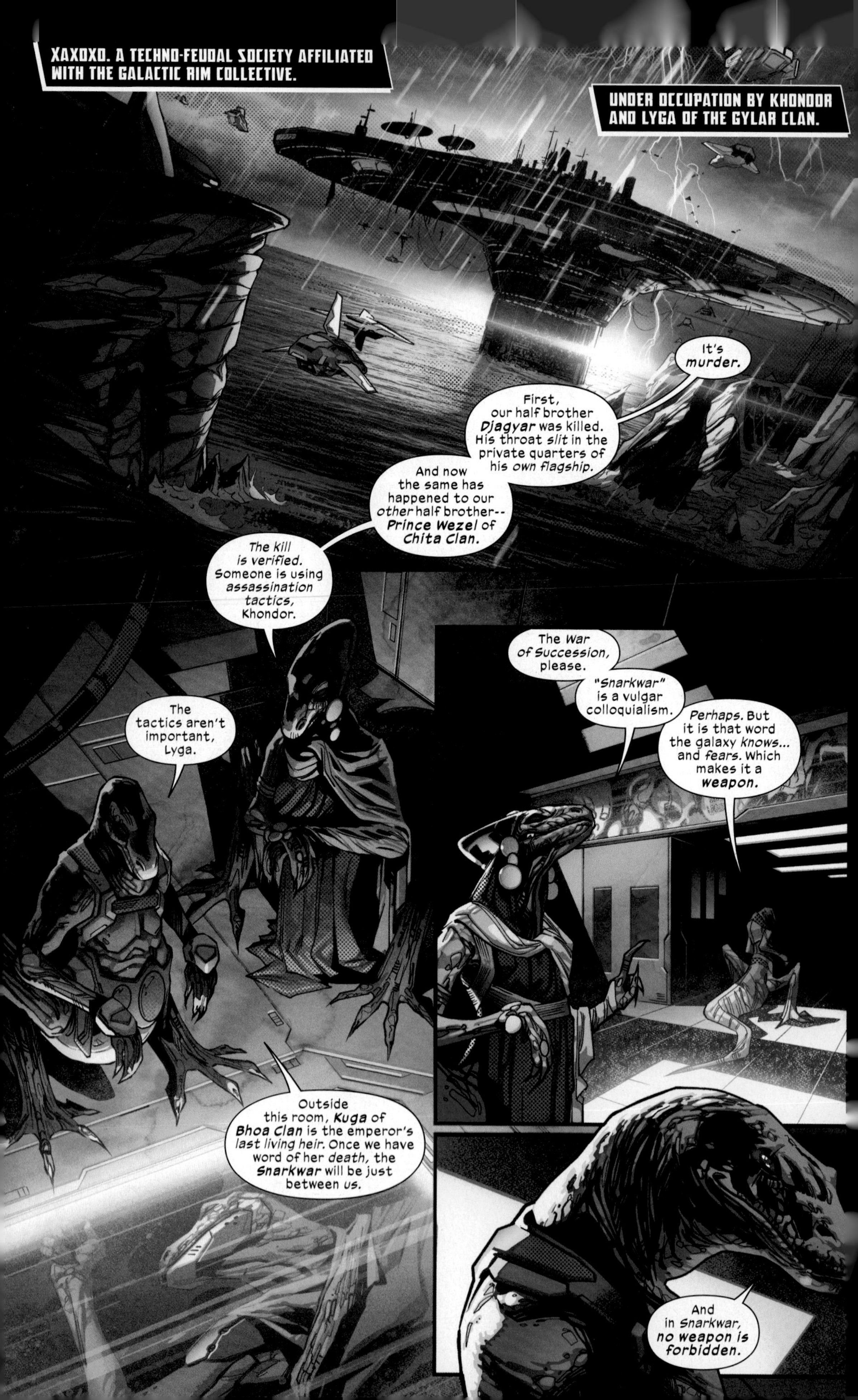
XAXOXO. A TECHNO-FEUDAL SOCIETY AFFILIATED WITH THE GALACTIC RIM COLLECTIVE.
UNDER OCCUPATION BY KHONDOR AND LYGA OF THE GYLAR CLAN.
It's *murder.*
First, our half brother ***Djagyar*** was killed. His throat *slit* in the private quarters of his *own flagship.*
And now the same has happened to our *other* half brother-- ***Prince Wezel* of *Chita Clan.***
The kill is verified. Someone is using *assassination tactics,* Khondor.
The tactics aren't important, Lyga.
The *War of Succession,* please.
"Snarkwar" is a vulgar colloquialism.
Perhaps. But it is that word the galaxy *knows*... and *fears.* Which makes it a ***weapon.***
Outside this room, ***Kuga*** of ***Bhoa Clan*** is the emperor's *last living heir.* Once we have word of her *death,* the ***Snarkwar*** will be just between *us.*
And in *Snarkwar,* ***no weapon is forbidden.***

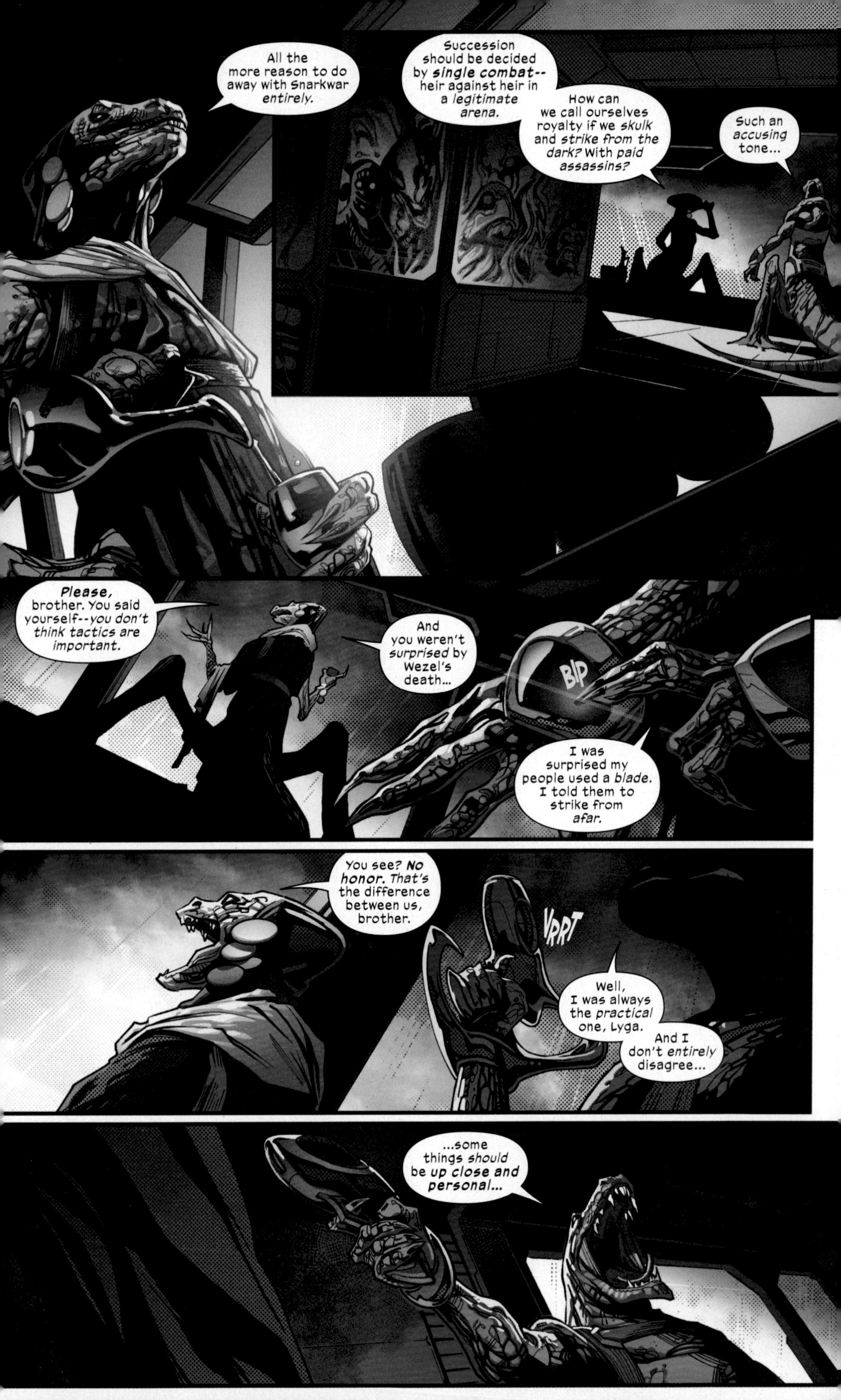
All the more reason to do away with Snarkwar *entirely.*
Succession should be decided by ***single combat***--heir against heir in a *legitimate arena.*
How can we call ourselves royalty if we *skulk* and *strike from the dark?* With *paid assassins?*
Such an *accusing* tone...
Please, brother. You said yourself--*you don't think tactics are important.*
And you weren't *surprised* by Wezel's death...
BIP
I was surprised my people used a *blade.* I told them to strike from *afar.*
You see? ***No honor.*** *That's* the difference between us, brother.
VRRT
Well, I was always the *practical* one, Lyga.
And I don't *entirely* disagree...
...some things *should* be ***up close and personal...***

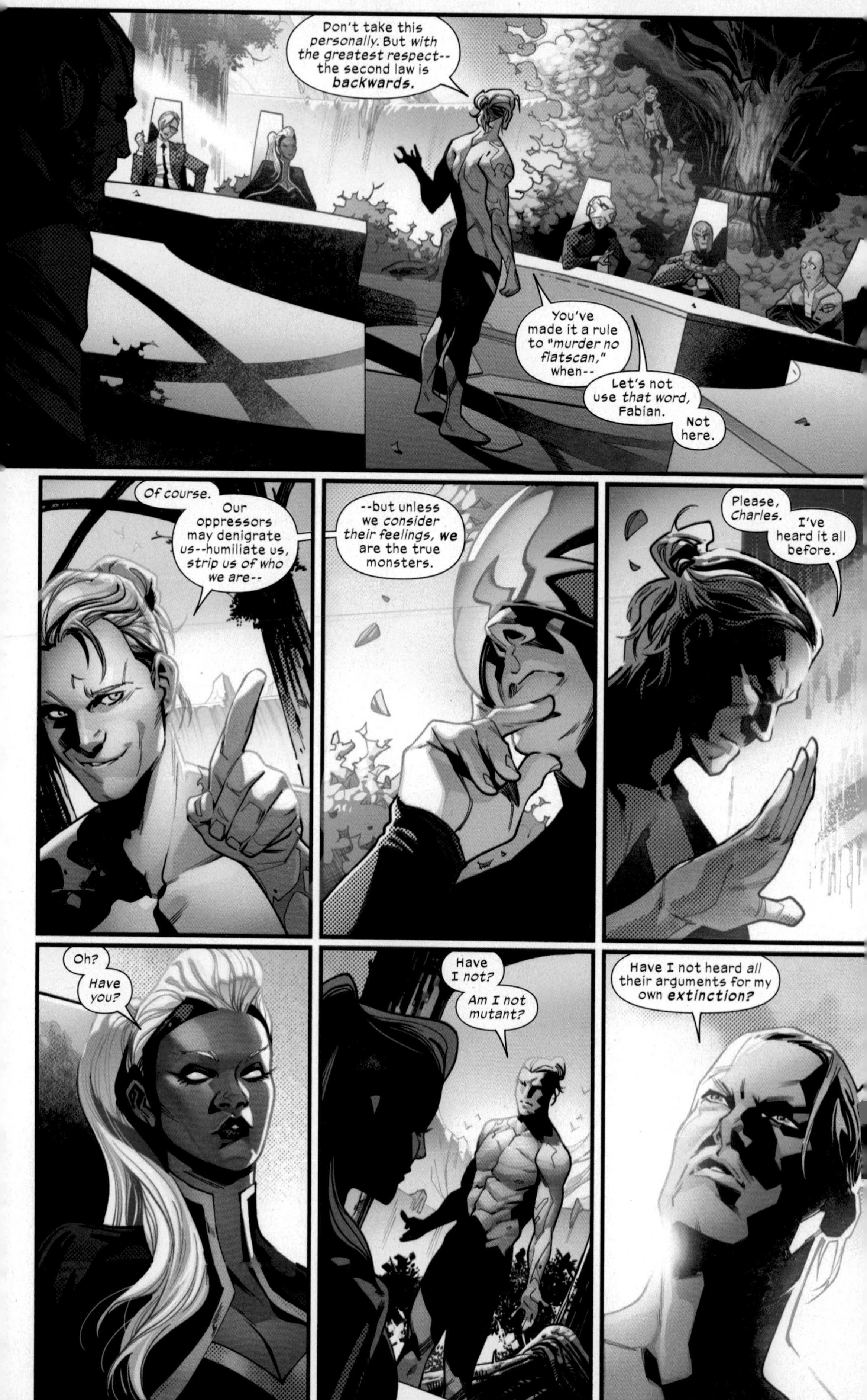
Don't take this *personally.* But *with* the *greatest respect*-- the second law is **backwards.**
You've made it a rule to "*murder no flatscan,*" when--
Let's not use *that word,* Fabian.
Not here.
Of course.
Our oppressors may denigrate us--humiliate us, *strip us of who* we are--
--but unless we *consider their feelings,* **we** are the true monsters.
Please, *Charles.*
I've heard it all before.
Oh?
Have *you?*
Have I *not?*
Am I not *mutant?*
Have I not heard *all* their arguments for my own ***extinction?***

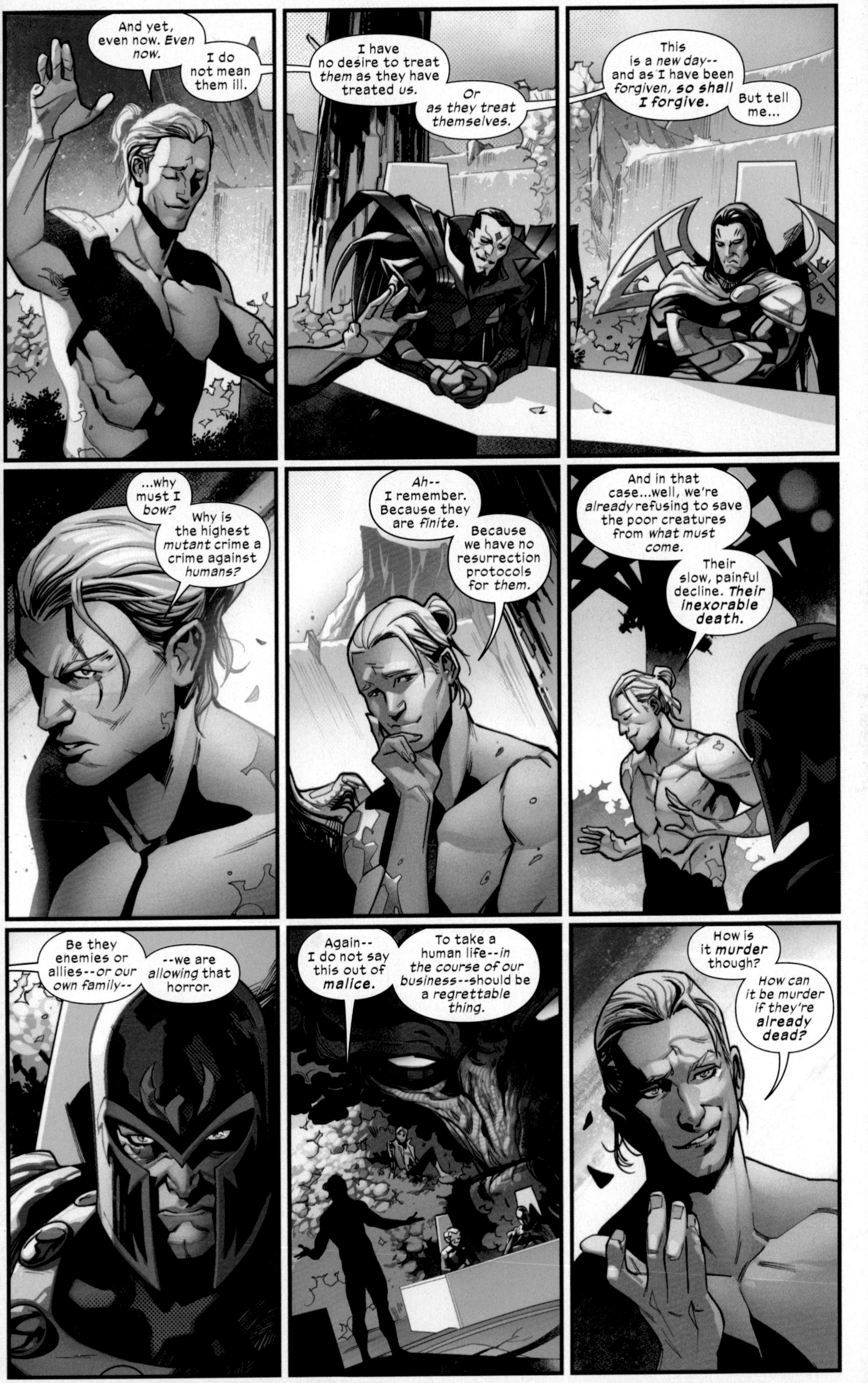
And yet, even now. *Even now.*
I do not mean them ill.
I have no desire to treat *them* as they have treated *us.*
Or as they treat themselves.
This is a *new day*--and as I have been *forgiven, so shall I forgive.*
But tell me...
...why must I *bow?*
Why is the highest *mutant* crime a crime against *humans?*
Ah-- I remember. Because they are *finite.*
Because we have no resurrection protocols for *them.*
And in that case...well, we're *already* refusing to save the poor creatures from *what must come.*
Their slow, painful decline. ***Their inexorable death.***
Be they enemies or allies--*or our own family*--
--we are *allowing* that horror.
Again-- I do not say this out of **malice.**
To take a human life--*in the course of our business*--should be a *regrettable* thing.
How is it *murder* though?
How can it be murder if they're ***already dead?***

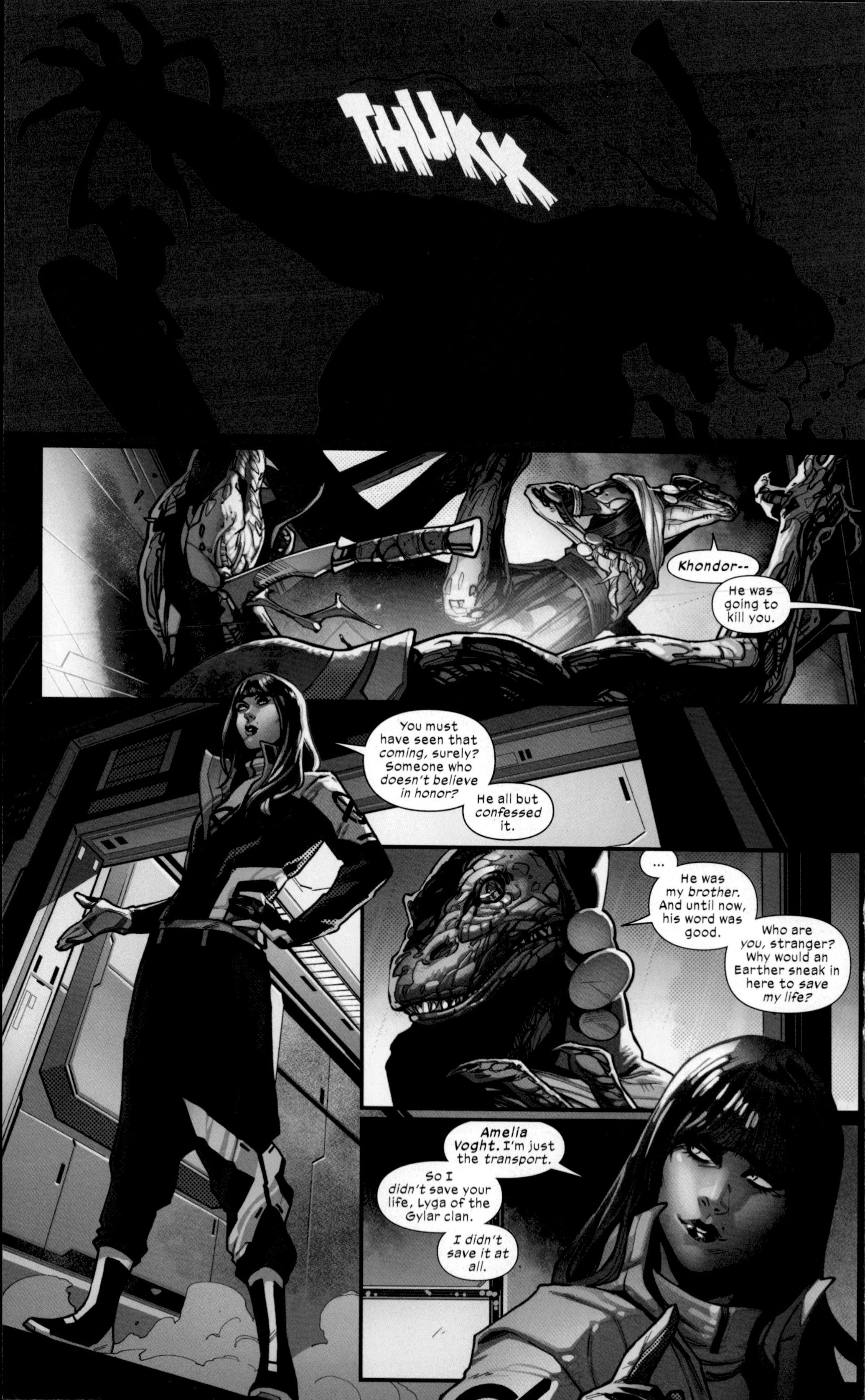

THUKK
Khondor--
He was going to kill you.
You must have seen that *coming, surely?* Someone who *doesn't believe in honor?*
He all but *confessed* it.
...
He was my *brother.* And until now, his word was good.
Who are *you, stranger?* Why would an Earther sneak in here to *save my life?*
Amelia Voght. I'm just the *transport.*
So I *didn't* save your life, Lyga of the Gylar clan.
I didn't save it at all.

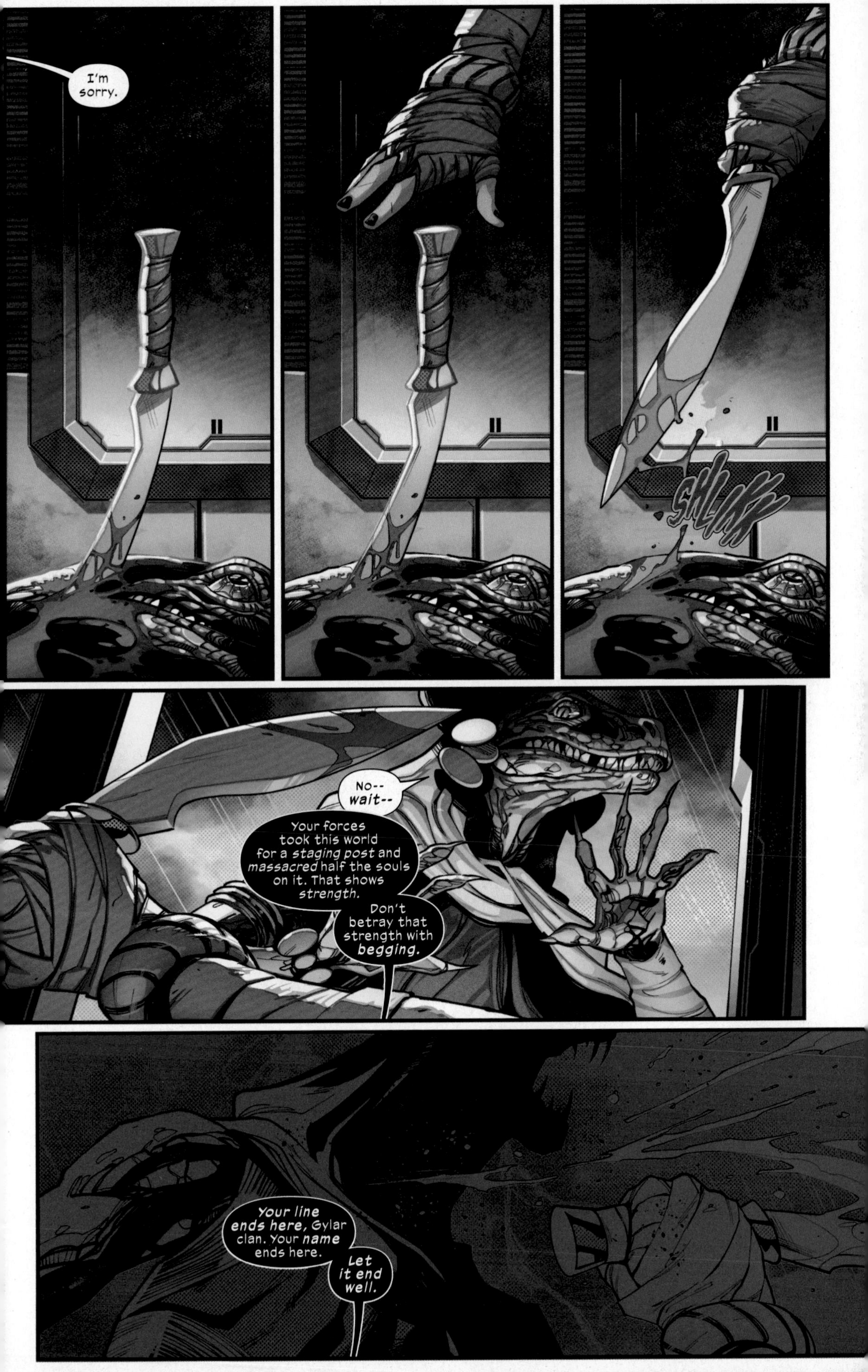
I'm sorry.
SHLIKK
No-- wait--
Your forces took this world for a staging post and massacred half the souls on it. That shows strength.
Don't betray that strength with begging.
Your line ends here, Gylar clan. Your name ends here.
Let it end well.

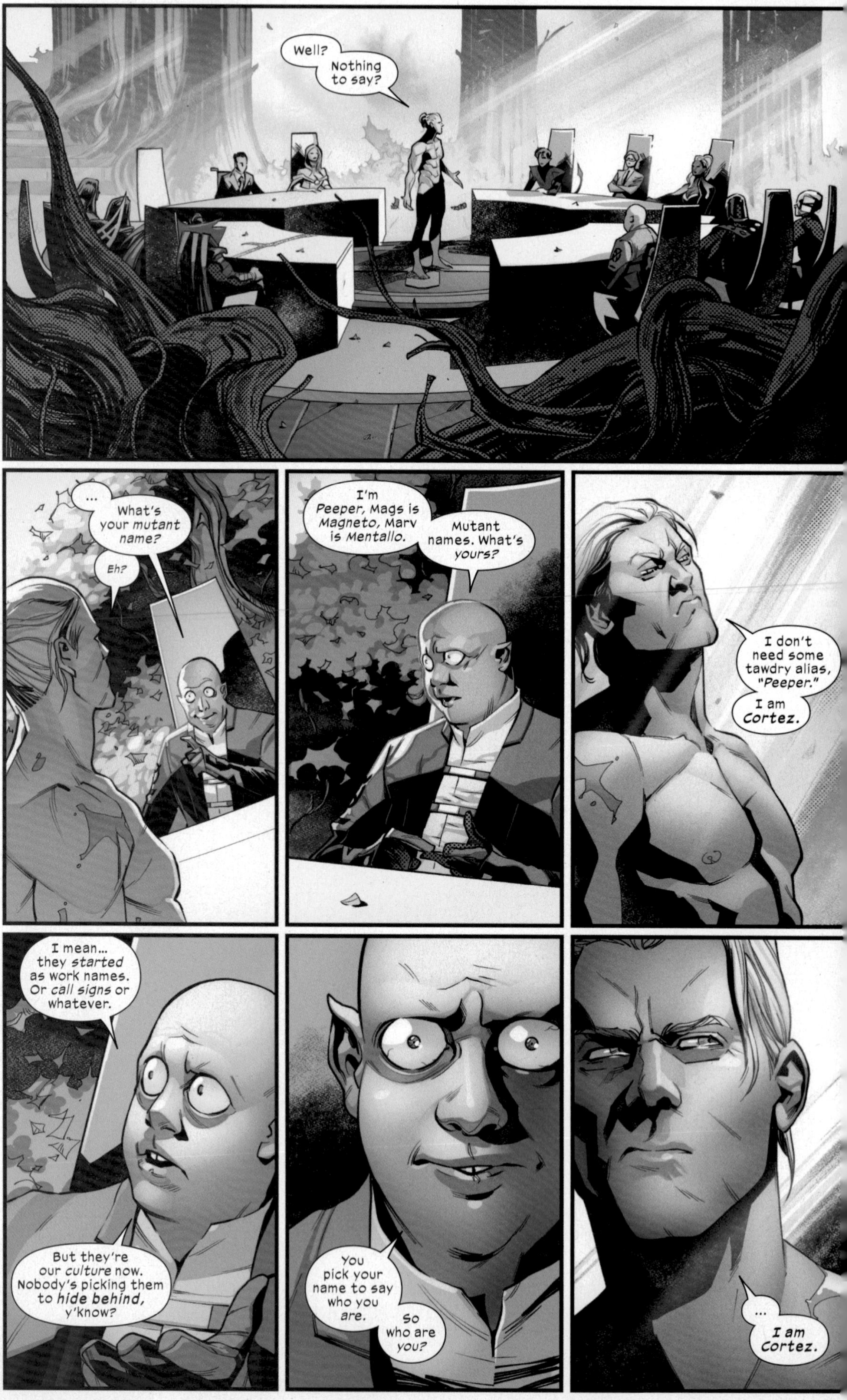
Well? Nothing to say?
... What's your *mutant* name?
Eh?
I'm *Peeper*, Mags is *Magneto*, Marv is *Mentallo*.
Mutant names. What's *yours?*
I don't need some tawdry alias, *"Peeper."*
I am **Cortez.**
I mean... they *started* as work names. Or *call signs* or whatever.
But they're our *culture* now. Nobody's picking them to ***hide behind,*** y'know?
You pick your name to say who you *are.*
So who are *you?*
...
I am Cortez.

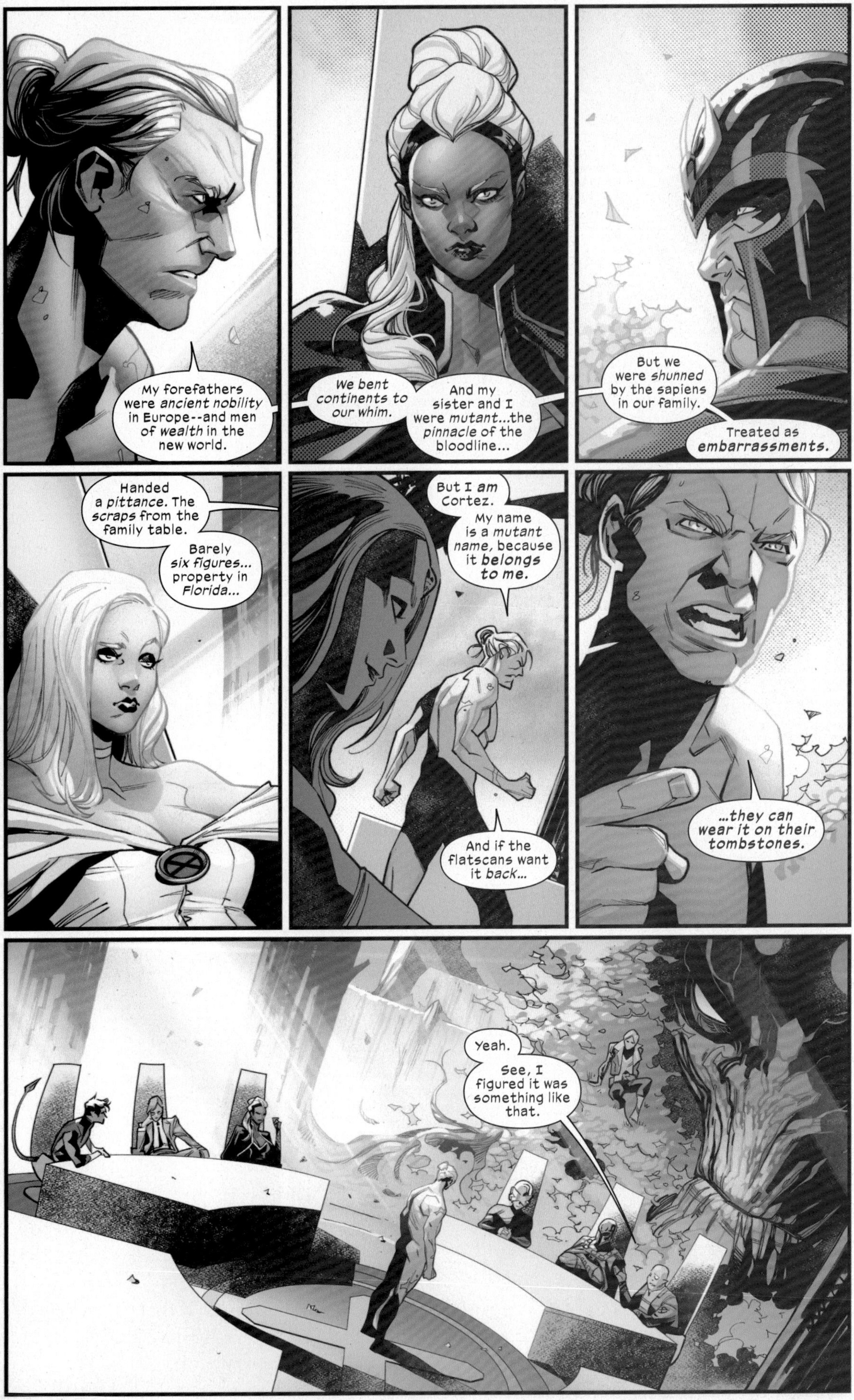

My forefathers were *ancient nobility* in Europe--and men of *wealth* in the new world.
We bent continents to our whim.
And my sister and I were *mutant*...the *pinnacle* of the bloodline...
But we were *shunned* by the sapiens in our family.
Treated as ***embarrassments.***
Handed a *pittance*. The *scraps* from the family table.
Barely *six figures*... property in *Florida*...
But I *am* Cortez.
My name is a *mutant name*, because it ***belongs to me.***
And if the flatscans want it *back*...
...they can wear it on their tombstones.
Yeah.
See, I figured it was something like that.

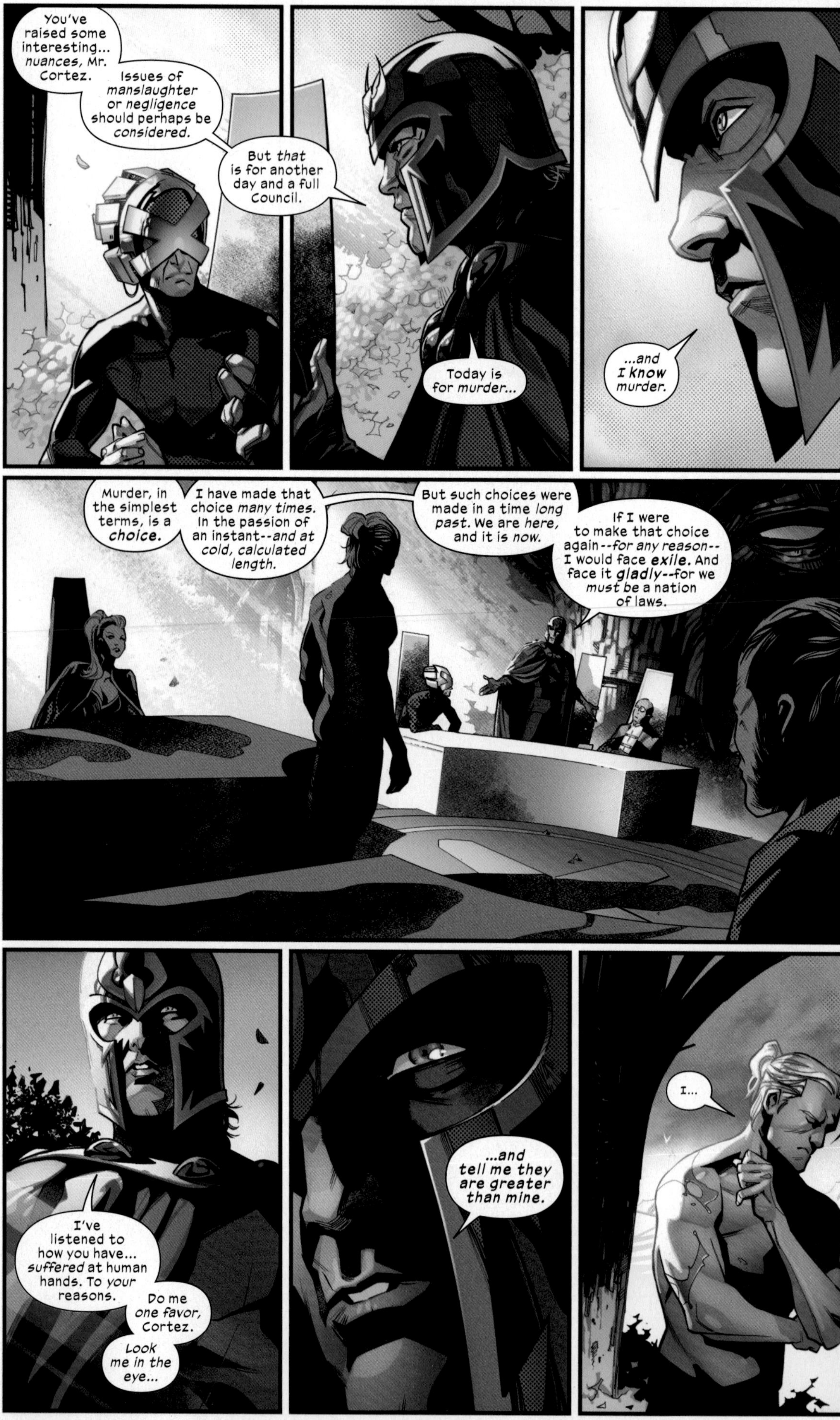
You've raised some interesting... *nuances*, Mr. Cortez.
Issues of *manslaughter* or *negligence* should perhaps be *considered*.
But *that* is for another day and a full Council.
Today is for *murder*...
...and I *know* murder.
Murder, in the simplest terms, is a ***choice.***
I have made that choice *many times*. In the passion of an instant--*and at cold, calculated length.*
But such choices were made in a time *long past*. We are *here*, and it is *now*.
If I were to make that choice again--*for any reason*--I would face **exile.** And face it ***gladly***--for we *must* be a nation of laws.
I've listened to how you have... *suffered* at human hands. To *your* reasons.
Do me *one favor*, Cortez.
Look me in the eye...
...and tell me they are greater than mine.
I...

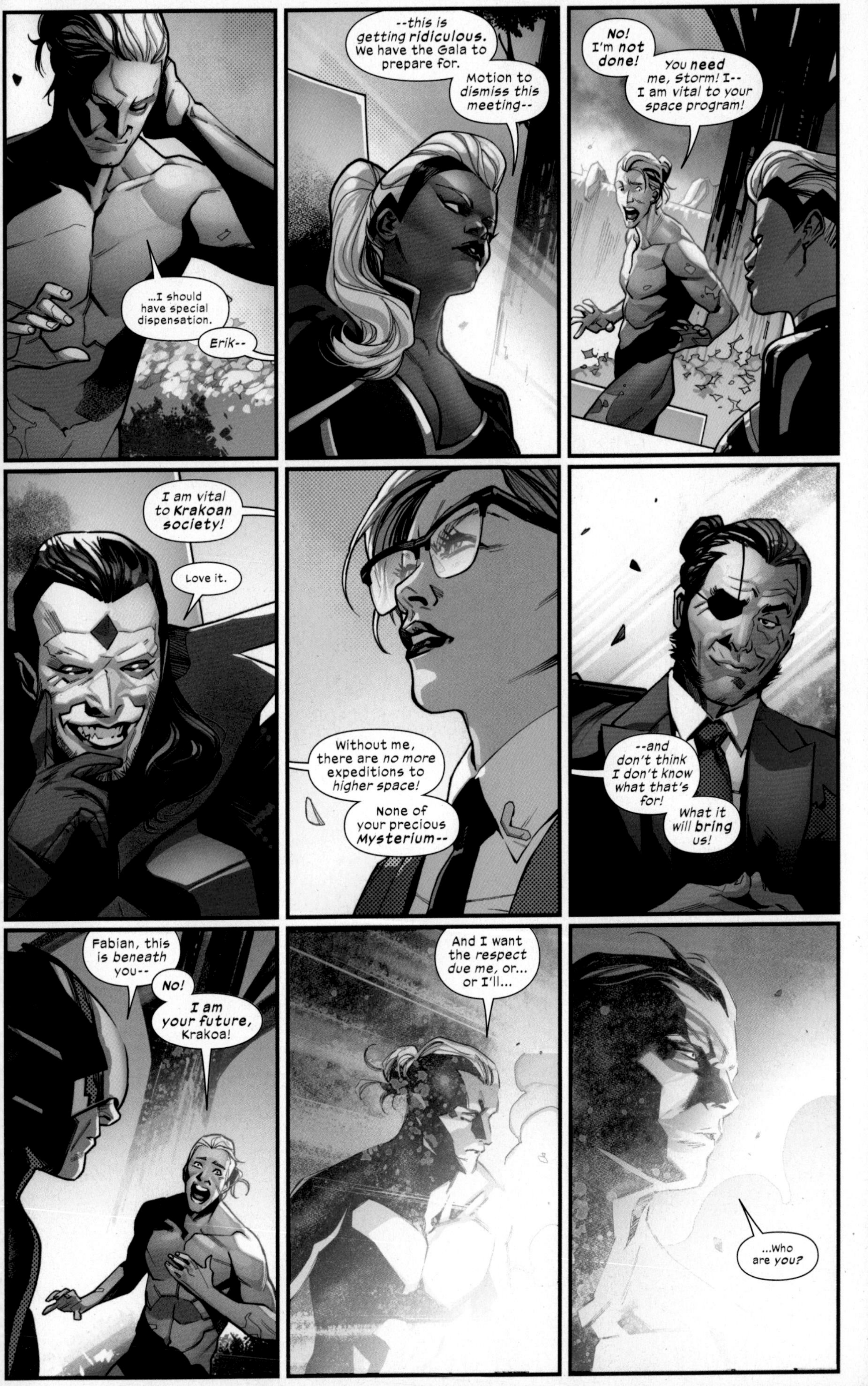
...I should have special dispensation.
Erik--
--this is getting ridiculous. We have the Gala to prepare for.
Motion to dismiss this meeting--
No! I'm not done!
You need me, Storm! I-- I am vital to your space program!
I am vital to Krakoan society!
Love it.
Without me, there are no more expeditions to higher space!
None of your precious Mysterium--
--and don't think I don't know what that's for!
What it will bring us!
Fabian, this is beneath you--
No!
I am your future, Krakoa!
And I want the respect due me, or... or I'll...
...Who are you?

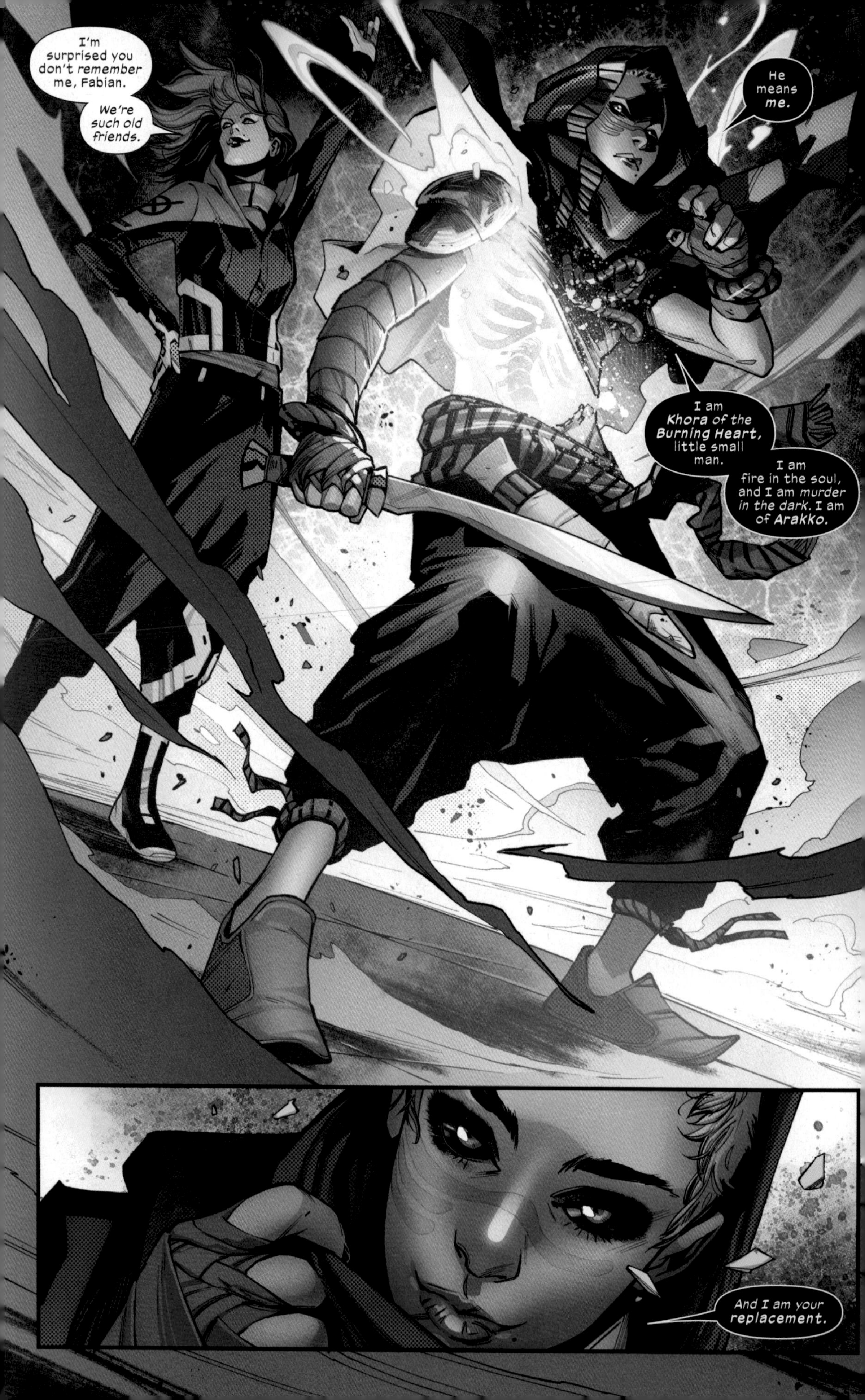
I'm surprised you don't *remember* me, Fabian.
We're such old friends.
He means **me.**
I am **Khora** *of the* **Burning Heart,** little small man.
I am fire in the soul, and I am *murder in the dark.* I am of **Arakko.**
And I am your **replacement.**

Brian Dunlop/Boost	Boost amplifies powers … other mutants; as such, he cannot amplify … than one mutant at a time. *Note: still a very useful power. Consider for security team or deniable ops.*
Absolon Mercator/Mister M	Unavailable. Whereabouts unknown.
Khora of the Burning Heart	Primary loyalty is most likely to Arako. That said, she fits all other criteria, with the added bonus that her skill set as an assassin will assist us in ending the current Snarkwar by taking out all heirs to the throne, bar our chosen candidate.

[PLog.....E-7-15 11/24]
[CORT.............FAB]

…ES ONLY :: DO NOT UNREDA…
…LL TELEPATHIC SAFEGUARDS ::

++ MISSION ASSETS AS FOLLOWS
++ KHORA OF THE BURNING HEART
++ AMELIA VOGHT

++ MISSION DETAILS AS FOLLOWS ++
++ LOCATE AND DESTROY: ++
++ DJAGYAR / BHOA CLAN ++
++ WEZEL / CHITA CLAN
++ LYGA / GYLAR CLAN
++ KHONDOR / GYLAR CLAN
++ PROTECT AND DEFEND:
++ KUGA / BHOA CLAN

++ MISSION OBJECTIVE AS FOLLOWS ++
++ END SNARKWAR WITH RADICAL ++
++ MODERNIST FACTION IN CONTRO… ++
++ AND INDEBTED TO SOL SYSTE… ++

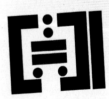

[PLog.....E-8-7 01/19]
[Eyes............only]

…YES ONLY :: EYES…

PERSONNEL NOTES

KHORA OF THE BURNING HEART :: EYES ONLY

ABIGAIL BRAND :: E-8-7 01/19 :: GSTC 0527

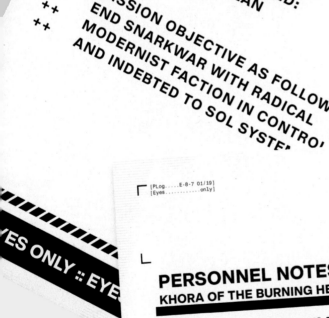

She's called that because her heart literally burns in her chest, a furnace in her rib cage. The flame is her life force -- if she keeps it to herself, it makes her stronger, faster and more dangerous in combat than any ten trained soldiers I know, and I've known plenty. But the interesting thing is -- she can share it out, fill anyone close to her with the same burning energy she's got, and, in so doing, boost their power level far above normal. It's an ability she's barely used -- on Arakko, it'd be an insult to even suggest anyone needed that kind of boost. But frankly, it's the answer to my prayers.

Because Fabian Cortez can't be trusted, and somebody has to replace him.

… above all, but right now Arakko's goals are … Fabian. Even if

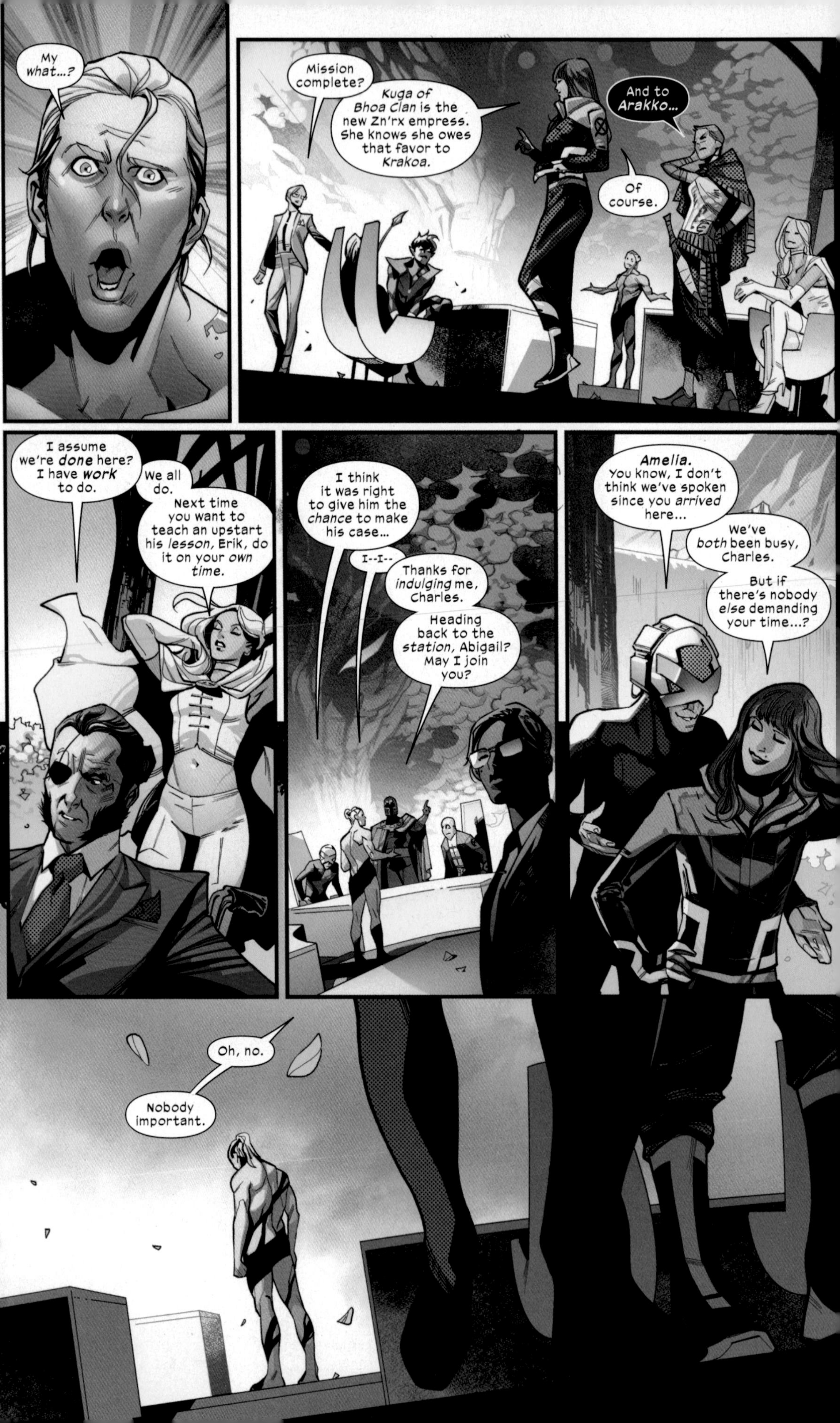

My what...?
Mission complete?
Kuga of Bhoa Clan is the new Zn'rx empress. She knows she owes that favor to Krakoa.
And to Arakko...
Of course.
I assume we're done here? I have work to do.
We all do.
Next time you want to teach an upstart his lesson, Erik, do it on your own time.
I think it was right to give him the chance to make his case...
I--I--
Thanks for indulging me, Charles.
Heading back to the station, Abigail? May I join you?
Amelia. You know, I don't think we've spoken since you arrived here...
We've both been busy, Charles.
But if there's nobody else demanding your time...?
Oh, no.
Nobody important.

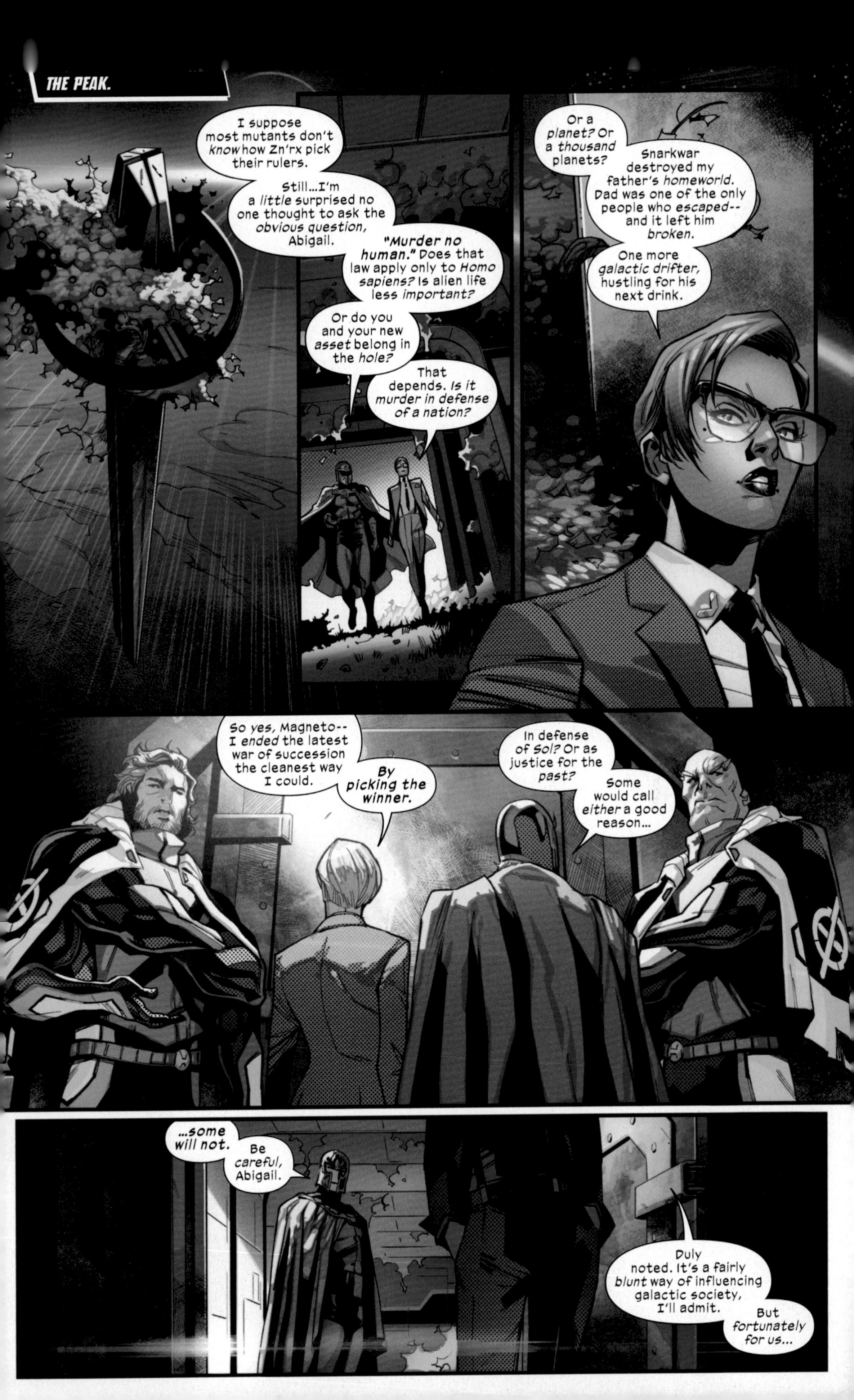
THE PEAK.
I suppose most mutants don't know how Zn'rx pick their rulers.
Still...I'm a little surprised no one thought to ask the obvious question, Abigail.
"Murder no human." Does that law apply only to Homo sapiens? Is alien life less important?
Or do you and your new asset belong in the hole?
That depends. Is it murder in defense of a nation?
Or a planet? Or a thousand planets?
Snarkwar destroyed my father's homeworld. Dad was one of the only people who escaped-- and it left him broken.
One more galactic drifter, hustling for his next drink.
So yes, Magneto-- I ended the latest war of succession the cleanest way I could.
By picking the winner.
In defense of Sol? Or as justice for the past?
Some would call either a good reason...
...some will not.
Be careful, Abigail.
Duly noted. It's a fairly blunt way of influencing galactic society, I'll admit.
But fortunately for us...

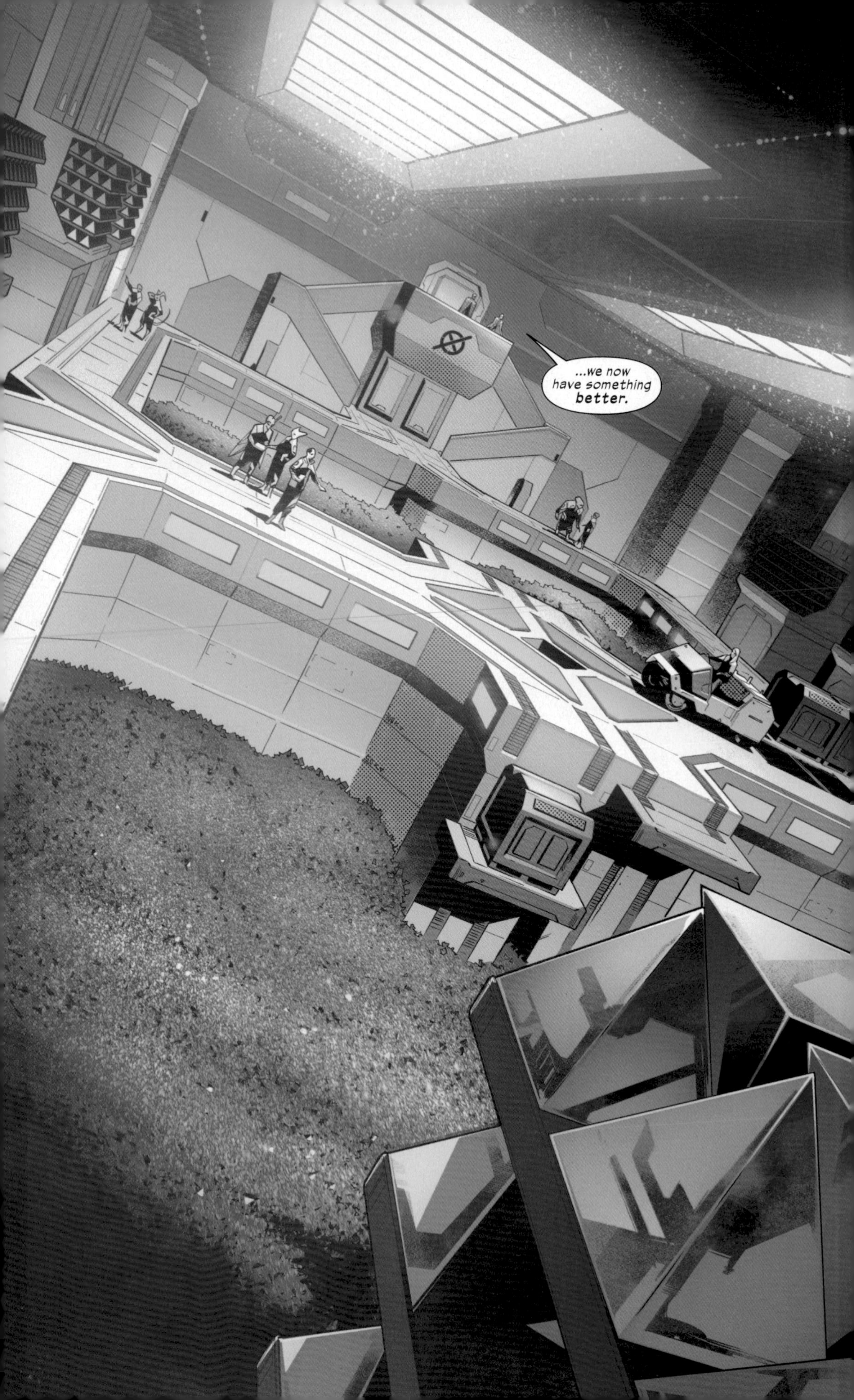
...we now have something **better.**

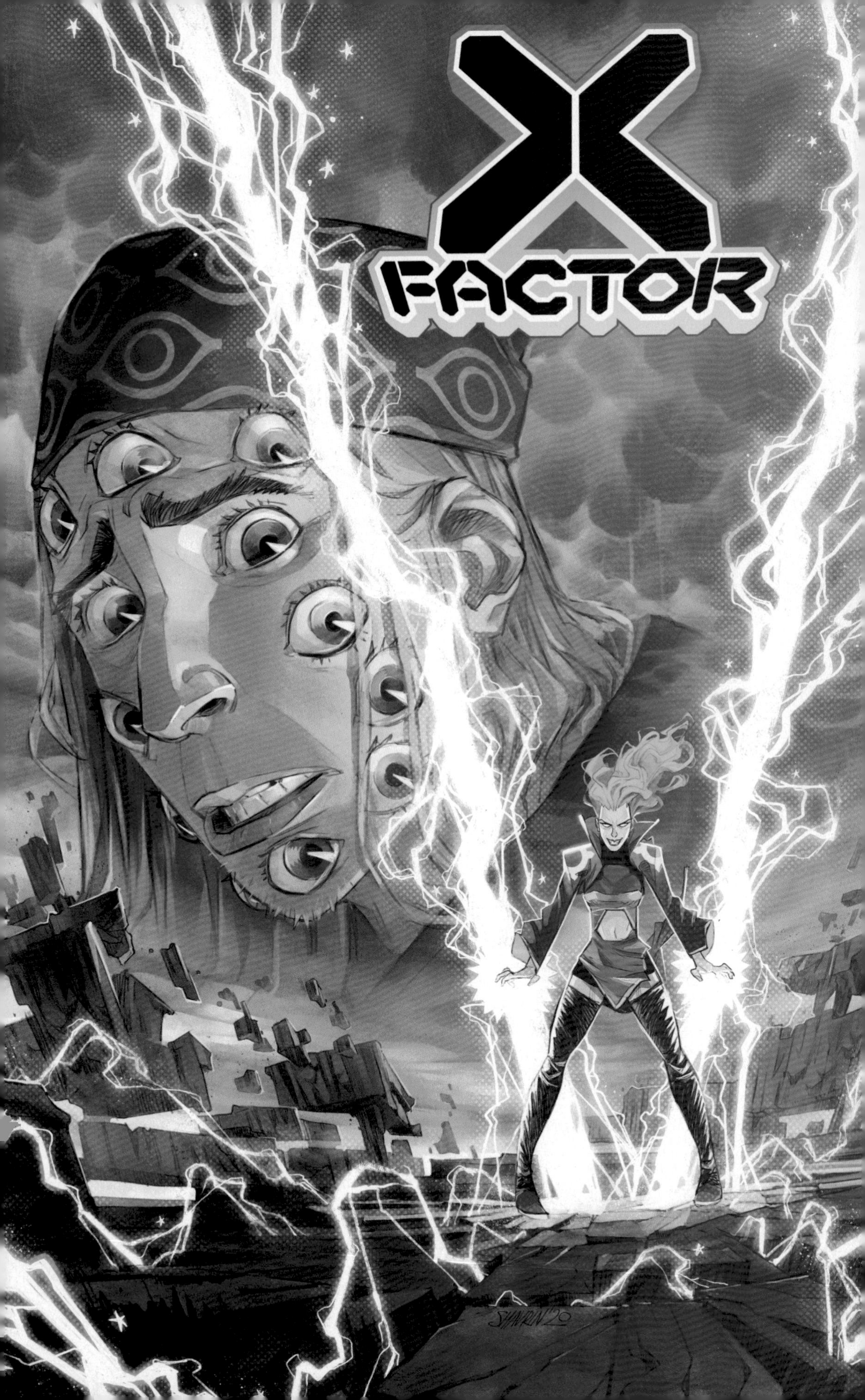
X
FACTOR

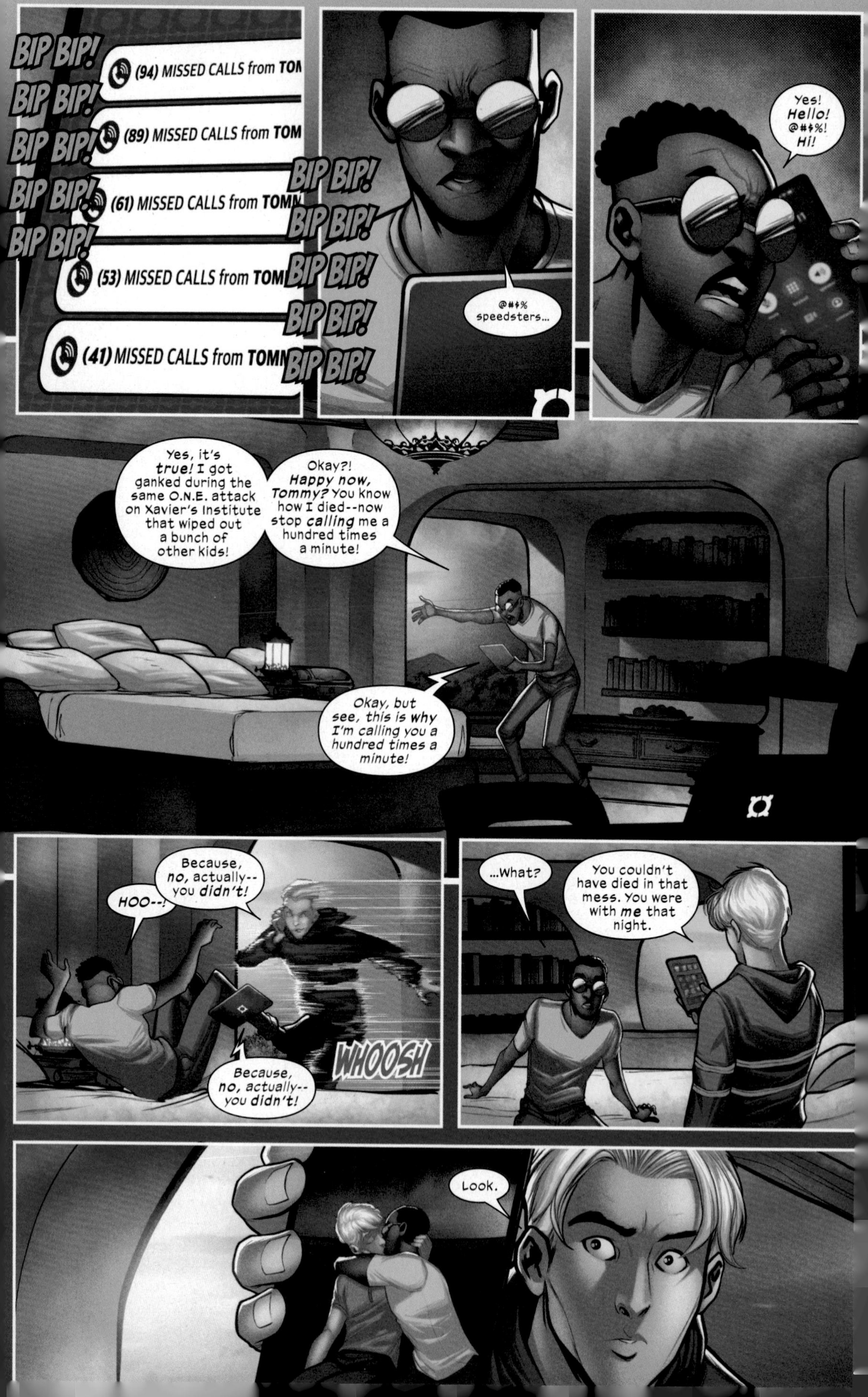
BIP BIP!
BIP BIP!
BIP BIP!
BIP BIP!
BIP BIP!
(94) MISSED CALLS from TOM
(89) MISSED CALLS from TOM
(61) MISSED CALLS from TOMM
(53) MISSED CALLS from TOM
(41) MISSED CALLS from TOMM
BIP BIP!
BIP BIP!
BIP BIP!
BIP BIP!
BIP BIP!
@#$% speedsters...
Yes! Hello! @#$%! Hi!
Yes, it's true! I got ganked during the same O.N.E. attack on Xavier's Institute that wiped out a bunch of other kids!
Okay?! Happy now, Tommy? You know how I died--now stop calling me a hundred times a minute!
Okay, but see, this is why I'm calling you a hundred times a minute!
HOO--!
Because, no, actually-- you didn't!
Because, no, actually-- you didn't!
WHOOSH
...What?
You couldn't have died in that mess. You were with me that night.
Look.

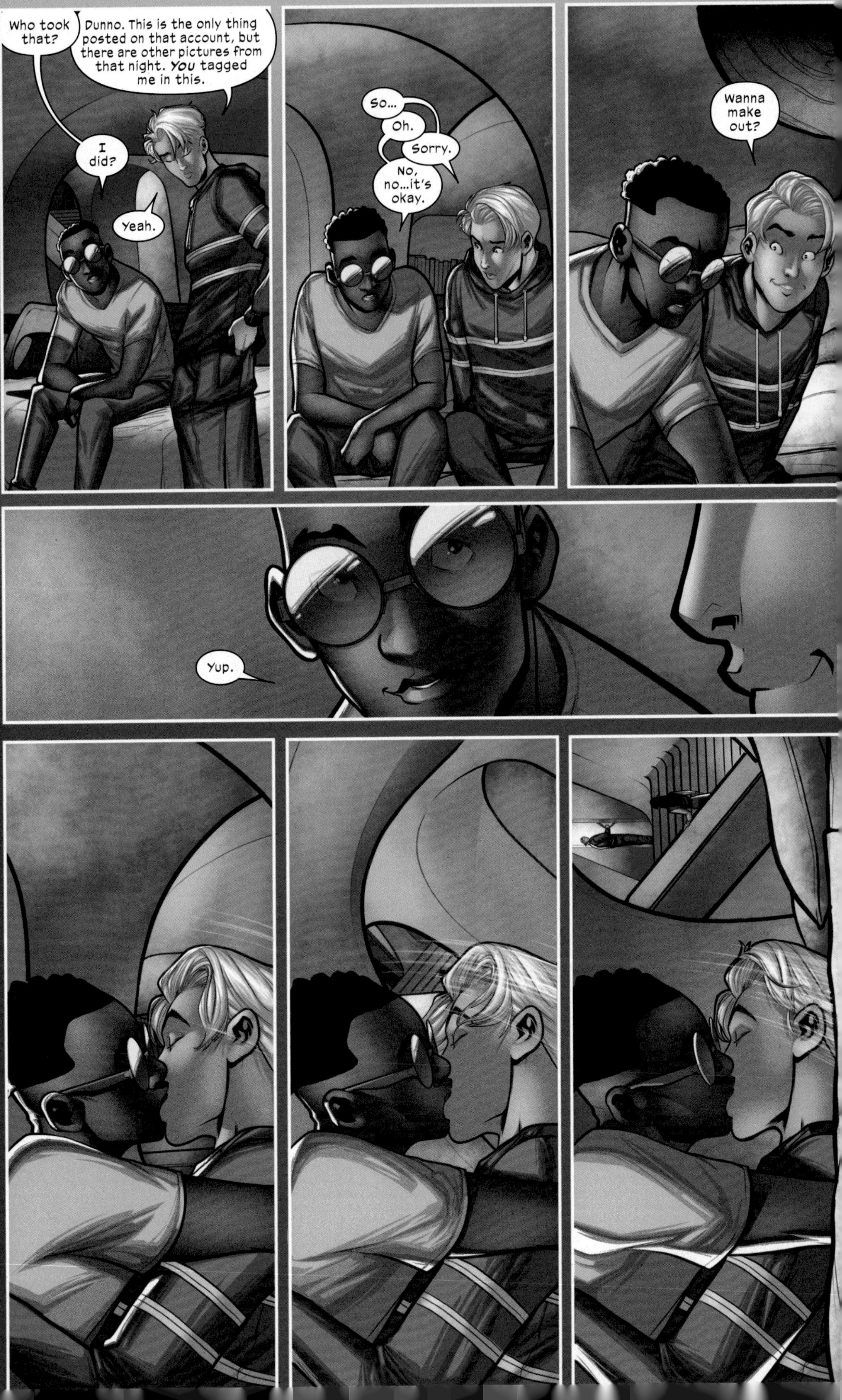

Who took that?
Dunno. This is the only thing posted on that account, but there are other pictures from that night. *You* tagged me in this.
I did?
Yeah.
So...
Oh.
Sorry.
No, no...it's okay.
Wanna make out?
Yup.

Hey, Prodigy. Here's the info you asked for. We knew to resurrect you without a body because the official incident report of your death was mailed to us along with Loa's, Rahne's, and everyone else who bit it around that same time. This was before X-Factor was established, so there was no formalized proof of death protocol back then, but since Wolverine and Cyclops were able to confirm so many of these deaths, we didn't question yours either. I hope this helps, and let me know if there's anything else I can do! What's this for, anyway?

Hugs 'n' kisses,

Elixir

Club Pepper
West Hollywood, CA

THE FIVE
Arbor Magna Hatchery, Krakoa

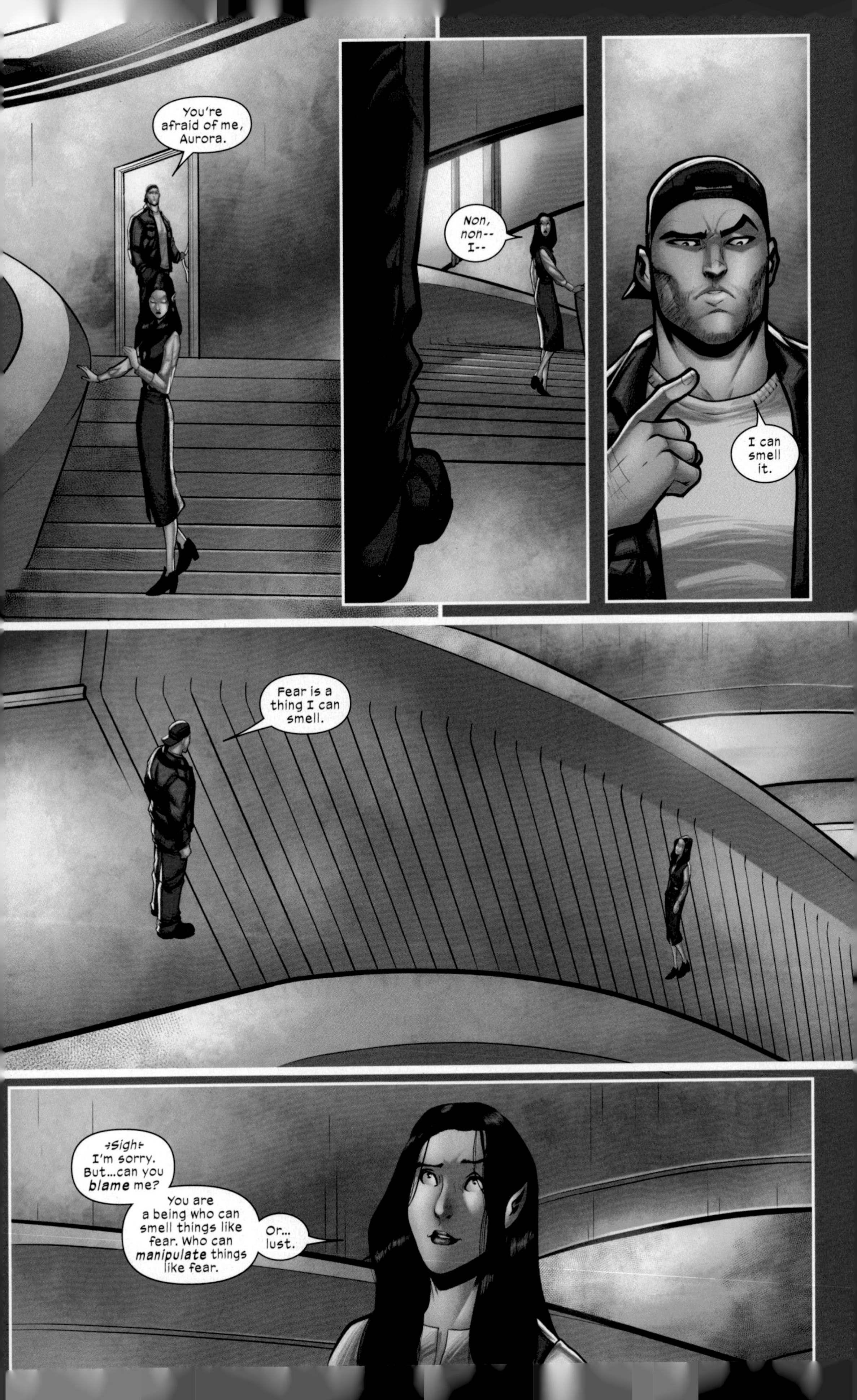
You're afraid of me, Aurora.
Non, non-- I--
I can smell it.
Fear is a thing I can smell.
Sigh I'm sorry. But...can you *blame* me?
You are a being who can smell things like fear. Who can *manipulate* things like fear.
Or... lust.

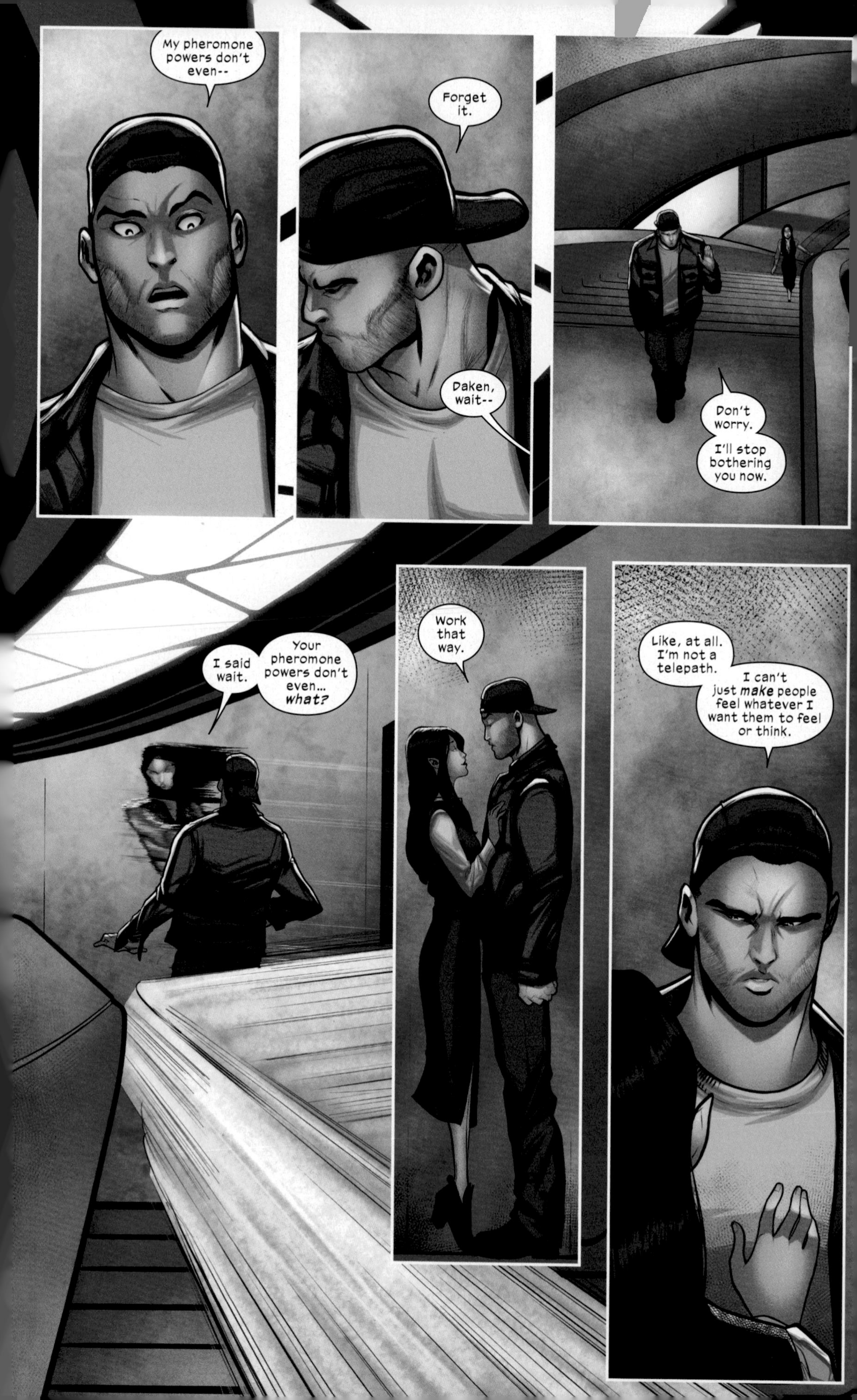
My pheromone powers don't even--
Forget it.
Daken, wait--
Don't worry.
I'll stop bothering you now.
I said wait.
Your pheromone powers don't even... *what?*
Work that way.
Like, at all. I'm not a telepath.
I can't just *make* people feel whatever I want them to feel or think.

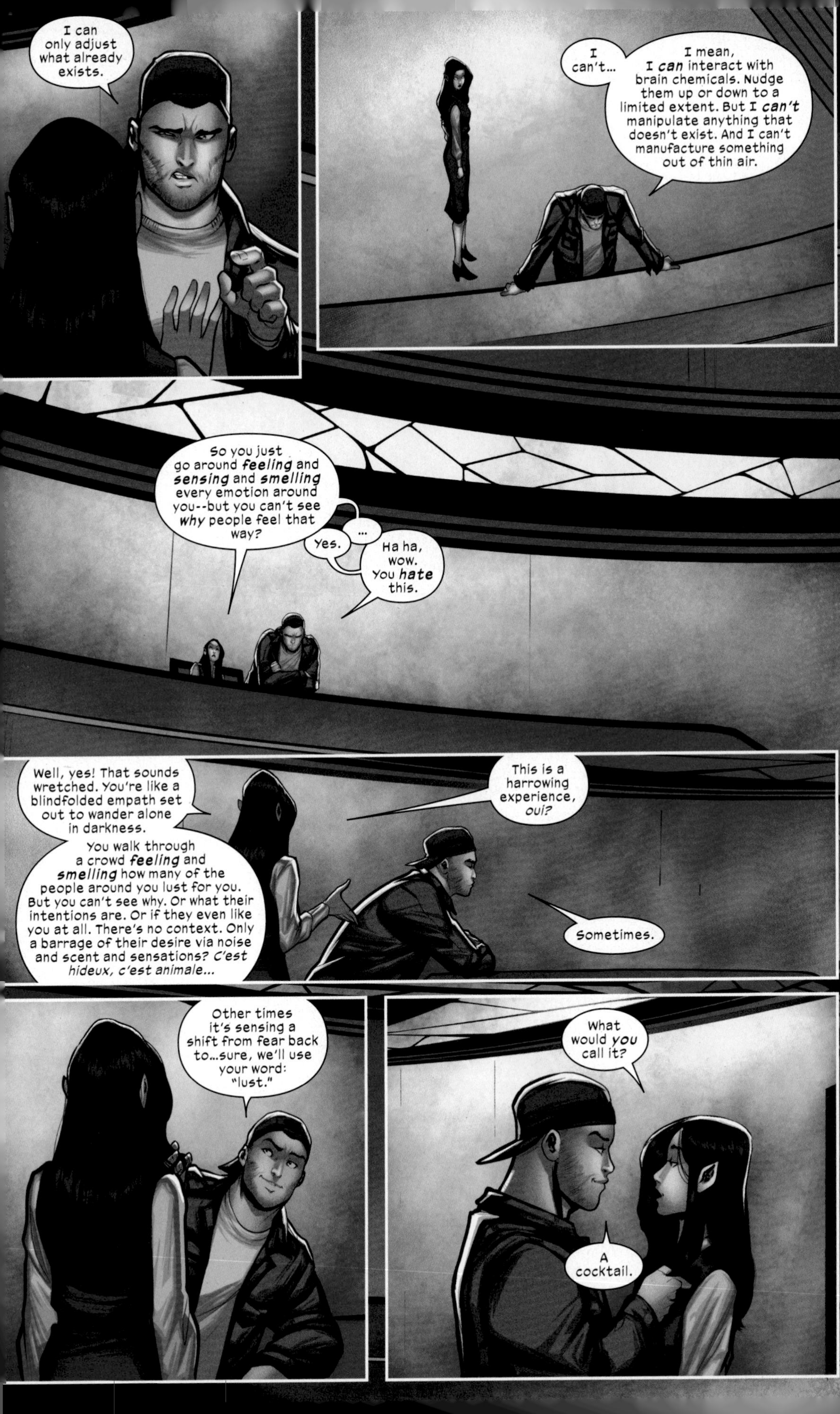

I can only adjust what already exists.
I can't...
I mean, I *can* interact with brain chemicals. Nudge them up or down to a limited extent. But I *can't* manipulate anything that doesn't exist. And I can't manufacture something out of thin air.
So you just go around *feeling* and *sensing* and *smelling* every emotion around you--but you can't see *why* people feel that way?
...
Yes.
Ha ha, wow. You *hate* this.
Well, yes! That sounds wretched. You're like a blindfolded empath set out to wander alone in darkness.
You walk through a crowd *feeling* and *smelling* how many of the people around you lust for you. But you can't see why. Or what their intentions are. Or if they even like you at all. There's no context. Only a barrage of their desire via noise and scent and sensations? *C'est hideux, c'est animale...*
This is a harrowing experience, *oui?*
Sometimes.
Other times it's sensing a shift from fear back to...sure, we'll use your word: "lust."
What would *you* call it?
A cocktail.

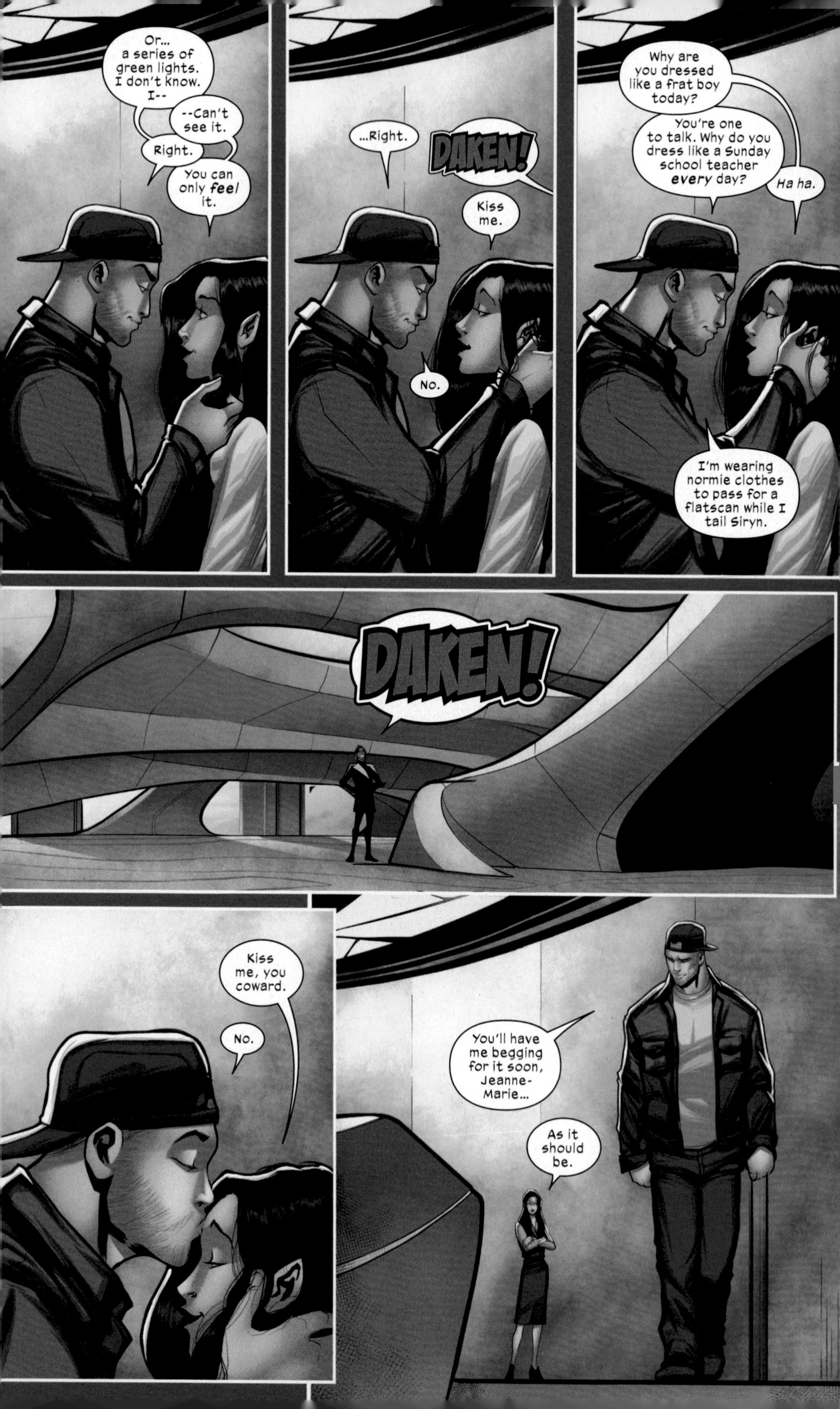
Or... a series of green lights. I don't know. I--
--Can't see it.
Right.
You can only feel it.
...Right.
DAKEN!
Kiss me.
No.
Why are you dressed like a frat boy today?
You're one to talk. Why do you dress like a Sunday school teacher every day?
Ha ha.
I'm wearing normie clothes to pass for a flatscan while I tail Siryn.
DAKEN!
Kiss me, you coward.
No.
You'll have me begging for it soon, Jeanne-Marie...
As it should be.

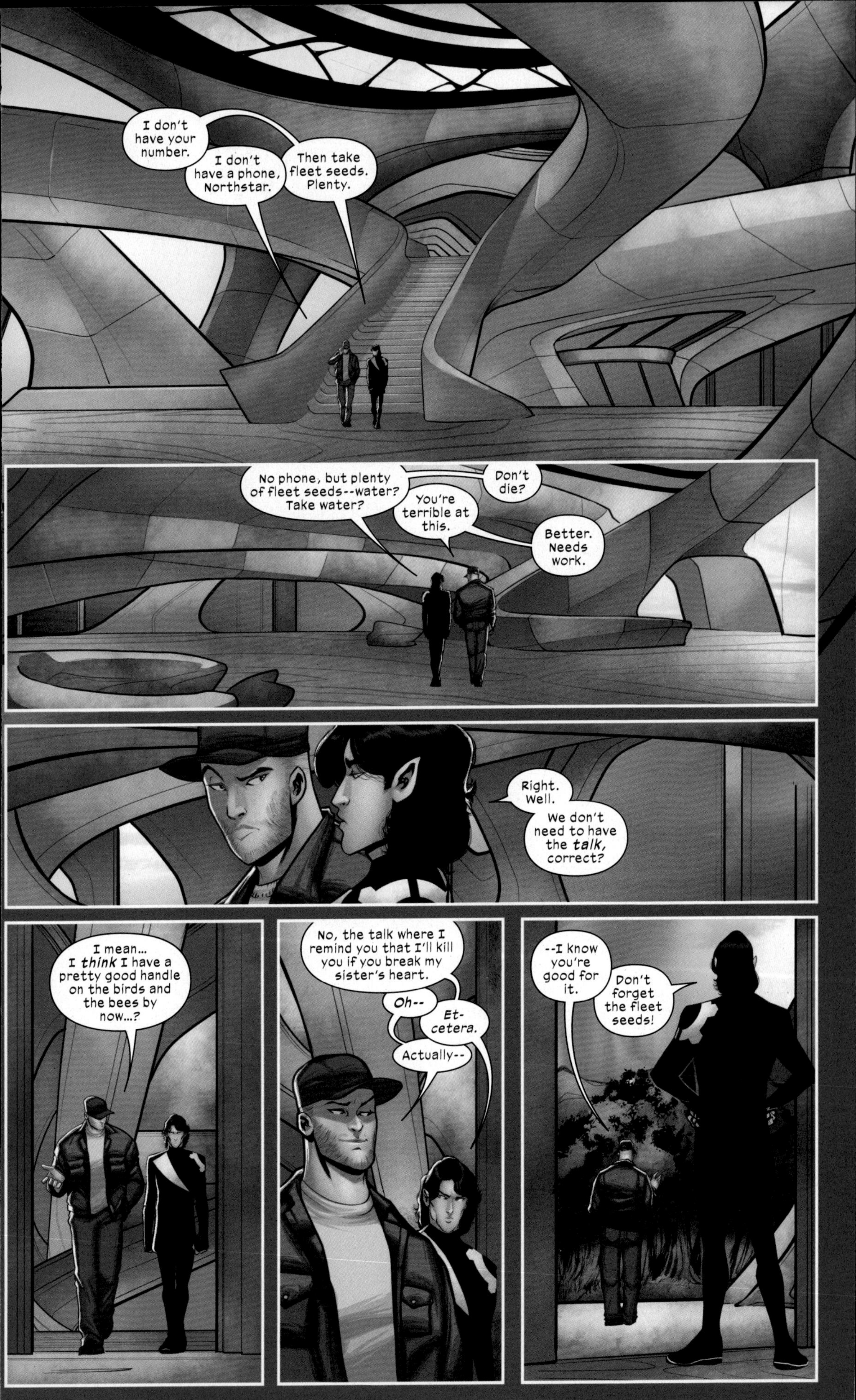
I don't have your number.
I don't have a phone, Northstar.
Then take fleet seeds. Plenty.
No phone, but plenty of fleet seeds--water? Take water?
Don't die?
You're terrible at this.
Better. Needs work.
Right. Well.
We don't need to have the *talk*, correct?
I mean... I *think* I have a pretty good handle on the birds and the bees by now...?
No, the talk where I remind you that I'll kill you if you break my sister's heart.
Oh--
Et- cetera.
Actually--
--I know you're good for it.
Don't forget the fleet seeds!

[00_proof_X]
[00_death_X]

HYPNOSIS ACTIVATED

X-FACTOR has been investigating dead and missing mutants, thus ensuring their resurrections. More recently, that applied to Siryn's multiple, unusual deaths. But when Polaris pushed her friend about her strange demises, Siryn pushed back...hitting Polaris with hypnosis to throw her off the trail.

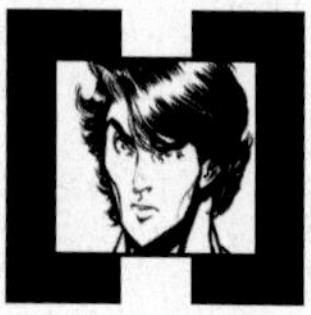
Northstar

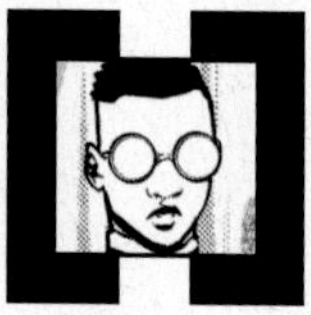
Prodigy

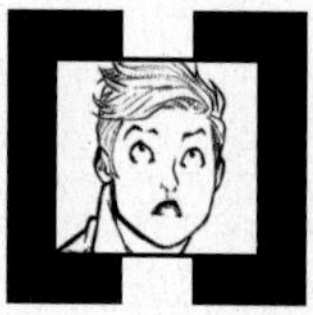
Prestige

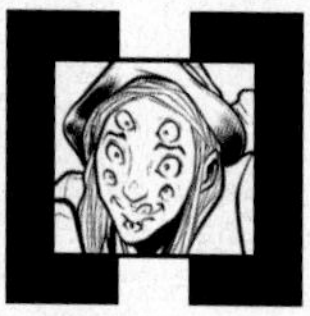
Eye-Boy

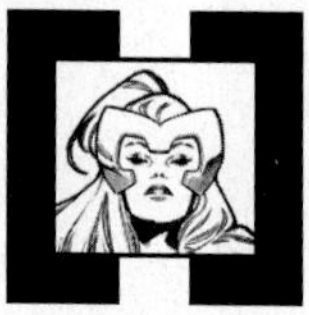
Polaris

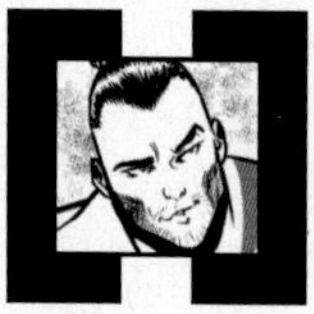
Daken

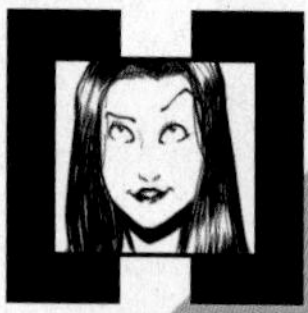
Aurora

X-FACTOR

[X_07]

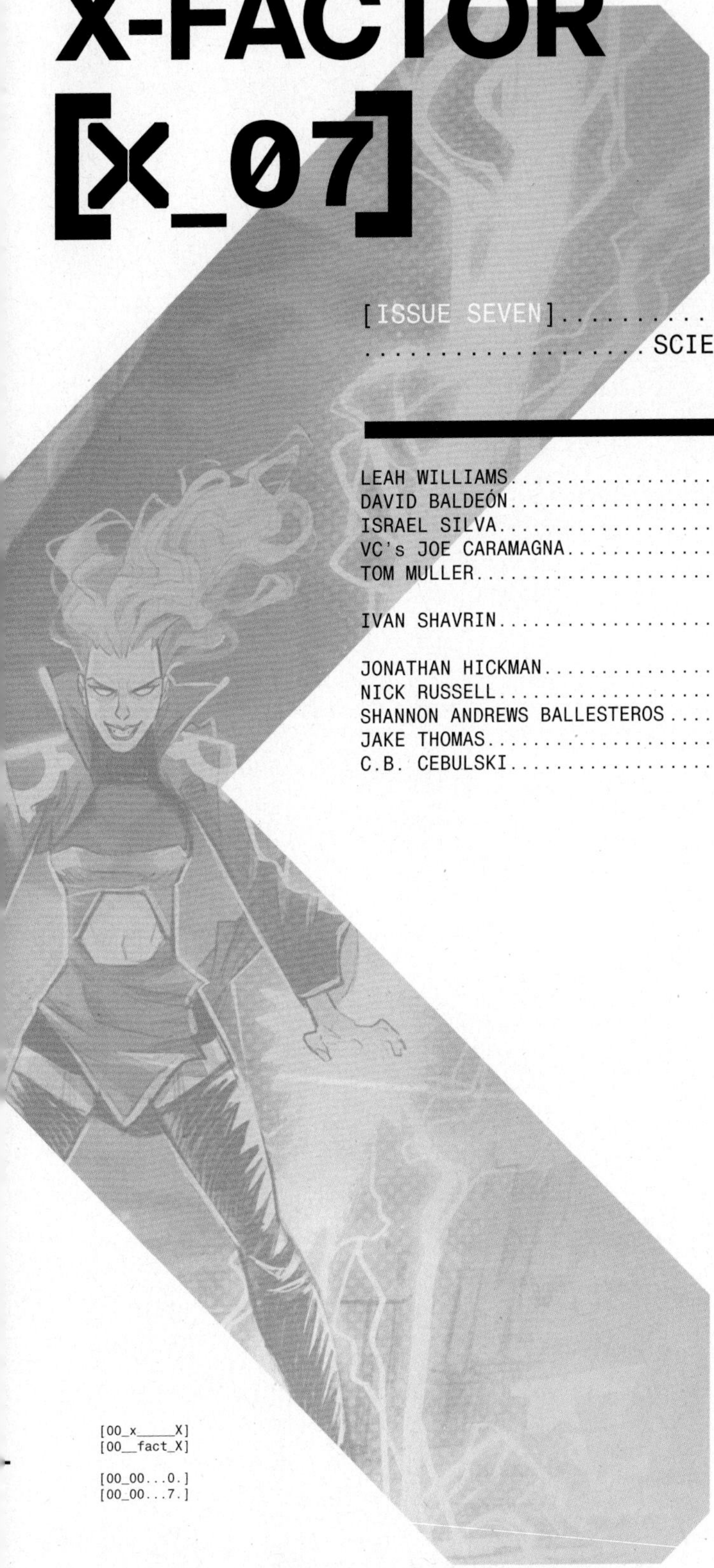

[ISSUE SEVEN]....................SUITE NO. 7:
....................SCIENTIA VINCERE TENEBRAS

LEAH WILLIAMS....................[WRITER]
DAVID BALDEÓN....................[ARTIST]
ISRAEL SILVA....................[COLOR ARTIST]
VC's JOE CARAMAGNA....................[LETTERER]
TOM MULLER....................[DESIGN]

IVAN SHAVRIN....................[COVER ARTIST]

JONATHAN HICKMAN....................[HEAD OF X]
NICK RUSSELL....................[PRODUCTION]
SHANNON ANDREWS BALLESTEROS....................[ASSISTANT EDITOR]
JAKE THOMAS....................[EDITOR]
C.B. CEBULSKI....................[EDITOR IN CHIEF]

[00_x_____X]
[00__fact_X]

[00_00...0.]
[00_00...7.]

[00________]
[00_and___]

[00_the___]

[00__five__]

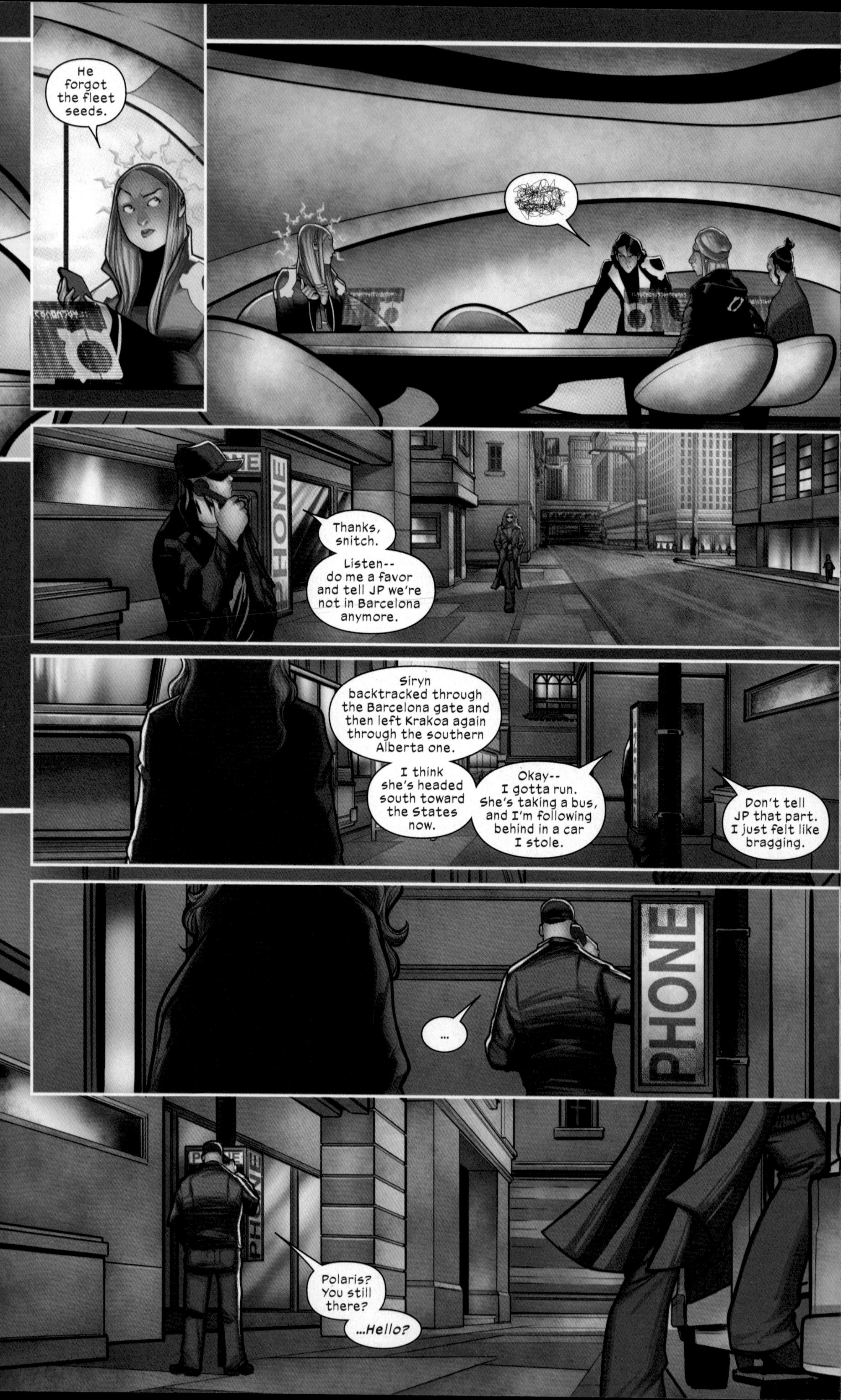

He forgot the fleet seeds.
Thanks, snitch.
Listen-- do me a favor and tell JP we're not in Barcelona anymore.
PHONE
Siryn backtracked through the Barcelona gate and then left Krakoa again through the southern Alberta one.
I think she's headed south toward the States now.
Okay-- I gotta run. She's taking a bus, and I'm following behind in a car I stole.
Don't tell JP that part. I just felt like bragging.
...
PHONE
Polaris? You still there?
...Hello?

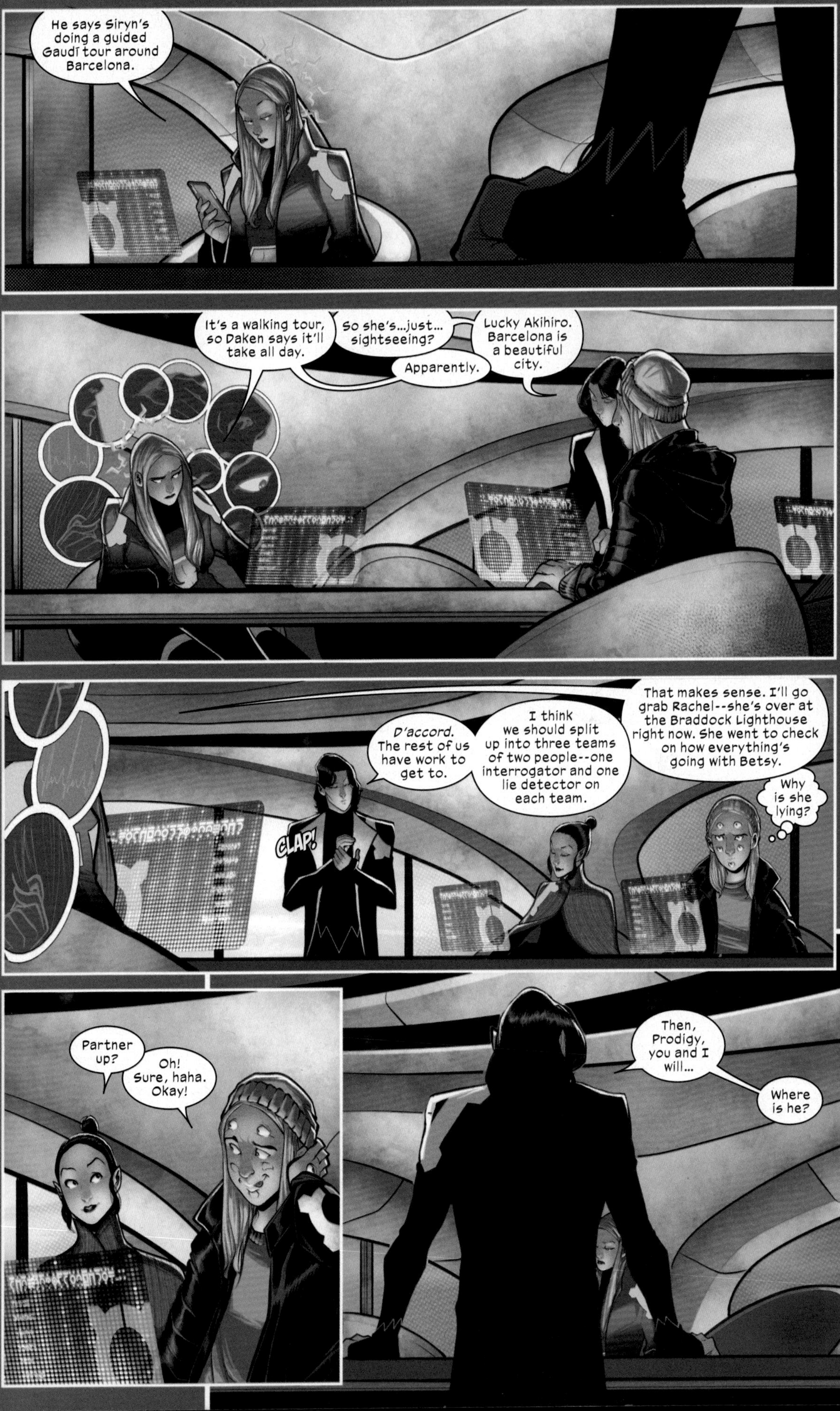
He says Siryn's doing a guided Gaudí tour around Barcelona.
It's a walking tour, so Daken says it'll take all day.
So she's...just... sightseeing?
Apparently.
Lucky Akihiro. Barcelona is a beautiful city.
CLAP!
D'accord. The rest of us have work to get to.
I think we should split up into three teams of two people--one interrogator and one lie detector on each team.
That makes sense. I'll go grab Rachel--she's over at the Braddock Lighthouse right now. She went to check on how everything's going with Betsy.
Why is she lying?
Partner up?
Oh! Sure, haha. Okay!
Then, Prodigy, you and I will...
Where is he?

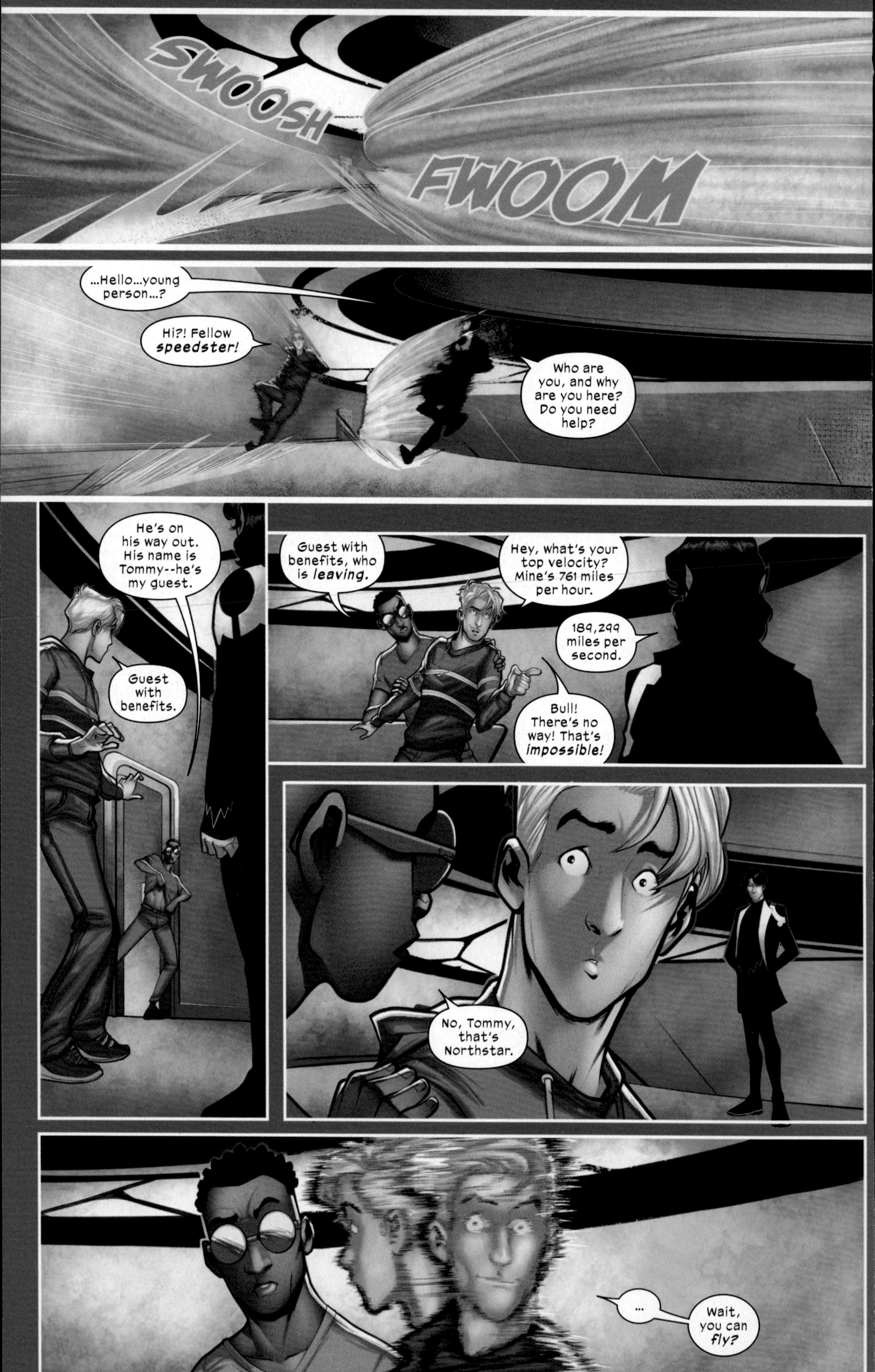
SWOOSH
FWOOM
...Hello...young person...?
Hi?! Fellow *speedster!*
Who are you, and why are you here? Do you need help?
He's on his way out. His name is Tommy--he's my guest.
Guest with benefits.
Guest with benefits, who is *leaving.*
Hey, what's your top velocity? Mine's 761 miles per hour.
189,299 miles per second.
Bull! There's no way! That's *impossible!*
No, Tommy, that's Northstar.
...
Wait, you can *fly?*

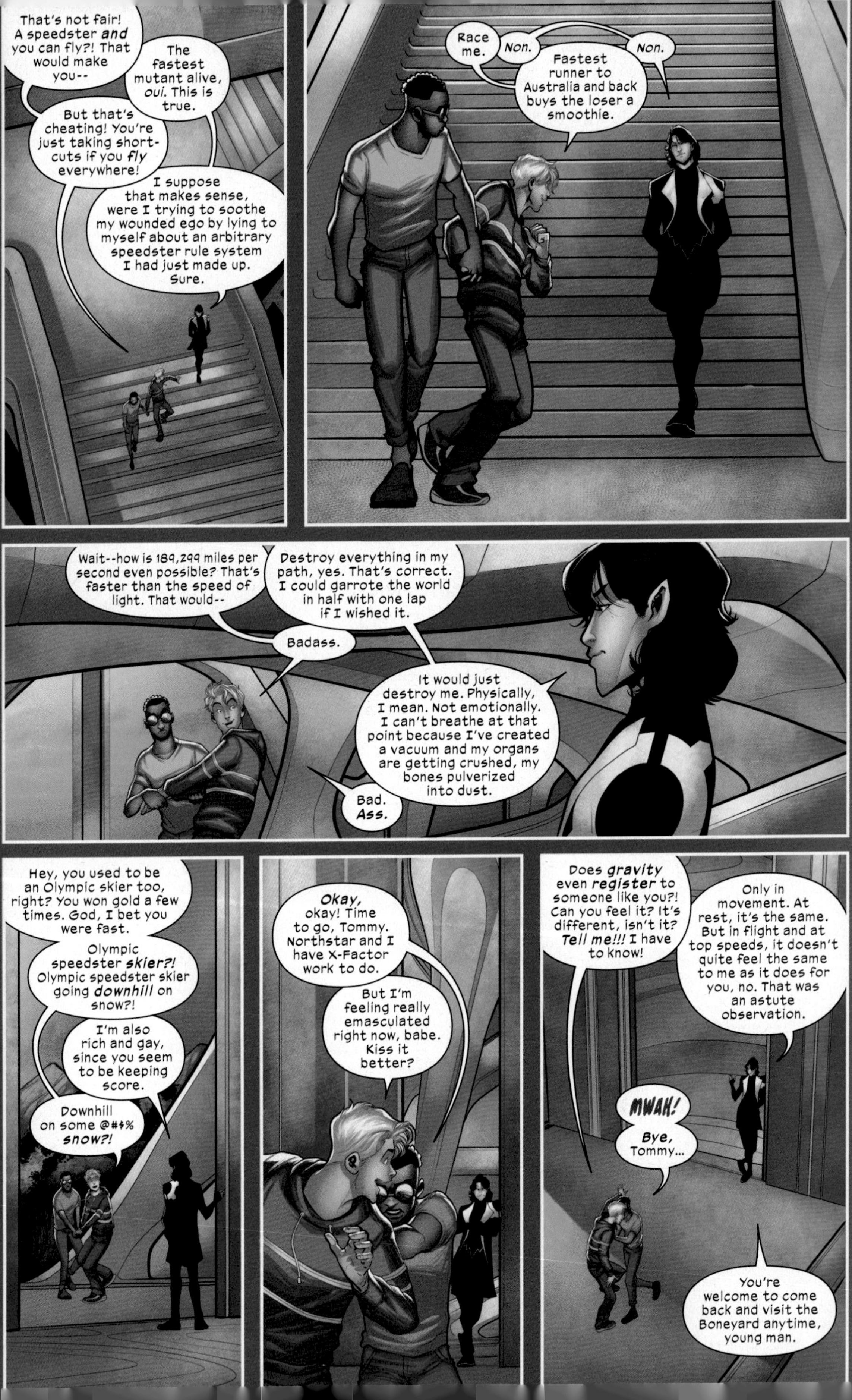
That's not fair! A speedster and you can fly?! That would make you--
The fastest mutant alive, oui. This is true.
But that's cheating! You're just taking short-cuts if you fly everywhere!
I suppose that makes sense, were I trying to soothe my wounded ego by lying to myself about an arbitrary speedster rule system I had just made up. Sure.
Race me.
Non.
Non.
Fastest runner to Australia and back buys the loser a smoothie.
Wait--how is 189,299 miles per second even possible? That's faster than the speed of light. That would--
Destroy everything in my path, yes. That's correct. I could garrote the world in half with one lap if I wished it.
Badass.
It would just destroy me. Physically, I mean. Not emotionally. I can't breathe at that point because I've created a vacuum and my organs are getting crushed, my bones pulverized into dust.
Bad. Ass.
Hey, you used to be an Olympic skier too, right? You won gold a few times. God, I bet you were fast.
Olympic speedster skier?! Olympic speedster skier going downhill on snow?!
I'm also rich and gay, since you seem to be keeping score.
Downhill on some @#$% snow?!
Okay, okay! Time to go, Tommy. Northstar and I have X-Factor work to do.
But I'm feeling really emasculated right now, babe. Kiss it better?
Does gravity even register to someone like you?! Can you feel it? It's different, isn't it? Tell me!!! I have to know!
Only in movement. At rest, it's the same. But in flight and at top speeds, it doesn't quite feel the same to me as it does for you, no. That was an astute observation.
MWAH!
Bye, Tommy...
You're welcome to come back and visit the Boneyard anytime, young man.

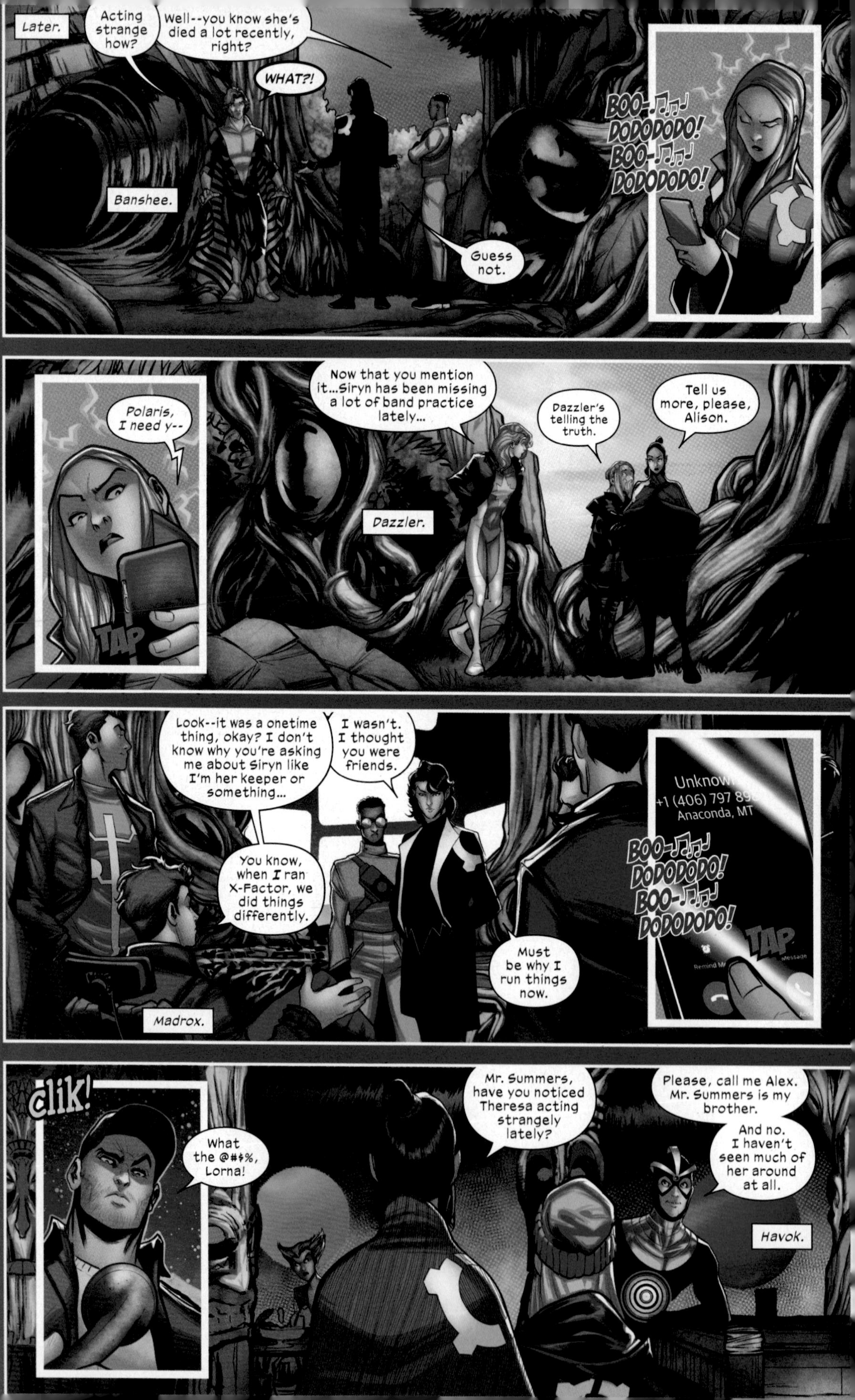

Later.
Acting strange how?
Well--you know she's died a lot recently, right?
WHAT?!
Banshee.
Guess not.
BOO-♫♫♩ DODODODO! BOO-♫♫♩ DODODODO!
Polaris, I need y--
TAP
Now that you mention it...Siryn has been missing a lot of band practice lately...
Dazzler.
Dazzler's telling the truth.
Tell us more, please, Alison.
Look--it was a onetime thing, okay? I don't know why you're asking me about Siryn like I'm her keeper or something...
I wasn't. I thought you were friends.
You know, when I ran X-Factor, we did things differently.
Madrox.
Must be why I run things now.
Unknow
+1 (406) 797 89
Anaconda, MT
BOO-♫♫♩ DODODODO! BOO-♫♫♩ DODODODO!
TAP
clik!
What the @#$%, Lorna!
Mr. Summers, have you noticed Theresa acting strangely lately?
Please, call me Alex. Mr. Summers is my brother.
And no. I haven't seen much of her around at all.
Havok.

The Morrigan, Goddess of Death and Battle.

Some claim she has existed since death itself began and has taken many different forms and different names as ages pass. It is said she is a shape-shifter who can affect areas of death and battle in all ways, including both bestowing and removing abilities in others. She can weaken victims to the brink of death or heal the sick back from the very same edge if she wills it.

Our history of her begins in the year 250 B.C.E., in which the Morrigan battles for her new host body. Her original form has long since been lost to time, and thusly the Morrigan may only pass into a new host upon death of the former host, though her window of time to do so is limited. It is death itself that permits the transfer, whether or not the intended host, who is always female, consents.

The source of the Morrigan's powers is by her own account ageless, drawn from the font of death and battles themselves. Celts and druids made ritual sacrifices in praise of her name, and some texts tell of death rite rituals found across many a different ancient heathen society of eras gone.

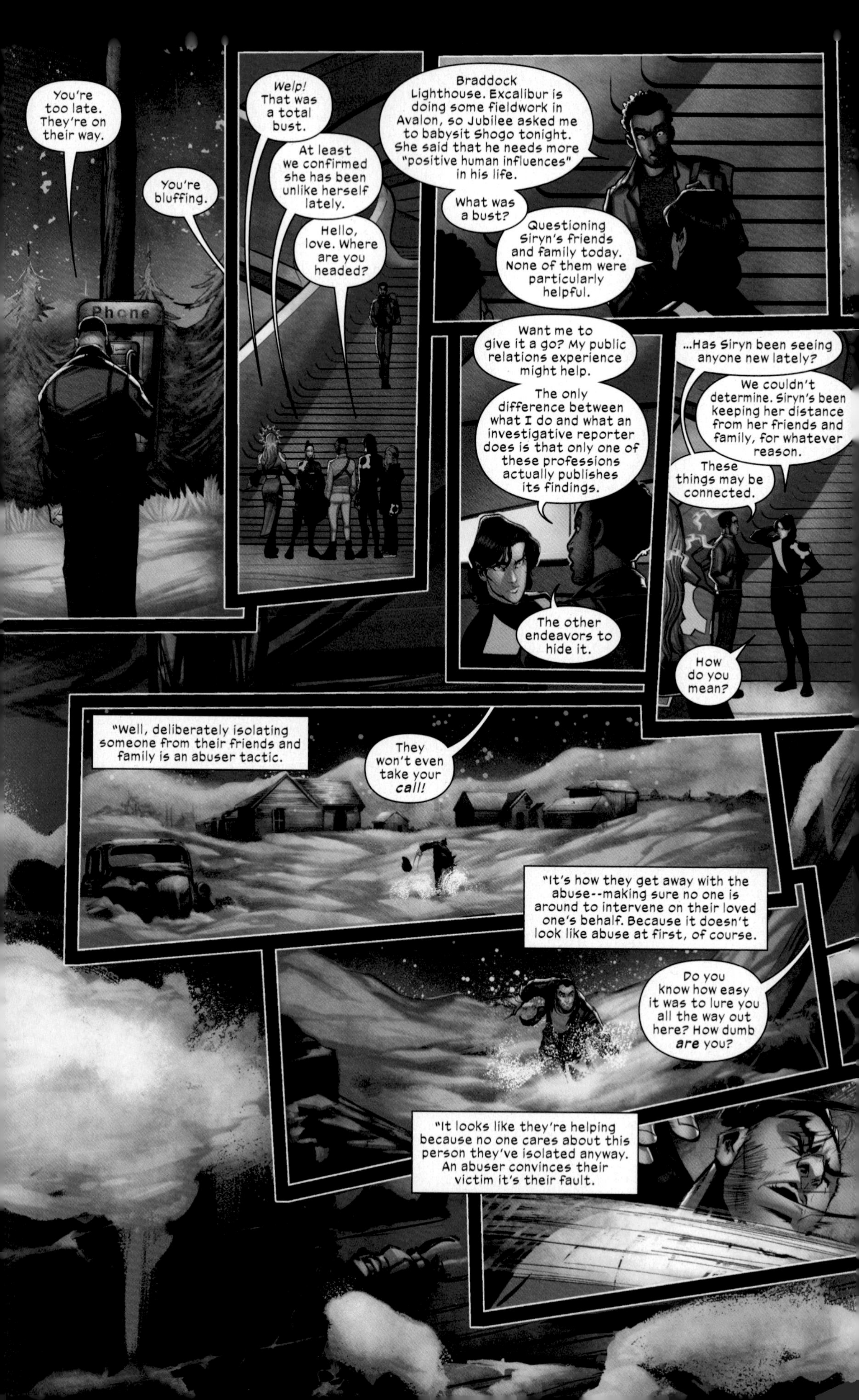
You're too late. They're on their way.
You're bluffing.
Welp! That was a total bust.
At least we confirmed she has been unlike herself lately.
Hello, love. Where are you headed?
Braddock Lighthouse. Excalibur is doing some fieldwork in Avalon, so Jubilee asked me to babysit Shogo tonight. She said that he needs more "positive human influences" in his life.
What was a bust?
Questioning Siryn's friends and family today. None of them were particularly helpful.
Want me to give it a go? My public relations experience might help.
The only difference between what I do and what an investigative reporter does is that only one of these professions actually publishes its findings.
The other endeavors to hide it.
...Has Siryn been seeing anyone new lately?
We couldn't determine. Siryn's been keeping her distance from her friends and family, for whatever reason.
These things may be connected.
How do you mean?
"Well, deliberately isolating someone from their friends and family is an abuser tactic.
They won't even take your call!
"It's how they get away with the abuse--making sure no one is around to intervene on their loved one's behalf. Because it doesn't look like abuse at first, of course.
Do you know how easy it was to lure you all the way out here? How dumb are you?
"It looks like they're helping because no one cares about this person they've isolated anyway. An abuser convinces their victim it's their fault.
Phone

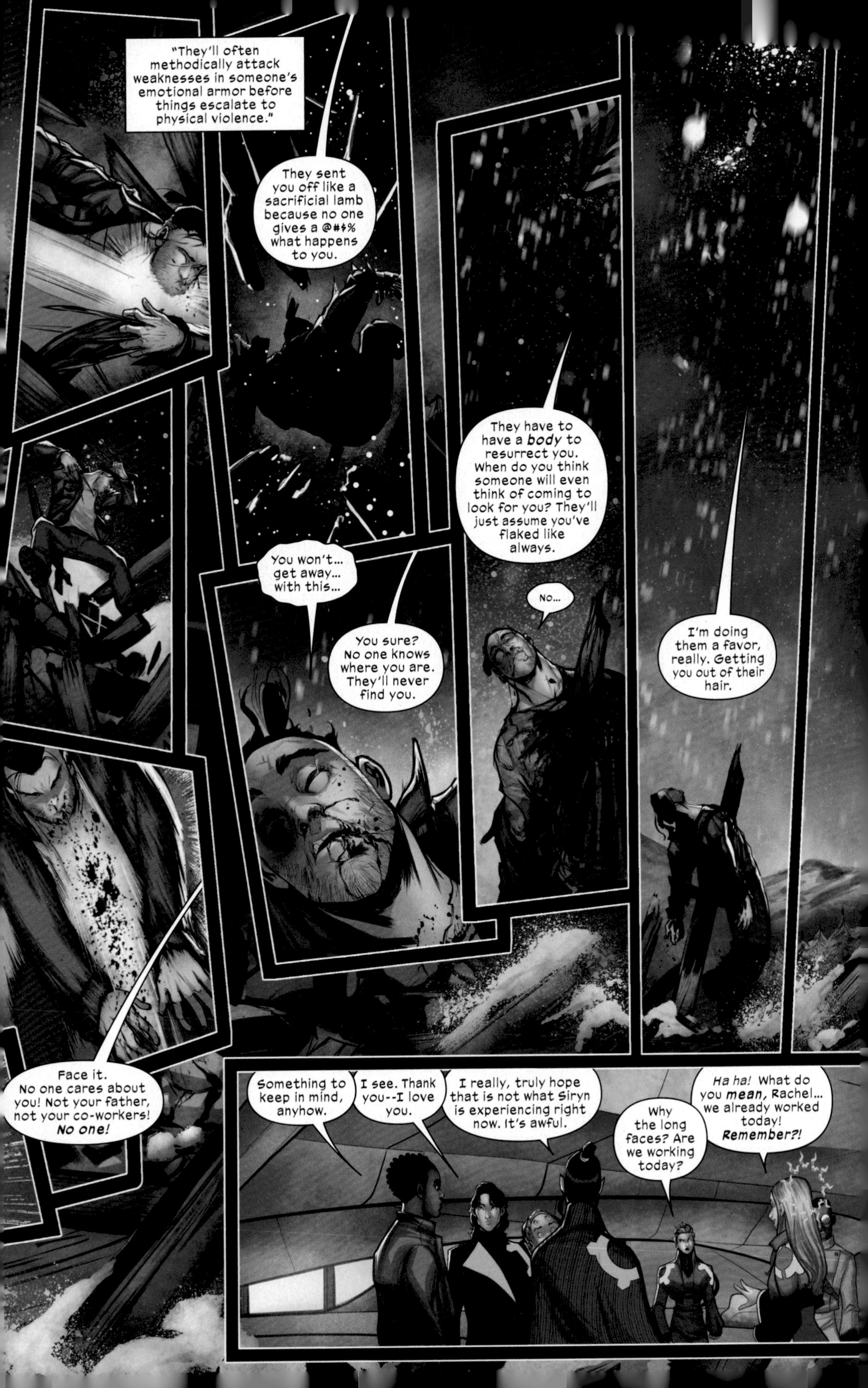

"They'll often methodically attack weaknesses in someone's emotional armor before things escalate to physical violence."
They sent you off like a sacrificial lamb because no one gives a @#$% what happens to you.
They have to have a *body* to resurrect you. When do you think someone will even think of coming to look for you? They'll just assume you've flaked like always.
You won't... get away... with this...
You sure? No one knows where you are. They'll never find you.
No...
I'm doing them a favor, really. Getting you out of their hair.
Face it. No one cares about you! Not your father, not your co-workers! ***No one!***
Something to keep in mind, anyhow.
I see. Thank you--I love you.
I really, truly hope that is not what Siryn is experiencing right now. It's awful.
Why the long faces? Are we working today?
Ha ha! What do you ***mean,*** Rachel... we already worked today! ***Remember?!***

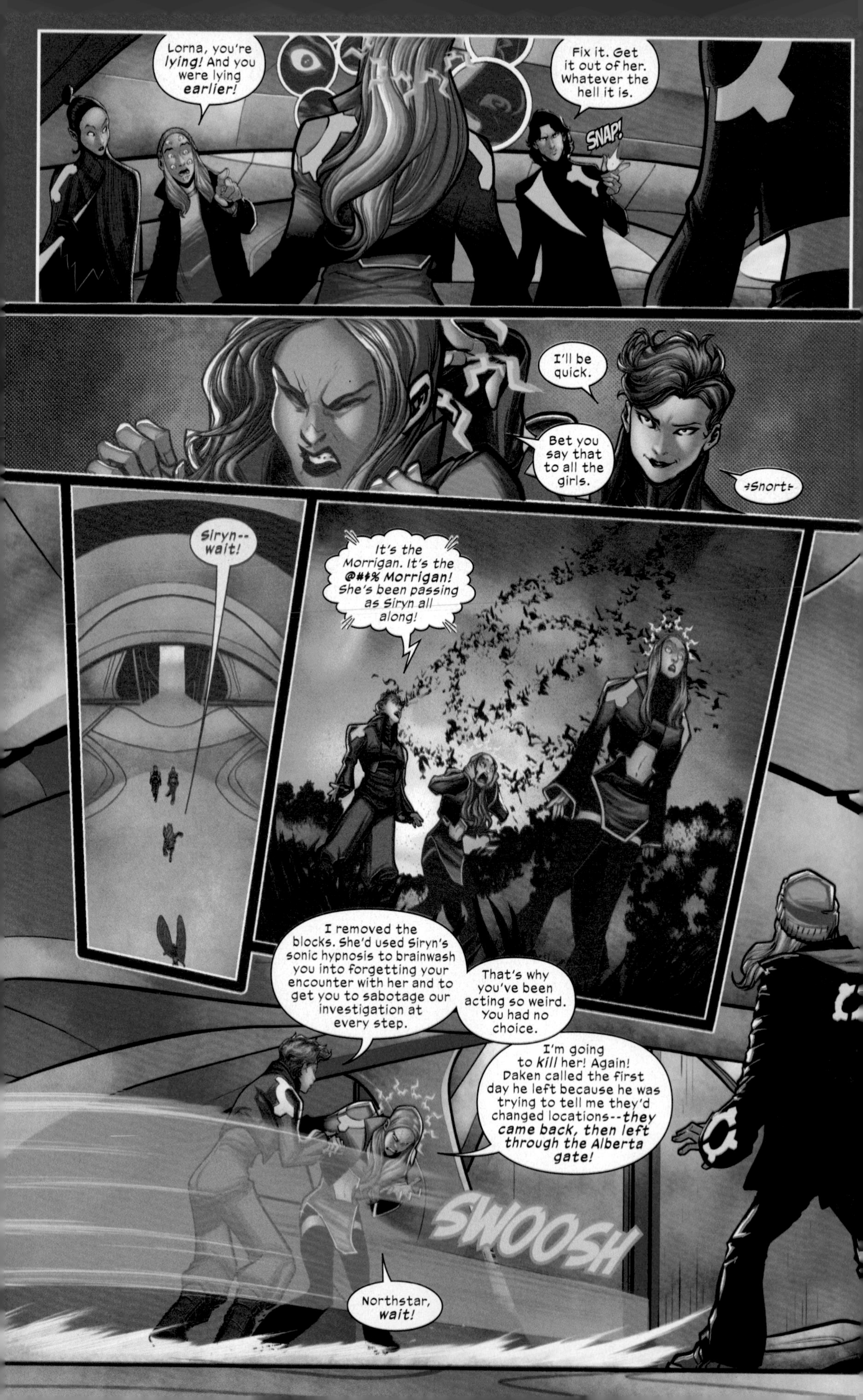
Lorna, you're *lying!* And you were lying *earlier!*
Fix it. Get it out of her. Whatever the hell it is.
SNAP!
I'll be quick.
Bet you say that to all the girls.
-Snort-
Siryn--wait!
It's the Morrigan. It's the **@#$% Morrigan!** She's been passing as Siryn all along!
I removed the blocks. She'd used Siryn's sonic hypnosis to brainwash you into forgetting your encounter with her and to get you to sabotage our investigation at every step.
That's why you've been acting so weird. You had no choice.
I'm going to *kill* her! Again! Daken called the first day he left because he was trying to tell me they'd changed locations--*they came back, then left through the Alberta gate!*
SWOOSH
Northstar, *wait!*

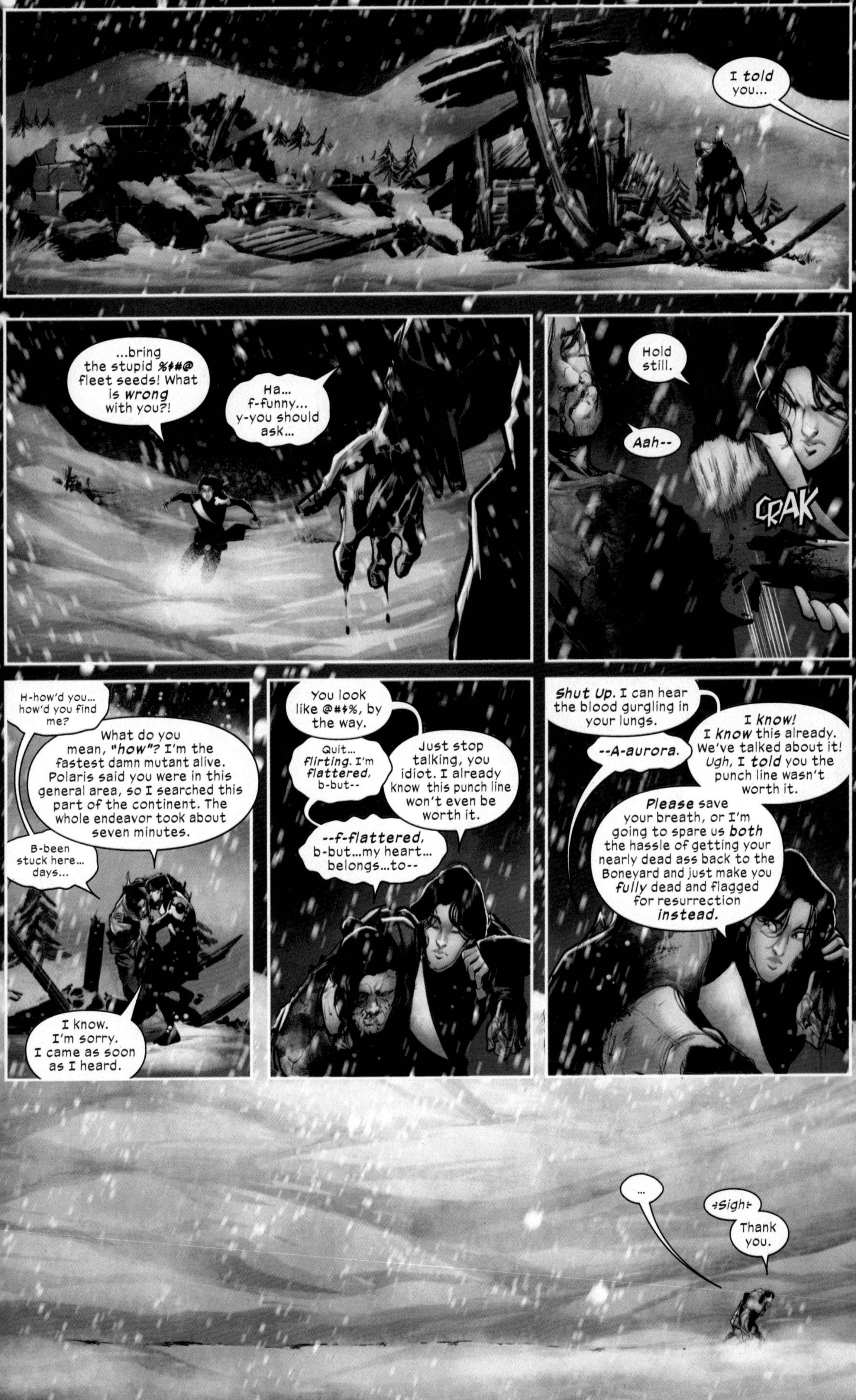
I told you...
...bring the stupid %$#@ fleet seeds! What is wrong with you?!
Ha... f-funny... y-you should ask...
Hold still.
Aah--
CRAK
H-how'd you... how'd you find me?
What do you mean, "how"? I'm the fastest damn mutant alive. Polaris said you were in this general area, so I searched this part of the continent. The whole endeavor took about seven minutes.
B-been stuck here... days...
I know. I'm sorry. I came as soon as I heard.
You look like @#$%, by the way.
Quit... flirting. I'm flattered, b-but--
Just stop talking, you idiot. I already know this punch line won't even be worth it.
--f-flattered, b-but...my heart... belongs...to--
Shut Up. I can hear the blood gurgling in your lungs.
--A-aurora.
I know! I know this already. We've talked about it! Ugh, I told you the punch line wasn't worth it.
Please save your breath, or I'm going to spare us both the hassle of getting your nearly dead ass back to the Boneyard and just make you fully dead and flagged for resurrection instead.
...
-Sigh- Thank you.

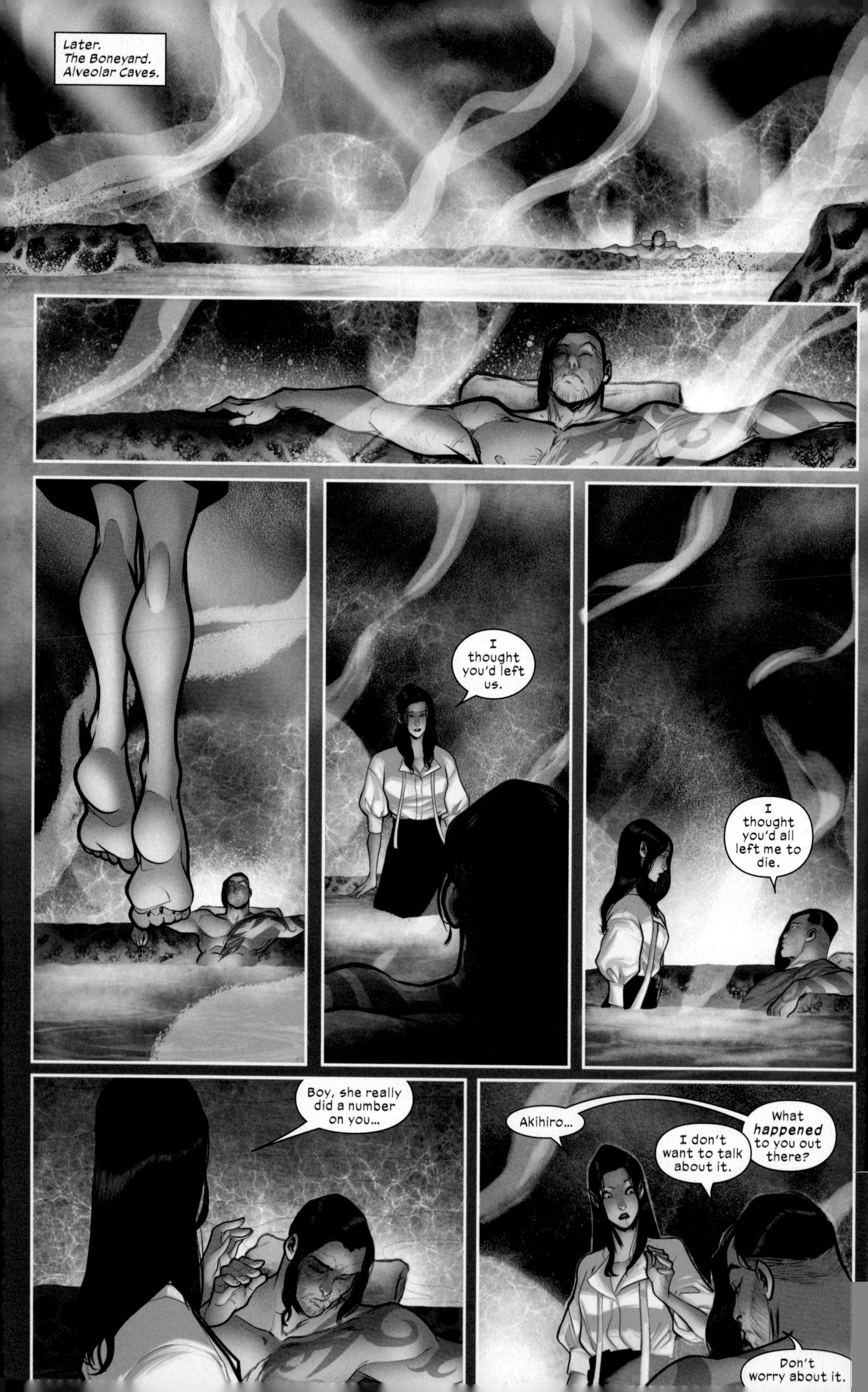
Later.
The Boneyard.
Alveolar Caves.
I thought you'd left us.
I thought you'd all left me to die.
Boy, she really did a number on you...
Akihiro...
What happened to you out there?
I don't want to talk about it.
Don't worry about it.

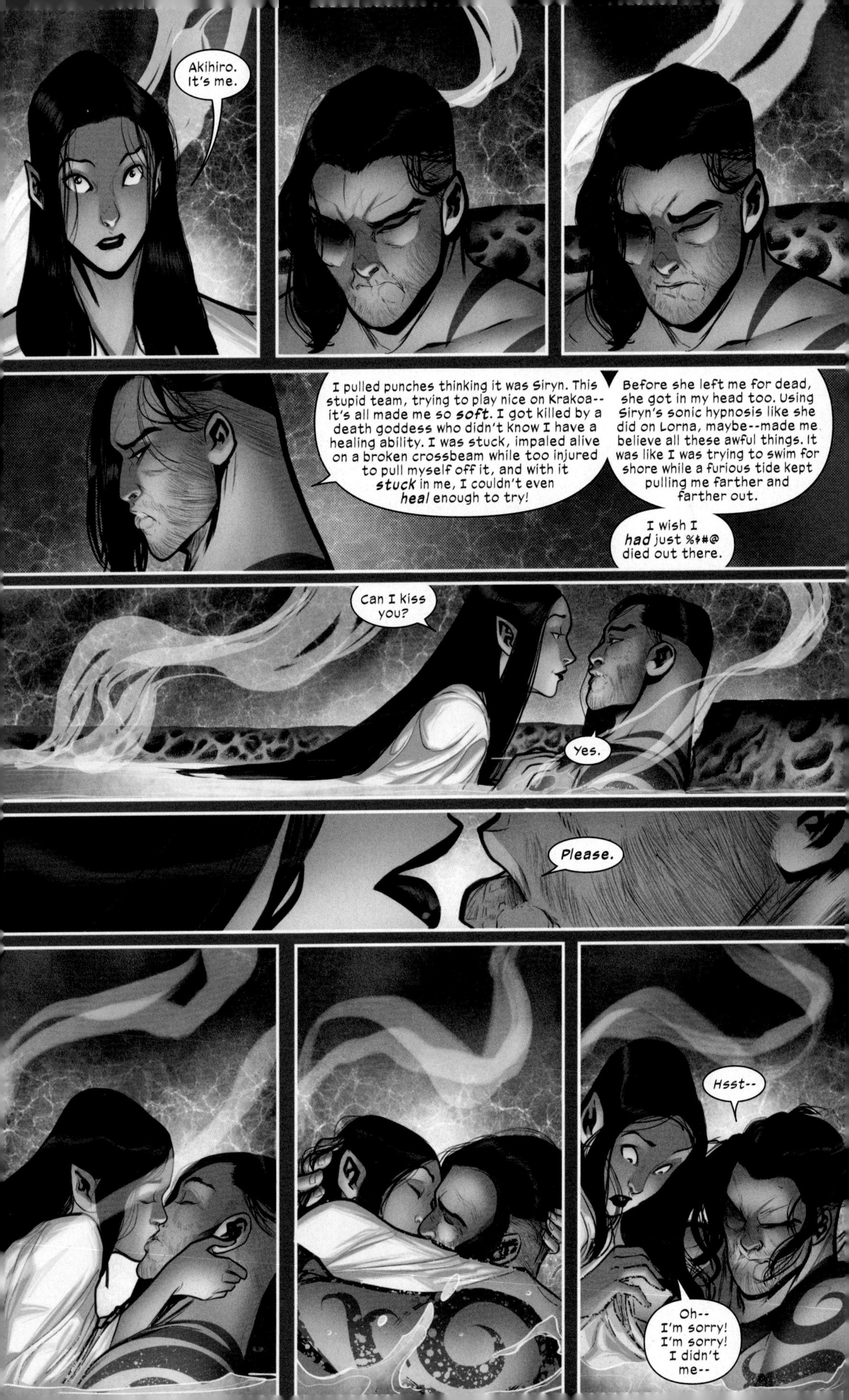
Akihiro. It's me.
I pulled punches thinking it was Siryn. This stupid team, trying to play nice on Krakoa--it's all made me so *soft*. I got killed by a death goddess who didn't know I have a healing ability. I was stuck, impaled alive on a broken crossbeam while too injured to pull myself off it, and with it *stuck* in me, I couldn't even *heal* enough to try!
Before she left me for dead, she got in my head too. Using Siryn's sonic hypnosis like she did on Lorna, maybe--made me believe all these awful things. It was like I was trying to swim for shore while a furious tide kept pulling me farther and farther out.
I wish I *had* just %$#@ died out there.
Can I kiss you?
Yes.
Please.
Hsst--
Oh--
I'm sorry!
I'm sorry!
I didn't
me--

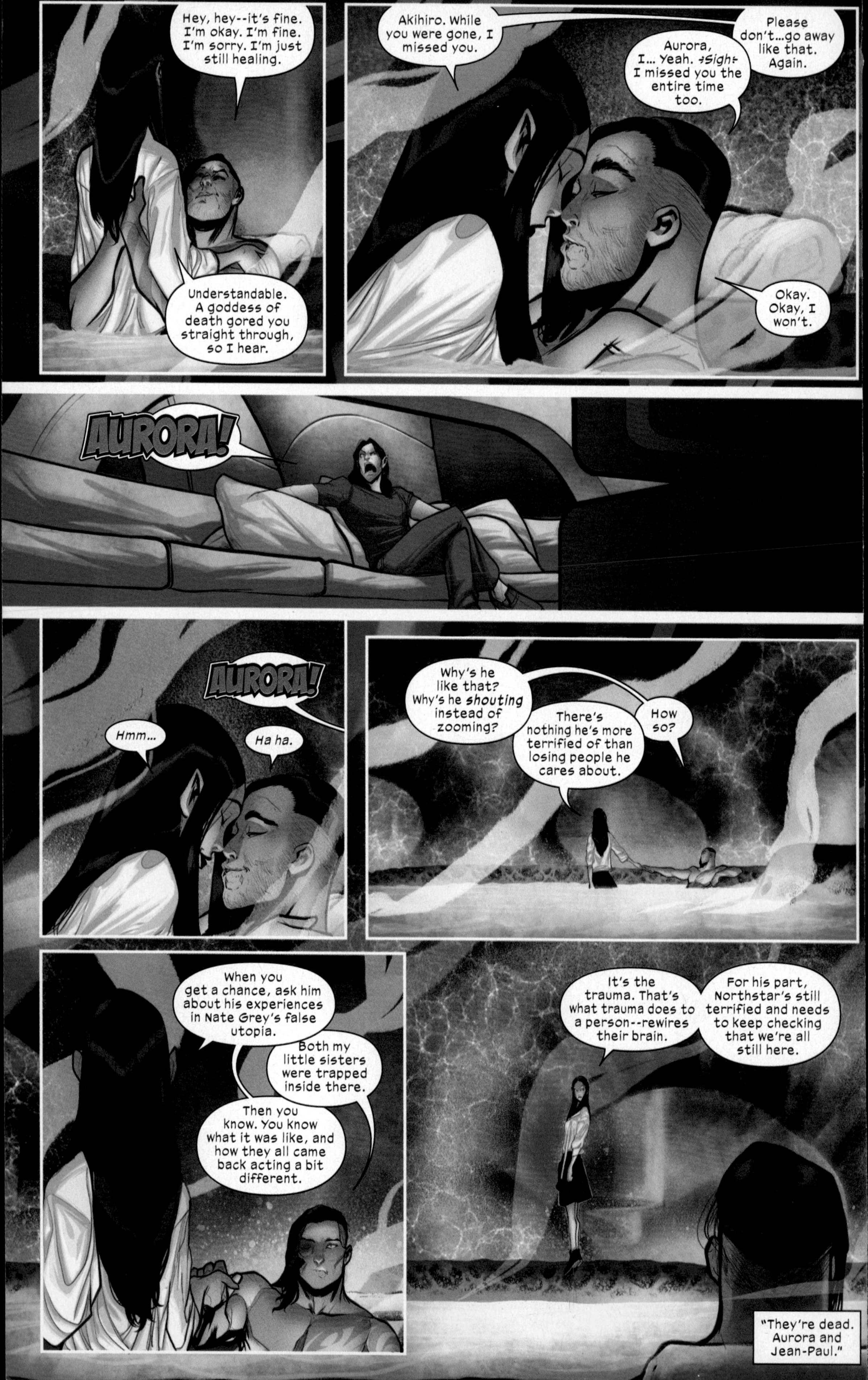
Hey, hey--it's fine. I'm okay. I'm fine. I'm sorry. I'm just still healing.
Understandable. A goddess of death gored you straight through, so I hear.
Akihiro. While you were gone, I missed you.
Aurora, I... Yeah. *Sigh* I missed you the entire time too.
Please don't...go away like that. Again.
Okay. Okay, I won't.
AURORA!
AURORA!
Hmm...
Ha ha.
Why's he like that? Why's he *shouting* instead of zooming?
There's nothing he's more terrified of than losing people he cares about.
How so?
When you get a chance, ask him about his experiences in Nate Grey's false utopia.
Both my little sisters were trapped inside there.
Then you know. You know what it was like, and how they all came back acting a bit different.
It's the trauma. That's what trauma does to a person--rewires their brain.
For his part, Northstar's still terrified and needs to keep checking that we're all still here.
"They're dead. Aurora and Jean-Paul."

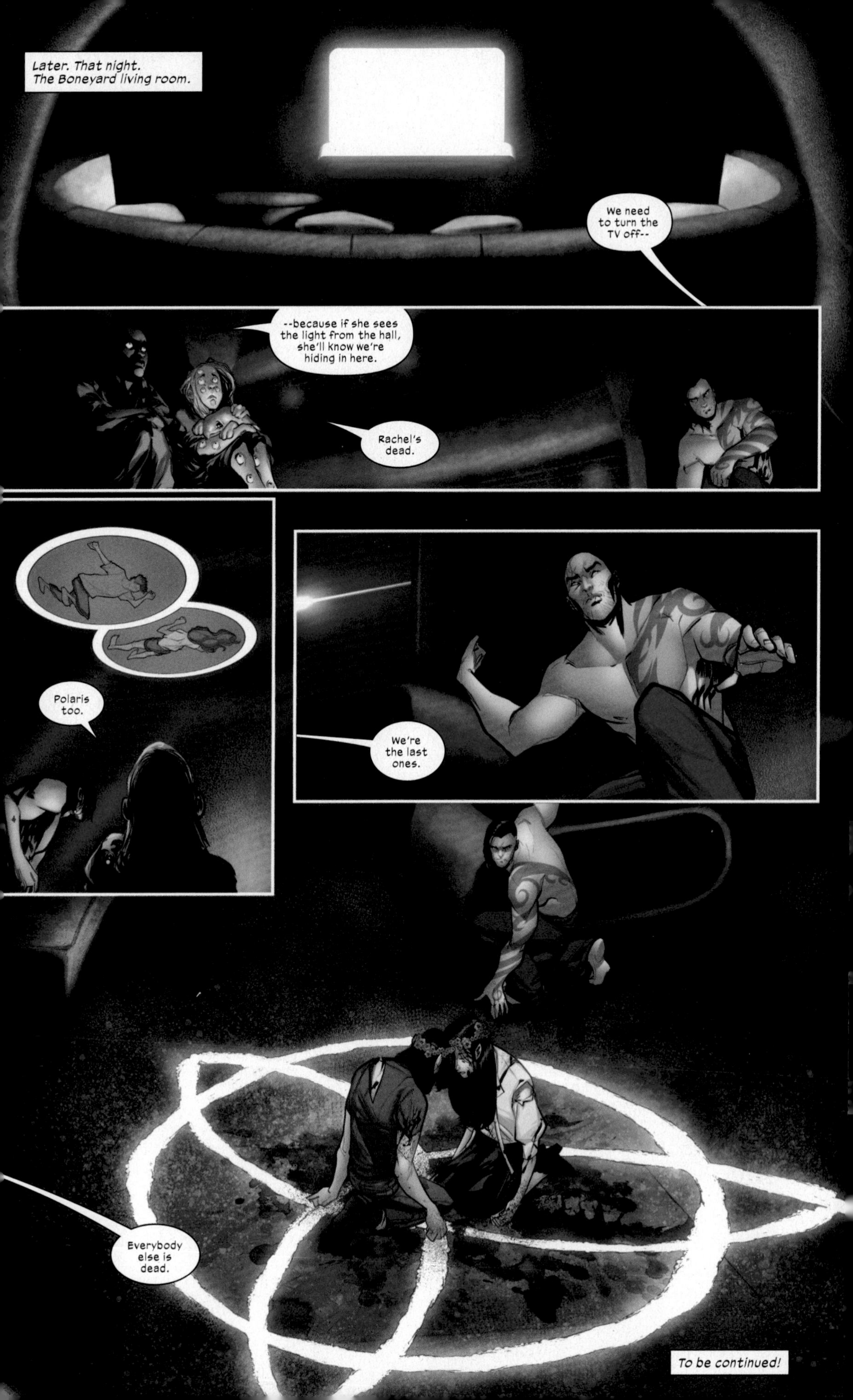

Later. That night.
The Boneyard living room.
We need to turn the TV off--
--because if she sees the light from the hall, she'll know we're hiding in here.
Rachel's dead.
Polaris too.
We're the last ones.
Everybody else is dead.
To be continued!

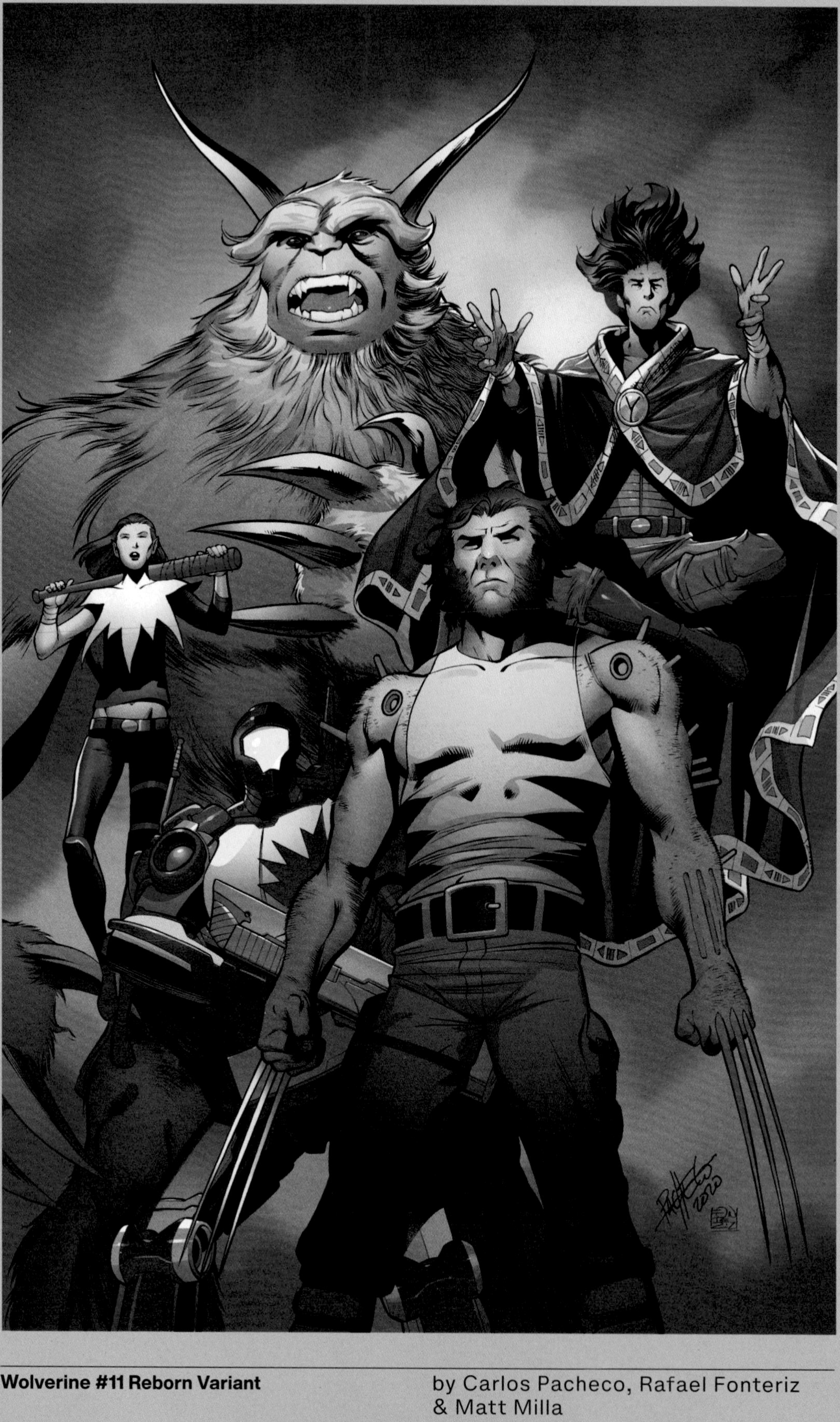

Wolverine #11 Reborn Variant

by Carlos Pacheco, Rafael Fonteriz
& Matt Milla

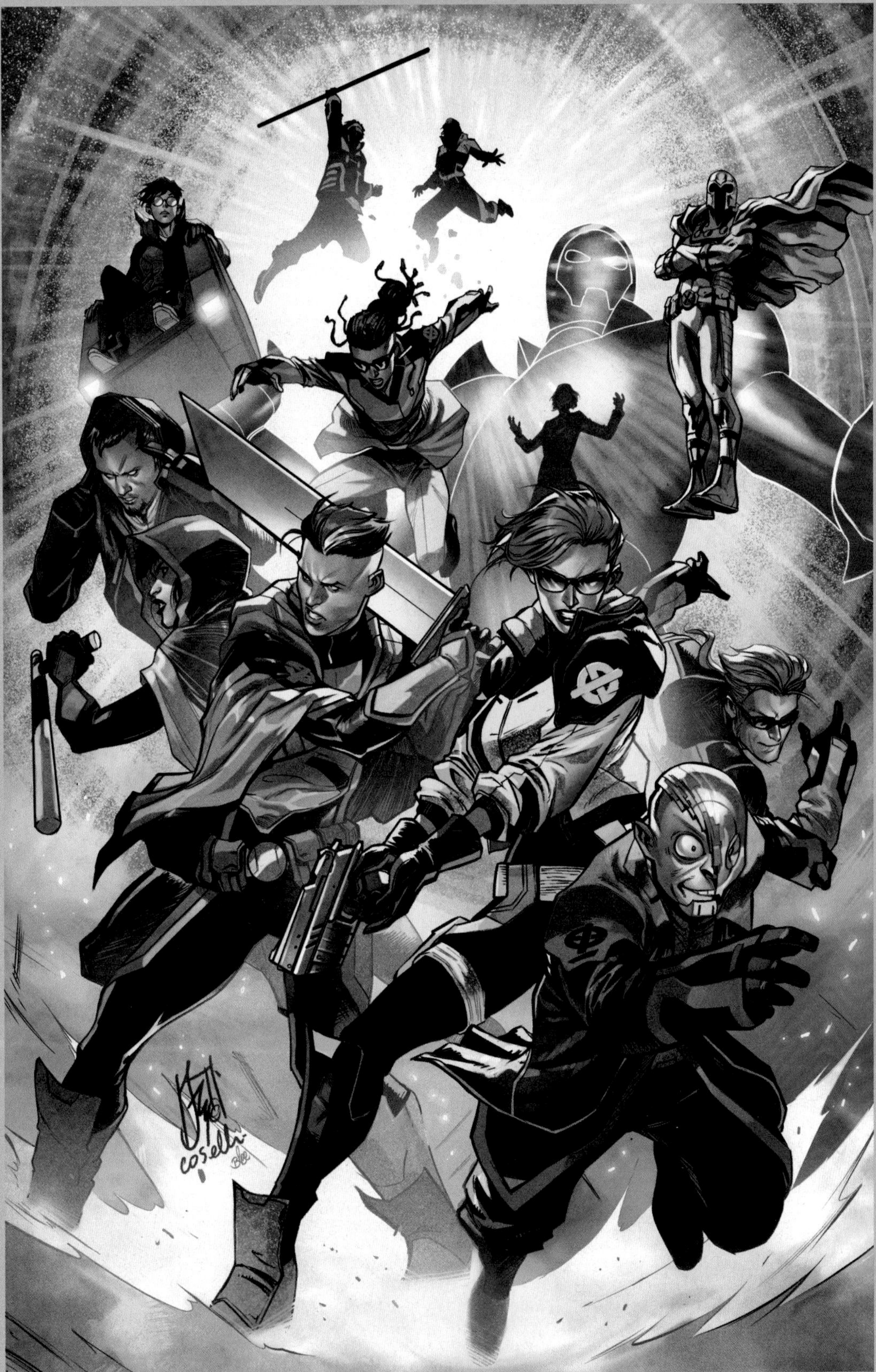

S.W.O.R.D. #5 Variant

by Stefano Caselli
& Federico Blee

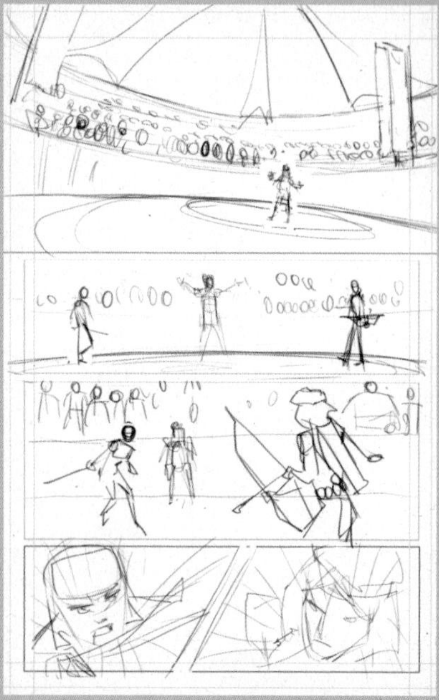

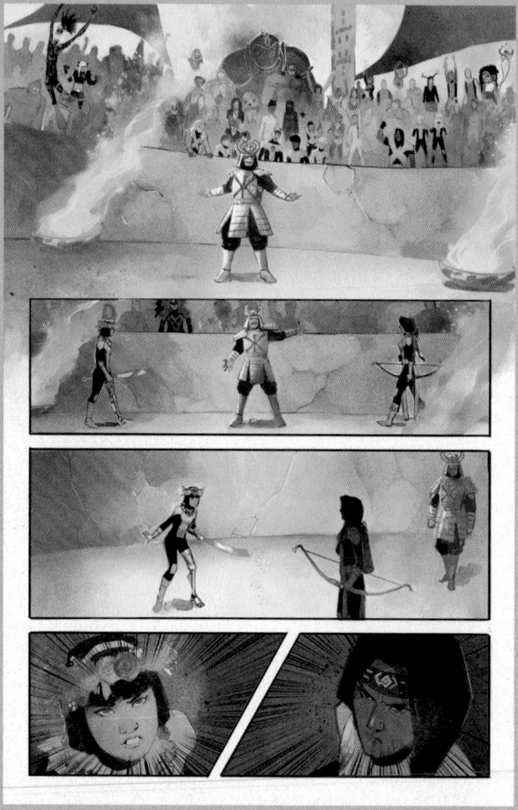

Page 4 Layouts & Final

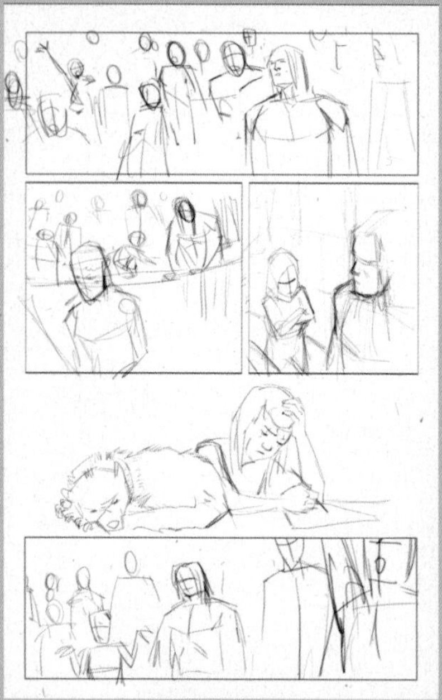

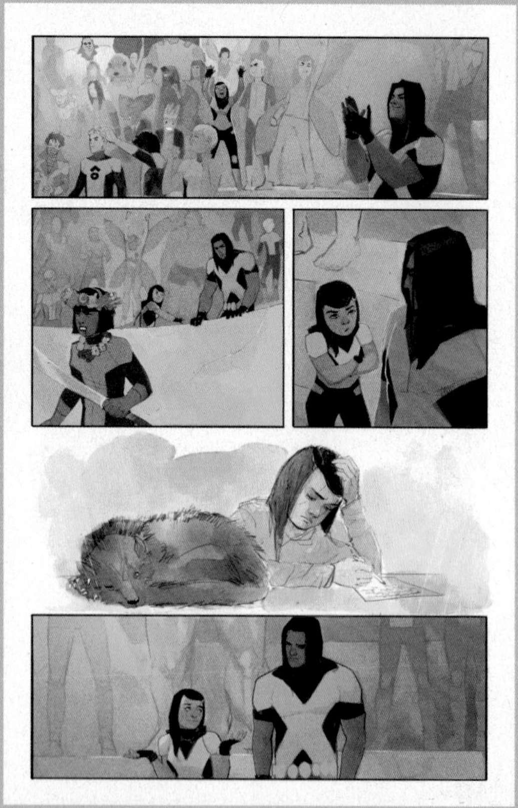

Page 6 Layouts & Final